THE FILMS OF TOD BROWNING

Black Dog Publishing

THE FILMS OF TOD BROWNING

EDITED BY BERND HERZOGENRATH

I dedicate this book to Frank, my beloved and courageous "little brother".

"Das ist nicht die Sonne die untergeht, sondern die Erde die sich dreht..."
(Tomte, "Die Schönheit der Chance")

FILMS

PLATES

INTRODUCTION

Bernd Herzogenrath

"When I hear the word 'culture', I reach out for my Browning!"—this quotation from Hans Johst's Nazi-play *Schlageter*, performed on Adolf Hitler's birthday in 1933, has been variously associated with both Hitler's Field Marshal Herman Göering, and the aesthetics and politics of Dadaism.

Here, "When I hear the word 'culture,' I reach out for my Browning!" should serve as the starting point for a meditation not on the interrelation of war and cinema—see Paul Virilio on that—but on the relation between culture and its other which I see as fundamental in the work of a particular American cult filmmaker. Thus, the Browning in question is neither John Moses Browning, the 'patron saint of automatic fire', who designed and developed many rifles, shotguns and pistols—among his 128 gun patents, one of the most famous is the Browning M1910 handgun that bears his name—nor the English poets Robert or Elizabeth Barrett Browning, but Charles Albert Browning Jr, much better known as Tod Browning.

With a significant number of his movies set in the world of the circus and the sideshow, Browning knew very well the milieu he was talking about. Born in Louisville, Kentucky, in 1880, Charles Albert left home early and ran away with a travelling carnival when he was only 16. Legend has it that he not only worked as a manager and roustabout there, but also started performing as a spieler and contortionist for the Manhattan Fair and Carnival Company. In 1920, the *Motion Picture News* state that in 1901, Browning "was an entertainer—singing, dancing and otherwise adding to the general gaiety in a 'river show' on the Mississippi and Ohio rivers".[1]

In Gatsby-like fashion, Charles Albert baptised and reinvented himself as 'Tod' Browning. True to the implications of his new identity (*tod* is also the German word for 'death'), Browning performed as "the Living Hypnotic Corpse", buried alive in a box with a secret ventilation system. People paid to watch 'un-dead' Tod in his coffin through a tube.

In 1909, Browning made the transition from the carnival to Hollywood, where he started as an actor in Edward Dillon's slapstick shorts. In 1913 he appeared in *Scenting a Terrible Crime* at the Biograph Studios, (playing an undertaker). There he met DW Griffith, and both men left Biograph for the Reliance-Majestic Studio in 1913. Browning soon worked as an assistant director on Griffith's *Intolerance* (where he even had a small role in the 'modern story' sequence). By 1919, after profitable movies such as *Jim Bludso*, Browning was an established and successful director and script writer. This was also the year he started collaborating with Lon Chaney, the "Man of a Thousand Faces". Browning and Chaney were brought together by Irving Thalberg; for Universal, Browning directed *The Wicked Darling*, 1919, with Priscilla Dean and Chaney—their first of a highly productive series of collaborations which include *Outside the Law*, 1920, which so successful that it was remade in 1930 as a talkie; *The Unholy Three*, 1925—a crook film set in the circus milieu; *The Blackbird*, 1926; *The Road to Mandalay*, 1926; *The Unknown*, 1927; *London After Midnight*, 1927, a famous 'lost film'; and the final collaboration *Where East is East*, 1929. Chaney, with his genius for startling make-up (usually of his own invention) and performances that made use of his physique as a tool to be contorted and deformed into almost every (in)conceivable pose, "gave body to the macabre figments of Browning's carnival background".[2] Together with his ability to completely change his outward appearance, Chaney was able to equip his characters with an extreme emotional intensity when it came to the depiction of suffering, mainly due to his almost masochistic will to perfection.

In the years after Chaney's death in 1930, Browning directed four movies which have become classics of the horror genre—and since murkiness seemed to be Browning's natural habitat, these films betray an elective affinity to the horror films of German Expressionist cinema (such as Paul Wegener's *The Golem*, or Robert Wiene's *The Cabinet of Dr Caligari*, both 1920) with their chiaroscuro lighting, forced perspectives, and weird angles and shadows. 1931's *Dracula* introduced Bela Lugosi (with whom Browning had already worked in *The Thirteenth Chair*, 1929) as 'the Count', and forever set the standard for 'the Dracula Look'. In 1932, Browning and Thalberg set out "to make a more ambitious version of the many successful circus films then being produced"—the result being the (in)famous *Freaks*.[3] Two years later, *Mark of the Vampire*, 1935, teamed Browning with Lugosi again in a movie that, in a way, infuses the genre with a substantial dose of ironic self-reflection—even if vampires shun mirrors!

Keeping his hands clean from controversial material after the scandal that *Freaks* had caused, Browning shot some 'lighter' movies after that, but 1936 saw him back on good form with the release of *The Devil Doll*, scripted with Erich von Stroheim, with whom Browning had already collaborated as assistant director for Griffith's *Intolerance*.

After his final film *Miracles for Sale*, 1939, Browning slowly said goodbye to Hollywood, except for some occasional scenario writing for MGM. In 1942, Browning retired to Malibu. Two years later, his wife Alice died. By that time, Browning had become so successfully reclusive that *Variety* mixed up his wife's death with Browning's own and published an obituary in 1944. 18 years later, on 6 October 1962, Browning died alone in the bathroom of his house at Malibu Beach.

Mostly known for successes and (financial) disasters such as *Dracula* and *Freaks*, Browning's work shows an interest—even an obsession—with mutilation and an almost 'cultic' and ritualistic (self-)sacrifice; with the *ab*normal, the *de*formed, the abject, that which has been 'thrown out' and rejected, that which exists on the outer limits of culture. It is by this very quality that Browning's films have become *cult* themselves. In staging the inherent antagonism between cult and culture, Browning's work often centres on the clash of different codes of behaviour, of different 'cultures', indeed—captured in terms of 'children' against 'adults', 'primitives' against 'civilised' cultures, instinct against reason, or 'abnormal' against 'normal'. Browning's movies display an amount of energy, libidinousness, otherness, of an intensity that is regarded as 'unorthodox', something almost too energetic for a culture based on repression to bear. Browning's work has such a cult status (and cult following) because it deals with and displays the very mechanisms and processes in which culture defines itself— but also in which culture's cultic other acts in this process. *Acts*, and not only *reacts*, because Browning is particular in taking sides with that other, but without just simply reversing the direction of the culture-formula, by presenting the other to culture as the more valuable side of the equation. Browning constantly folds both extremes into each other, creating a 'middle ground' in-between the binarisms, both on the level of content, and on the level of form. Thus, Browning's obsession with the abnormal and deformed, with the margins of culture (and culturally constructed ideas of 'humanity'), is not mere sideshow claptrap (although it is that, too), but an investigation into the workings and abysses of cult(ure).

"When I hear the word 'culture', I reach out for my Browning!"—the essays that follow reach out for *their* Browning in full force. The last few of years have seen an increase of interest in actor/writer/director Tod Browning. The 2002 complete retrospective at the Musée d'Orsay was a landmark, and it seems only in France that Browning's work has been analysed to any great extent (the much-awaited volume by Charles Tesson has been postponed again and again). Apart from that, there is a diaspora of scattered writings on Browning in the English-speaking world, as well as Stuart Rosenthal's volume on Browning in the *Hollywood Professionals* series, and the seminal biography by David J Skal and Elias Savada, *Dark Carnival. The Secret World of Tod Browning, Hollywood's Master of the Macabre*. This present volume deals with Browning's work from a multiplicity of vantage points—film history, film studies, philosophy, colonial studies, psychoanalysis—tackling not only Browning's most popular films, but also lesser known ones. Broader topics, such as the importance of the body in his oeuvre, the various transitions implicit in his work (from stage to screen, from silent to sound films), his work as an actor, his partnership with Lon Chaney, among others, are introduced alongside analyses of particular films.

The first essay by Vivian Sobchack, "The Films of Tod Browning: An Overview Long Past", can in many ways be considered the introduction proper to this volume. Dating from the mid-1970s, it not only presents a thorough overview of Browning's work and its reception by contemporaneous reviewers —even better, it perfectly captures the enthusiasm of discovering a cinematic outsider, the 'gold-digger spirit' of hitting on something big, the joy and laughter of finding.

As Boris Henry in his essay on "Tod Browning and the Slapstick Genre" argues, many of Browning's movies have a comic element. Laughter seems to both revive and/or continue Browning's beginnings in cinema: before he was a director, he acted in about 50 slapstick movies. Even if Browning's movies as director are not considered slapstick movies, he nevertheless maintains a peculiar connection with this genre, as is shown by his quotation of and borrowing from those in which he acted. Some of the main figures, procedures and themes of Browning's own movies are those used by slapstick: the liveliness of the elaboration of a situation, the taste for repetition, the double and the duality, the importance of gesture, the physical changes, the dressing-up, the small people and the miniaturisation, the loneliness of the main character and his failure to adjust to the world, as well as some ferocity against middle-class values. It is perhaps with regard to his slapstick past that Browning chooses to structure some of his stories—and some of his movies as well—and to think about the characterisation of a body, and about what a body can do.

Using Browning's purported professional beginnings as a magician's assistant and one-time handcuff escape artist as a point of departure, Matthew Solomon's essay examines the ways several of Browning's silent films thematise and represent illusionism. While discussing the highly theatricalised deceptions of *The Unknown*, and the lost *London After Midnight*, Solomon's "Staging Deception: Theatrical Illusionism in Browning's Films of the 1920s" also sets two lesser-known Browning films, *White Tiger*, 1923, and *The Show*, 1927, in historical context, juxtaposing them with the work of Edgar Allan Poe and PT Barnum, as well as the performances of early twentieth century vaudeville magicians. The essay considers how the spectacular set-pieces of these films, which take place, respectively, in a wax museum and sideshow palace of illusions, both extend and complicate modes of illusion that would have been familiar to Browning from his early experience in the realm of small-time and itinerant American entertainment. The essay demonstrates the many affinities between Browning's films and what James W Cook describes as the American tradition of "artful deception", which always offset apparent mystification—the magician's stock-in-trade—with selected demystifying revelations.

In "The Spectator's Spectacle: Tod Browning's Theatre", Stefanie Diekmann and Ekkehard Knörer attempt to place Tod Browning's films in a theatrical context. In a first approach they show Browning's affinity in subject, mood, and style with the French Grand Guignol, which flourished from the beginning of the twentieth century well into the 1920s, when it began to decline from a genuinely sensational theatre of fear to a relic that was out-spectacled by, among other things, the horror films of the 1930s. Similarities between Browning and the Grand Guignol include a definitive sense of the grotesque, and an intermingling of melodrama and rather naturalistic and graphic descriptions of violence and mutilation. In a second approach they argue that Browning's films also have a more general affinity to certain forms of theatre, especially the vaudeville. Browning's cinema is focused on the spectator in a manner that predates his or her immobilisation as an audience in front of the traditional stage or the cinema screen. Browning's films are at once pre-theatrical and meta-theatrical as they restage the stage as a means of multiplying plots and glances, of starting, unfolding and finishing all kinds of intrigue, tricks, sleights of hand and double-crossing. In Browning's films, the stage is not yet closely separated from the space of the spectator—who, then, is literally or allegorically drawn into the scene from which he or she can never really achieve a distance.

Horror films, and B-movies in general, are of course notorious for their production flaws and narrative discrepancies. As Alec Charles in "Double Identity: Presence and Absence in the Films of Tod Browning" shows, Browning's films are hardly immune to these discontinuities and aporia. However, in the insights which these apparent errors offer into the films' underlying themes, neuroses and desires, these anxious and monstrous disturbances may act upon audiences (consciously or otherwise) in ways which Freud would have dubbed 'uncanny'. The dark and problematic undercurrents which they reveal mirror the doubling effects upon which so many of Browning's plots turn. These (no)things expose the endless emptinesses upon which cinema's (and indeed patriarchy's) essential myths of power, presence, endurance, satisfaction and closure are impossibly founded.

In 1919, Browning started his collaboration with Lon Chaney, a partnership that was to last until Chaney's death in 1930. With Chaney, Browning made a series of very successful movies focusing on the themes of obsessive revenge and sexually charged mutilations of the body—Browning and Chaney became a successful tandem. Nicole Brenez, in her essay "Body Dreams: Lon Chaney and Tod Browning—Thesaurus Anatomicus", focuses on this partnership and argues that Browning's films can be aptly described as deep adventures of the body. What does the actor's acting reveal when it uses the body as a subject? One finds three significant answers in the American silent movie: Douglas Fairbanks, Buster Keaton and Lon Chaney. Reviewing the fictions of euphoric control typical of Fairbanks, or those of the art of affective objectivation invented by Keaton, Lon Chaney's research with Tod Browning inscribes itself in a perspective which can only be called 'negative'—that of the body's disintegration. Chaney is a plastic artist who has methodically invented visual practices through which he intensifies the treatment of the body as a fantastic anatomy: typage, make-up, scripts of psychosomatic phenomena. The plastic diversity of appearances may be remarkable, but it does not, however, constitute the whole of Chaney's art. To consider this work in its entirety, one must at least observe the different sites of multiplicity, the constancy of somatic scenarios and the symbolic constancy of acting as well—in short, the figurative economy created by Chaney.

Robin Blyn, in "Between Silence and Sound: Ventriloquism and the Advent of the Voice in *The Unholy Three*", shows how, in its exploration of the representation of the human voice, figured most explicitly in the silent acts of ventriloquism that motivate its plot, Browning's *The Unholy Three* is emblematic of a kind of self-reflexive performance. This, Blyn argues, allows for both a reevaluation of the strange body of Browning's work and of the interregnum period between the silent and sound eras, roughly between 1925 and 1932, when cinema anticipates and responds to the emergence of the technology of recorded sound in its earliest deployments. Loosing the voice from the body of the speaker, *The Unholy Three* draws attention to the film's own awareness of the artificiality of the cinematic medium and to its own irreverent play with the conventions of Hollywood cinema. Rather than paving the way for the synchronous sound recording and autonomous subject that were to become the very signatures of the 'classic' mode in the sound era, films such as *The Unholy Three* convey the extent to which popular film served as a significant vernacular discourse about new conceptions of subjectivity, conceptions inspired by the prospect of sound recording. If, as James Lastra has recently demonstrated, such vernacular discourses shape both the technological development and the aesthetic history of the cinema, then popular films like *The Unholy Three* participate in a cultural conversation that both registers the multivalent potentials of sound technologies and actively informs the representational practices cinematic history has come to understand as the "advent of the voice".

Where East is East, the last co-production of director Tod Browning with Lon Chaney, illustrates Browning's life-long tendency to interweave images of sex and race, creating an ambivalent narrative of sensual fulfillment and frantic disillusionment. According to Stefan L Brandt's "White Bo(d)y in Wonderland: Cultural Alterity and Sexual Desire in *Where East is East*", this film's dilemma is epitomised by the figure of Bobby, the 'white boy', who finds himself torn between his fiancée Toyo and her mother Madame de Sylva, an oriental beauty whose scheming nature threatens to tear the whole family apart. By situating the narrative in the borderland of Western civilisation and Eastern tradition ("a colorful spot of French rule and Chinese custom"), the movie alludes to those "curious interrelationships between figures for sexual and racial Otherness" which have been described in postcolonial theory as the pivotal features of Western colonial discourse. Paradoxically, the film both essentialises the East as a universal and homogeneous entity ("Where East is East") and deconstructs it as a Western myth consisting of nothing but colourful [male] fantasies. Criticised by contemporary reviewers as being filmed "in the mood of a cheap magazine sex tale of the Orient", the movie goes well beyond stereotype and cliché, confronting the audience with an uneasy mixture of elements of boundary-subversion and boundary-maintenance. It meticulously stages cultural alterity in the form of desiring, rebellious, mutilated, and threatening bodies, rendering the coloniser a problematic figure full of inconsistencies and at the same time bestowing the colonised with a sense of agency and spectatorship.

In her essay "Speaking with Eyes", Elisabeth Bronfen explores the multifaceted trope of the vampire in Tod Browning's *Dracula*. This first talkie horror film is read here within its historic context, as an expression of fascination for political leader personalities, with Van Helsing and Count Dracula performing a will to power in which a dialectic of the Enlightenment emerges. For the superstition of Van Helsing not only marks the moment when modernity falls back into mythical thinking; his victory over the vampire is presented in such a way as to illustrate that the force used to combat the cultural Other is infected by that which it seeks to contain. At the same time Tod Browning's vampire is clearly also staged as the phantom of those young Westerners who feel themselves to be on the margin; the travelling solicitor Renfield, the women Mina and Lucy, travelling with their desires. Finally, Browning's fascination with Stoker's Count Dracula also serves to disclose the medium of cinema itself as vampiristic.

Browning's boxing drama *Iron Man* is one of the rarely discussed movies of this cinematic *auteur*. Leger Grindon's essay "Tod Browning's Thematic Continuity and Stylistic Development in *Iron Man*" explores key questions regarding Browning's authorship. First, the essay argues for the thematic continuity between Browning's more famous tales of grotesque horror and this boxing film. The moral and sexual frustrations that Stuart Rosenthal argues are central to Browning's work are readily apparent. Furthermore, Browning's portrayal of suffering and vulnerability to predatory sexuality in *Iron Man* are also closely related to earlier films. Second, *Iron Man* arises at an important juncture in the evolution of Browning's *mise-en-scène*. Critics have noted that during the silent era Browning maintained a stationary camera and depended upon editing and composition as expressive tools. However, his collaboration on Dracula with the famous German cinematographer Karl Freund resulted in the conspicuous use of camera movement. In his first production after the Freund collaboration, Browning continues to make camera movement a key expressive device that results in a transformation of his style. *Iron Man* is not an anomaly in Browning's career, rather it is a work that testifies to the continuity of his worldview, and also features a shift in his cinematic style as camera movement gains prominence. This neglected film serves as an example of the director's achievement in the maturity of his career.

Bernd Herzogenrath's essay on "The Monstrous Body/Politic of *Freaks*" focuses on one of Browning's best-known movies, the notorious *Freaks*. Bodily deformation—in particular those of circus people, or side-show freaks —frequently took centre stage in Browning's films. 'Freaks' by birth, or by self-mutilation, Browning's scenarios reveal these deformations as socially constructed. Thus, one might read them as a comment upon the political reality of America in the 1930s, as (in)directly referring to the social circumstances of the Depression Era. Browning's movies present 'filmic test arrangements', a virtual acting out of the possibility that those who do not belong to the well-knit body politic might form a parallel society within it. This thematic thread is repeated on the formal/aesthetic level of Browning's films, which fold elements of culture's *other* into their narrative and formal texture, and present a critique not only of the perfect Body/Politic, but also of the idea of the classical film as a 'well-made urn'.

In his reading of *Mark of the Vampire*, Matthew Sweney points out the film's Bohemian setting, and argues that the 'unsatisfying' ending of the film in fact strengthens its dream logic. The exposition of the vampires as faked by a theatre company also puts the film into the category of Browning's films about the carnival, where monsters are made to satisfy the desire for voyeurism on the part of the audience. For its magnificent tracking shot on the stairwell, for its introduction of 'the Look' for female screen vampires, for giving us more Lugosi and Lionel Barrymore, for its eerie soundtrack, for the invention of 'bat thorn', *Mark of the Vampire*, like a good carnival sideshow, is a film greater than the sum of its parts, and at just over an hour, one of Browning's most condensed works.

In 1953, in the only retrospective article dealing with Browning's work published in Browning's lifetime, George Geltzer praised the "unexpected scenes of sheer pictorial beauty in almost all of Browning's films". He goes on to observe that Browning's "techniques and devices for thrilling and chilling audiences have been copied by directors all over the world".[4] This is still true—50 years later, there's a case to be made for Browning's influence on directors—*auteurs*—such as David Lynch or John Waters. The freaks peopling the movies of Alejandro Jodorowsky seem to have sprung from Browning's cinematic universe, and the 'body horror' of David Cronenberg owes much to Browning's and Chaney's experiments with what a body can do. And some, but by far not all, of Browning's movies have been made accessible on DVD—thus, there is still plenty to be discovered in the cinema of Tod Browning.

⋈ NOTES

1. *Motion Picture News*, 25 December 1920 (no pagination).

2. Hardy, P T Milne, and P Willemen eds., *The Encyclopedia of Horror Movies*, New York: Harper and Row, 1986, p. 35.

3. Baxter, John, *Hollywood in the Thirties*, New York: Paperback Library (International Film Guide Series), 1970, p. 101.

4. Geltzer, George, "Tod Browning: He Made Great Horror Films Because He Believed Horror Is Naturally Cinematic", *Films in Review*, vol. 4, no. 8, October 1953, pp. 410–416, p. 416.

THEMES

TOPICS

APPROACHES

THE FILMS OF TOD BROWNING

Vivian Sobchack

AN OVERVIEW LONG PAST

⋈ EPILOGUE FIRST ⋈

The following essay was written over 30 years ago in 1974 as a research exercise for a graduate seminar at UCLA on American film history. It was part of a longer study that addressed both Tod Browning's films and his personal history (at least what I was able find out about it during an academic quarter in Los Angeles). Hard to imagine today, this was a period before videos and DVDs (or the *AFI Catalog of Feature Films* for 1911–1920), and Browning's extant films were not readily available for viewing. This was also the period just before the major shift in film studies to more theoretical concerns and methodologies informed by structuralism, psychoanalysis, post-structuralism, and gender studies. Thus, in the present context, perhaps what follows is most valuable for its use of contemporaneous reviews of Browning's films written upon their theatrical release. The essay's excesses and *lacunae* are testimony, therefore, not only to my scholarly naïveté but also to the discipline's. (In this regard, I have corrected errors of fact where possible.) Not exactly a disclaimer, these hindsight remarks are, at the least, an apologia for the essay's indiscriminate delight at every scrap of information I was able to find. At the most, they allow me to dedicate what follows to *The New York Times'* Mordaunt Hall, who, whether he appreciated Browning's films or not, reviewed them.

I was fascinated by Tod Browning's films long before I became conscious of their director. As Andrew Sarris notes of this *auteur*'s pantheon: "in every instance, the film[s] preceded the filmmaker in the critic's consciousness".[1] *Dracula*, 1931, intrigued me primarily because of Bela Lugosi's mesmerising performance, but I remember also three uncanny women drifting into a castle room toward a Renfield who later—mad—crouched in corners and ate insects. *Freaks*, 1932, astonished me because of its documentary straightforwardness in the midst of heightened melodrama, its revelation of a world usually hidden from view; and a wedding feast that was the strangest thing I'd ever seen on the screen. *The Devil Doll*, 1936, captured me with its superb special effects and its casual acceptance of Lionel Barrymore in drag. I also had seen *The Unholy Three*, 1925, with Lon Chaney in skirts and an absolutely rotten little dwarf—and then a few sequences of *The Unknown*, 1927, which presented Chaney armless, throwing knives and smoking cigarettes with his toes. Stunned by these few films, I began to wonder what kind of man this was who seemed so at home with the bizarre, the forbidden, the deformed. Indeed, before I began my research and actually saw a picture of Browning, I rather imagined him as Edgar Allan Poe, mustachios drooping, immersed in the dream world of his gothic imagination (and, perhaps, alcohol). Melodramatic? Certainly, but prompted by the films—and finally not so terribly far from the truth (except that he actually looked more like William Faulkner).[2]

⋈ THE FILMS, 1920–1939 ⋈

This overview of Browning's films relies on memories of the films I've seen and on secondary resources about the content and style of the ones I haven't. Thus, the extrapolations and observations to follow are somewhat suspect and open to present and future challenge and revision. Furthermore, given the paucity of information on most of Browning films before 1920, focus will be on those he directed from 1920 to 1939. A number of one and two reelers are attributed to Browning from 1914 to 1916, and the *AFI Catalog* indicates he directed 17 features from 1917 to 1920.[3] Available information on these early features suggests most were melodramas, although there were some Westerns, several comedies, and a number of mystery/crime dramas. (Many also involved the disguise and impersonation found in later Browning films.) Of the 31 films Browning directed between 1920 and 1939, only two might be considered serious dramas, two romantic comedies, and one a horror film. All the others are melodramas of various types. Reading plot synopses, one has the urge to laugh at their incredible premises (whether trite or bizarre), *deus ex machina* climaxes, and happy endings that prove love and justice will out. However, synopses of such classics as *The Unholy Three* or *Freaks* seem ludicrous too, abstracted from their powerful and disturbing realisations on the screen.

Most of Browning's melodramas fall into three major categories: 1) exotic melodramas, in which the film's physical setting generates much of the plot and action; 2) crook melodramas, whose main characters are criminals (primarily thieves and swindlers); and 3) bizarre melodramas, that focus on physically deformed or freakishly disguised characters in situations that go beyond even the melodramatically 'normative'. In addition, there is a fourth and minor group of films: *mystery melodramas*, that deal with solving a crime (usually a murder), often debunking supernatural explanations in the process.

Browning loved exotic settings. Six of his films seem to depend upon the physical strangeness of place for their effectiveness and plot movement. Browning's first big hit was *The Virgin of Stamboul*, 1920. "Carl Laemmle let

Browning spend money lavishly" on a studio 'Istamboul' that featured bazaars, harems, the desert, and elaborate costuming.[4] *Under Two Flags*, 1922, takes place in Algiers, again using harems, a French Foreign Legion encampment, and the desert. The reviewer for *The New York Times* (hereafter, *The Times*), while only mildly enthusiastic, ended with clear appreciation of the latter: "It is… the sort of film that makes over-frequent use of punctuation in the titles, but it atones for that in the sand storm scenes."[5] *Drifting*, 1923, is set in China: "There are compelling scenes of Shanghai, and also a series of pictures of studio-made villages of the Celestial domains, together with a fairly good idea of horse races in the country of the Yellow Man…. The 'Emperor Jones' idea of the incessant beating of drums is used in this film with some effect."[6] *The Road to Mandalay*, 1926, again uses street bazaars and the Singapore docks (although *The Times* reviewer felt the scenic effects left much to be desired).[7] *West of Zanzibar*, 1928, starts out in London but is set primarily in African swamps, jungle, and cannibal villages. Reviewing this "drama of pagan superstitions, hate and ivory", *The Times* commented: "The scenes sometimes appear to be a little cramped, but they are nonetheless frequently effective. There are the forbidding, dark waters, the comfortless shack, perspiring savages, and a generally clever conception of the depressing torrid temperature…. The men's once-white garments help to lend an impression of the heat and its consequent lethargy."[8] And released in two versions by MGM, one silent and one with sound effects, *Where East is East*, 1929, takes place in the jungles of Indochina where tigers are captured and sold to circuses.[9]

These exotic settings seem to drive and take precedence over the melodramatic plots and plentiful physical action. Nonetheless, one frequent minor theme worth noting in the exotic melodramas is that of sacrifice. The French-Arab waif (and "daughter of the regiment"), Cigarette, sacrifices herself to save Corporal Victor in *Under Two Flags*. Spurned, a Chinese girl plans suicide for love of Captain Jarvis in *Drifting*—although, to save him, she has to give up her knife and lives. Singapore Joe dies saving his daughter from a fate worse than death in *The Road to Mandalay*. Flint sacrifices his life so that his daughter can escape from the tropics in *West of Zanzibar*, and Tiger Haynes is mauled to death for love of his daughter in *Where East is East*. Many of Browning's other melodramas also use exotic settings to provide atmosphere rather than bearing the weight of the narrative: San Francisco's Chinatown (shot on location), South America, Bohemia, London, Budapest, Spain, Calcutta, Transylvania and Czechoslovakia. These films always take advantage of the 'ethnicity' of place—often determining Browning's minor, and stereotypical, characters (villainous Orientals, Bohemian villagers, and the like).

Browning was apparently fascinated with crooks, burglars, bank robbers, and conmen. Eight of his films from 1920 to 1939 are crook melodramas—but there are others that, while involving crooks and their schemes, are focused on more bizarre things than a straightforward robbery or scam. In almost every crook melodrama at least one of the crooks escapes punishment and/or is miraculously reformed or rehabilitated. This is generically unusual enough to have regularly irked Mordaunt Hall of *The Times*; however, it seems primarily a melodramatic convenience for, even if all the major characters in the films are crooks, one has to be around at the end to hold the heroine's hand. Nonetheless, the matter remains open to speculation, for in 13 of Browning's melodramas a criminal escapes imprisonment and/ or death.

Outside the Law, 1920, features Lon Chaney in a dual role: criminal and gang leader, Black Mike Sylva, and the ruthless Chinese villain, Ah Wing. Shot in San Francisco's Chinatown, Nob Hill, and waterfront district, the film's plot concerns jewel theft and multiple murders. *Motion Picture News* praised the film's realism: "Browning does not exaggerate his situations. He does not have to. He is too much a student of life; too much the keen observer to have to resort to the amateurishness of the device."[10] Browning, however, did use a 'device' in *Outside the Law* which "was much commented on in its day, for it involved a highly effective use of trick photography in which Chaney playing one character murders himself playing another".[11]

The Man Under Cover, 1922, deals with oil well swindlers and conmen, embezzlement and bank robbery, in a small town setting. *White Tiger*, 1923, is essentially a remake of *Outside the Law*. *Silk Stocking Sal*, 1924, is interesting because its townhouse burglar is a plucky young woman who subsequently saves the falsely accused hero from execution. *The Mystic*, 1925, opens in a carnival and features Hungarian gypsies who stage fake *séances* in a put-up spooky setting, but is essentially a crook melodrama about swindling and embezzlement. *The Times* praised the film, noting that "Browning has a distinctive bent for this special type of crook story."[12] *The Blackbird*, 1926, is also a crook melodrama in which Chaney again plays two roles: a thief who disguises himself as his own (bogus) crippled brother, a rescue mission worker named The Bishop. Despite this bizarre turn, the main emphasis seems to be on robbery and the rivalry between two thieves. Describing the film as "gripping" and Browning's direction as no "flash-in-the-pan", *The Times* said *The Blackbird* possessed "a streak of *Jekyll and Hyde*, glimpses of *Limehouse Nights* and incidents of Hornung's *Raffles*".[13]

The Big City, 1928, concerns a nightclub robbery and, again, the rivalry between two thieves. This time Chaney plays only one of them—"without a twisted limb or any facial disguise". Rather, as *The Times* reports: "He appears as a crook, a man of imagination, who enjoys outwitting other thieves almost as much as he does running his fingers through a pile of glistening loot." Although *The Times* faults the film's ending, it praises Browning, "who is in his element when presiding over an underworld story", and enthuses about one particular sequence: "Mr Browning depicts a night club in full swing, with two dancers, black hoods covering their heads, and soon these dancers whip out pistols and threaten the patrons of the place. It is not long before money and jewelry have been collected, and Mr Browning elects to show some of the gems hidden in a dish of spaghetti."[14] Chaney reforms by the film's end and, embraced by his long-suffering accomplice-girlfriend whom he has decided to finally marry, snarls (silently, of course): "Listen: I ain't going to buy you nothing. I'm just going to marry you."[15] Browning's only sound crook melodrama was a 1930 remake of *Outside the Law*, which retained the original title. It was unfavourably received by Hall who wrote, nearly yawning in print, "This is another crook yarn in which the criminals are for a time clever enough to pull the wool over the eyes of the slow-witted police. In the end, however, the law has its way, which is something in favor of this picture."[16] One scene, however (not in the earlier version), sounds visually intriguing: in it, thief "Fingers" O'Dell, planning a robbery, poses as an advertising automaton in a bank window in order to "case the joint".

The strange touches that often inform Browning's crook melodramas (particularly those with Chaney) are foregrounded in *The Unholy Three*. Indeed, the film contains major elements of Browning's bizarre melodramas. It starts in a circus sideshow, and its three central characters—a ventriloquist, a nasty dwarf, and a Strong Man—fascinate not because they are thieves, but because they look so strange and yet move so confidently through a *mise-en-scéne* where anything can and does happen. Leaving the circus with his two odd companions for a bigger scam, Echo (the male ventriloquist) impersonates an elderly woman, and takes over a pet shop to find and gain access to the homes of prospective robbery victims. "The scene", as Denis Gifford says,

> is mind-blowing. Echo, bearded and bombazined, sells a talking parrot to a rich client. When the client complains that the bird no longer talks (it never did; Echo was ventriloquising, of course), the Little Lady comes a-calling. She brings along her baby, who promptly clambers from his pram to stuff any spare jewelry down his diaper (the midget in disguise, you see). By way of a climax, Browning introduces a giant gorilla.[17]

As *The Times* (Hall, again) raved: "It is a stirring story, stocked with original twists and situations, a picture that teems with surprises."[18]

Georges Sadoul called *The Unholy Three* "a marvelous piece of fantasy and one of the most bizarre films in the history of the cinema, tinged with moments of black humor".[19] What is also humorous is that, in contrast, *The Times* praised the film for its *realism*. Hall writes, with what seems a certain bewilderment: "There is nothing ludicrous or slapstick about a single scene. It all seems plausible." And this statement comes after he describes the disguised Echo's visit with her 'baby' to a rich woman's home as she is examining an emerald necklace: "The… precious stones attract the 'baby', who cries for it, and the owner laughingly dangles it before the supposed child, being astounded when the 'baby' clings to the necklace with strange strength and only reluctantly parts with the jewels."[20]

This brings us to the last important film grouping: the bizarre melodramas. If one includes *The Unholy Three*, Browning made five. *The Show*, 1927, is set in a Budapest circus and a fairway show called the Palace of Illusions. Despite the negative *Times* review (focused on John Gilbert's performance), the film contains a number of extraordinary images and scenes.[21] George Geltzer mentions "some thrilling illusions of beheadings, especially one of John the Baptist in the Salome episode".[22] And a 1928 review credited to Paul Gilson tells us:

> It would be useless to describe this film where the intrigue is complicated by the murder of a sheep merchant, the misadventures of his daughter Lena, the illusions of an old blind man and some interventions by a venomous lizard. The film, through its magic, makes us accept the inventions of melodrama: it would be a disservice to recount them.

But Gilson does recount several, describing the enchanting yet seedy atmosphere of the fair: "On the stage… a living hand, 'the hand of Cleopatra', emerges from a velvet hanging and distributes tickets. How can we not be seduced? In this Palace of Illusions, the raised curtains reveal spider dancers, women aerialists, ballerinas smiling over the blade of a sword."[23]

The Unknown, 1927, also takes place in a circus. Originally conceived as an MGM vehicle for Chaney and Greta Garbo, which Browning would direct "from a story he had devised for their special and unique talents, tentatively called *Alonso, the Armless*", Joan Crawford actually played Estrellita.[24] *The Times* review was ambivalent:

> Although it has strength and undoubtedly sustains the interest, 'The Unknown'… is anything but a pleasant story. It is gruesome and at times shocking, and the principal character deteriorates from a more or less sympathetic individual to an arch-fiend. The narrative is a sort of mixture of Balzac and Guy de Maupassant with a faint suggestion of O Henry plus Mr Browning's colorful side-show background…. Mr Chaney really gives a marvelous idea of the Armless Wonder, for to act in this film he has learned to use his feet as hands when eating, drinking and smoking. He even scratches his head with his toes when meditating…. In one very clever scene Alonzo is perceived sitting in his cabin with his arms free. He is, nevertheless, using his toes to pour wine to drink and to hold a cigarette. Cojo calls Alonzo's attention to the fact that Alonzo is so accustomed to using his feet that he has forgotten that his arms are not strapped to his body. Alonzo has an idea of his own. He is trying to find out whether he could not do without arms.[25]

Shortly thereafter, both for love of Estrellita (who can't stand men touching her) and to avoid suspicion of murdering her father, he has them amputated. The film's climax occurs when, after Alonzo's long recovery, he returns to the circus to find Estrellita married to Malabar, the Strong Man, and enraged, attempts unsuccessfully to kill Malabar during an act involving two horses pulling the Strong Man in opposite directions. Exposed, the still raging Alonzo is finally trampled to death.

Browning's most notorious bizarre melodrama is *Freaks*, 1932. In relation to the film's frame story and horrifying denouement, Browning had conceived the image of a human with the body of a chicken well before August of 1930 (when Chaney died)—for, in Gifford's *A Pictorial History of Horror Movies*, there is a photograph of a grinning Chaney as a human chicken.[26] The idea was realised on screen in Freaks' terrifying final shot. Visually, the film combines the heightened chiaroscuro shadows and lightning bolts of Expressionism with a flat grey documentary style. As John Thomas writes:

> The crucial scenes in the movie are those which show the daily routine of the freaks, the individual adjustment… to their handicaps being almost clinically observed. We watch the armless woman drink beer from a glass grasped by a prehensile foot; while the human worm, both armless and legless, lights his own cigarettes with his teeth. Having selected a new dress, the pinhead Schlitzy flirts charmingly with the clown… one of the few normal characters who treats the freaks as equals…. We are first introduced to them during an outing in the country, when the camera, peering through the trees, comes upon a grotesque round dance of hopping, squirming, crawling things. Then, as the camera draws closer, the monsters resolve suddenly into people—'just children', as the normal woman with them explains— transformed from agents of terror to objects of compassion within moments.[27]

Not only does the film treat the freaks compassionately, it also allows for a humour that underscores their humanity and Browning's respect for them. The Bearded Lady gives birth to a bearded baby in a touching and funny scene whose emotional issue is both joy and laughter. The Siamese Twins quarrel comically about their respective paramours and the attraction of Joseph/Josephine (half-man, half-woman) toward Hercules, the Strong Man, is amusingly observed by a roustabout who taunts Hercules: "She likes you. But he don't!" Then, of course, there is the famous wedding feast for dwarf Hans and strapping Cleopatra, clips of which have circulated out of context for years. The scene starts by treating the freaks humanly, but proceeds—as they drink and are seen by an increasingly mobile and dizzy camera—to turn them into grotesques in contrast to the two 'normal' humans present: Cleopatra and Hercules. "Leading a macabre chant, 'We accept her, we accept her, gobble, gobble, one of us, one of us', a dwarf dances across the banquet table bearing a huge communal wine bowl, offering it at last to Cleopatra to drink from as her token of induction into the world of the freaks."[28] Her refusal is almost a relief; it is only when she humiliates Hans that the freaks again become human in comparison. The sequence is a masterpiece of sound and image, and utterly unique in conception and realisation. The freaks' revenge on Cleopatra and Hercules is visualised in near Expressionist style. As Thomas describes:

> Amidst a jumble of wrecked circus trailers, lightning splitting sky and sound track, the ground a muddy ooze, the darkness swarms with crawling, hopping shapes, lit grotesquely by momentary flashes, all humanity seemingly erased…. We are horrified, but we are simultaneously ashamed of our horror; for we remember that these are not monsters at all but people like us, and we know that we have again been betrayed by our own primal fears…. Each of them is one of us; each of us, one of them.[29]

Perhaps this recognition proved too much for the audience and most reviewers. The film was "too strong for some of its exhibitors, who flatly refused to run it after a disastrous preview in San Diego… during which a woman ran screaming up the aisle".[30] One of the most extreme reviews stated: "Not even the most morbidly inclined could possibly find this picture to their liking. Saying that it is horrible is putting it mildly. It is revolting to the extent of turning one's stomach, and only an iron constitution could withstand its affects…. Anyone who considers this entertainment should be placed in the pathological ward in some hospital."[31] Some criticism was sympathetic: "If *Freaks* has caused a furore [sic] in certain censor circles the fault lies with the manner in which it was campaigned to the public. I found it to be an interesting and entertaining picture, and I did not have nightmares, nor did I attempt to murder any of my relatives."[32] *The Times* was noncommittal and *Variety* gave the film a negative —and oddly remote—review: "Here the story is not sufficiently strong to get and hold the interest, partly because interest cannot easily be gained for a too fantastic romance."[33]

    The Devil Doll, 1936, Browning's last bizarre melodrama and penultimate film, is reminiscent of *The Unholy Three*. Lionel Barrymore is dressed through most of the film as Madame Mandelip, the elderly proprietor of a Paris doll shop. The premises on which the revenge plot rests are again incredible, but the visual realisation is so fascinating that we are drawn, nonetheless, into a world which seems quite credible and moving. When Paul Lavond (Barrymore), in disguise, visits the laundry where his daughter works and develops a disquieting friendship with her, some of their sequences together are disturbing enough to significantly temper melodramatic sentimentality. The scenes that involve the 'dolls' (really miniaturised people) as they attempt to carry out the murderous telepathic commands of a vengeful Lavond are often chilling, but most often also *interesting*—observed by a camera objectively recording the fascinating details of their progress. As Frank Nugent wrote in his *Times* review: "The picture relies mainly, and with understandable assurance, upon such ingenious bits as Miss Ford's demonstration of Alpine skill in climbing (via a slipper, footstool, bench and drawer handles) to the top of a dressing table; or Mr Hohl's ludicrous impersonation of a Christmas tree ornament; or the Apache dance with a table-top serving as a ballroom."[34] Although it has its horrific moments, like *Freaks*, *The Devil Doll* is not a horror film.

Indeed, there are some rather comic scenes in the film: Madame Mandelip visiting her 'victims' and their families at the bank or in their homes to sell them her marvellous 'living toys'. The humour arises from the extremely realistic domestic wheedling involved in these transactions and its juxtaposition with the almost fairytale quality of Barrymore's visits (reminding us of *Snow White*'s Wicked Queen with her basket of poisoned apples). Marked by "characteristic Browning elements—greed as a motive, transvestism", John Baxter sees *The Devil Doll* as "one of the 30s' most effective examples of atmospheric fantasy".[35] Certainly the film is a fantasy, with its miniaturised St Bernard, Great Dane, circus horse, and its assorted tiny humans who go about sticking poisoned little daggers into sleeping bankers. But the film also creates a world so full of carefully observed details that we cannot do other than accept it as 'real'.

Besides the constantly noted physical oddities of their major characters, another common element shared by the bizarre melodramas is a hint of perverse sexuality. There is, of course, the transvestism of *The Unholy Three*, but there is also the scatological dwarf who hides jewellery in his diaper, and the comic role-playing of a mother/son relationship between two consenting males. *The Show* focuses on the Salomé/John the Baptist 'illusion' that speaks of sadomasochism and symbolic castration. *The Unknown*'s Estrellita is horrified at being touched by men's hands and Alonzo's surgery for love of her (as well as to hide his crime) is, to say the least, excessive. *Freaks* forces us to contemplate the practicalities of the physical relationship between Hans and Cleopatra. As Ivan Butler writes: "There is indeed at times a nasty feeling that at the back of her [Cleopatra's] mind is an obscene desire to sink her gleaming teeth into the midget and gobble him up."[36] *The Devil Doll* once more uses transvestism to create an occasional sense of acute discomfort. Nonetheless, one wonders how much weight to place on the sexual 'perversity' in Browning's work for, in all the films, there are also conventional (and melodramatically generic) heterosexual romances. Furthermore, sexuality in the films seems less perverse than diverse: of a piece with all the other oddities of human being found in Browning's films.

Browning made only one true horror film: *Dracula*, 1931. Originally slated for Chaney, the film starred Bela Lugosi (who, in 1929, appeared in Browning's first sound film, *The Thirteenth Chair*). Much has been written by various critics about the static and stagy quality of the film (which was adapted from the hit stage adaptation of Stoker's novel). Nonetheless, every critic who emphasises the film's 'uncinematic' qualities goes on to describe those 'few' scenes that *are* cinematic. Indeed, there is quite a list. Roy Huss sees *Dracula* as a "film of missed opportunities" and yet describes in some detail the artistry of Renfield's carriage ride to Castle Dracula:

> [Browning] admirably composes a montage of shots to invoke a sense of speed and terror: (1) high-angle panoramic sighting of the vulnerably small black vehicle being dragged at breakneck pace through the desolate countryside, intercut with (2) shots of the bouncing interior of the coach showing Renfield's discomfort, followed by a cut to (3) a medium shot of the bat, into which the driver (Dracula himself) has been transformed, controlling the horses by flying over their heads; then a cut to (4) a medium reaction shot of Penfield leaning out of the carriage to chastise the driver and finding, the driver's seat empty; and ending with a cut to (5) the driverless carriage suddenly coming to a rattling halt in the somber blackness of the castle's court-yard.[37]

Calling it "Browning's only concession to cinema", Gifford discusses an earlier scene (also mentioned by Huss) in which the camera "creeps through the crypt, watching the bowed glidings of Dracula's three wraith-like wives, the scurrying of rats around their coffins, then cutting away as the Count rises from his, as if to spare his embarrassment".[38]

Huss praises a subsequent "scene in which Renfield, having fallen to the floor, is approached by the three figures trailing their white gowns as zombie-like they move toward him in their blood-thirst".[39] And he finds the sequence of the ship carrying Dracula's coffin to England reminiscent of German Expressionist cinema: "With the dramatic shot of merely the shadow of the dead captain strapped to the helm, magnified as it is projected on a wall, we have another inkling of what this film might have been."[40] Other 'exceptions' to the film's "static staginess" are "a shot in which Dracula's face, shown in close-up, slides down off the lower left-hand cornerof the frame as he bites Mina's neck for the first time", and a parallel close-up shot later of "Mina's immobile, trance-like face moving off-frame in the same manner, as her growing vampirism prompts a blood-lust movement toward her fiancé".[41] Butler adds to the list of the very 'few' cinematically 'effective moments': "the Count's invisibility, in a silver box, the un-dead Lucy wandering specter-like in the shadows, the dark arches of Dracula's Hampstead cellar, even the very unlikely London of swirling fogs. The mistiest parts are, in fact, the best."[42] Hardly uncinematic, there is only one sour note in the entire movie: the epilogue in which Edward van Sloan (as Dr Van Helsing) stands before a blank background and warns us that vampires really exist. The epilogue is of interest, however, when we place its superfluous (and deflating) empiricism in the context of Browning's total work.

Although fascinated by the grotesque, the deformed, and the perverse, Browning (a former magician) was a debunker of the occult and the supernatural. *The Mystic*, for example, uses clairvoyance, séances and spiritualism to dramatic effect but also reveals the fakery of such things. Indeed, Browning is more interested in tricks and illusions than in the supernatural. Thus, in the minor group of mystery melodramas, the occult and the supernatural are employed on one level for their dramatic value but are invariably revealed as tricks. Thus, *London After Midnight*, 1927, called by Gifford "the first true American vampire movie despite the twist in its tail", is not really a vampire film at all.[43] Rather, emphasis is on solving an old crime through the use of illusion, hypnotism and disguise. Chaney, as Inspector Burke, 'becomes' a vampire to get the murderer to reveal himself. Butler also comments that the film "contained too much 'comedy relief' for the sinister elements to obtain their full effect", and calls the ending weak; he does, however, mention that the film was "directed with considerable panache", with Chaney's "black-clad, high-hatted figure gliding, half-creeping, along a deserted hotel corridor", and "the vampirical mist billowing beneath a closed door, then clearing to reveal his crouching figure—at first only the black circle of his hat, gradually lifting as he raises his head and draws to his feet".[44]

In *The Thirteenth Chair*, 1929, Browning's first sound film, the police seek help from a supposedly successful medium. Although there are various scenes of séances, the murder is solved not by occult means, but by frightening the killer into a confession. *Mark of the Vampire*, 1935, is essentially a remake of *London After Midnight*, only here the Inspector and fake vampire are different people, the first played by Lionel Atwill and the second by Lugosi. An added character is Professor Zelen (Lionel Barrymore), who resembles *Dracula*'s empirical Dr Van Helsing. The film ends in the 'real' world of murder and detectives and there is no epilogue. The 'supernatural' scenes are shaped toward a realistic denouement—of which the actors ("playing the story as strict horror") had no knowledge and "reportedly balked at Browning's 'gimmick' ending".[45] Browning's last film, *Miracles for Sale*, 1939, is also a mystery melodrama set "smack-dab in the middle of a magicians' congress, with a demonologist in the spare bedroom, a psychic re-searcher in the attic and a bird named Tauro the Great pulling corpses, instead of rabbits, out of his silk hat". As *The Times* reviewer continued: "It isn't enough just to worry about the murderer: one must also do a little extra puzzling over disappearing cigarettes, spirit-invocation, card tricks and self-pounding typewriters."[46] But, again, the murder has an empirical solution.

The remaining seven films Browning made between 1920 and 1939 also contain many elements of the larger groupings discussed above. *The Day of Faith*, 1923, is an odd mixture of crook, newspaper, and romantic melodrama and the plot involves faith healing. However, given Browning's continuing fascination with physical deformity (generated, perhaps, by self-consciousness about his own badly scarred leg and limp, the result of an horrific automobile accident in 1915), what is particularly intriguing is that an intertitle describes one of the film's main characters as having "a limp in his foot and his soul".[47]

The Dangerous Flirt, 1924, is a romantic melodrama, but it is partially set in 'exotic' South America—the plot revolves around the heroine's sexual repression, and is suggestive of the various sexual concerns in other Browning films. Like the crook melodramas, both *Dollar Down*, 1925, and *Fast Workers*, 1933, involve swindles of some kind. *No Woman Knows*, 1921, is a family melodrama concerning a Jewish family set in Wisconsin and Dresden. *The Wise Kid*, 1922, seems a simple romantic comedy. And *The Iron Man*, 1931, a boxing drama, is —both in subject and plot—generally regarded as uncharacteristic of Browning's other work.

Overall, numerous questions are raised by the films, their plots, motifs, and visual style. Most can only be answered by viewing the films themselves. Nonetheless, using available materials, one can offer some tentative generalisations about Browning's work. Sarris, considering Browning as a potential *auteur*, writes: "The morbid cinema of Tod Browning seems to have been ahead of its time on some levels and out of its time on others." Comparing him to James Whale (director of *Frankenstein* and other Universal horror films), Sarris concludes that "Browning's career is more meaningful than Whale's in terms of a personal obsession."[48] Browning's morbidity is questionable however; his films often treat their bizarre characters and situations with a documentary coolness and acceptance, or a comic effect, that cannot be considered morbid. Beyond that, Browning does not seem deeply interested in the truly horrific or supernatural. While "obsession" may be too strong a word, however, Browning is clearly fascinated by the worlds of carnivals and circuses, by magicians and illusionists—and, by extension, by the criminal world, bent on deception: swindlers and thieves who disguise themselves and have aliases like "Fingers" O'Dell or "The Blackbird". A great many of his films concern characters in fear of being 'found out', and who willingly (or otherwise) assume roles and disguises that mask their true identity. Related to this is Browning's fascination with physical deformity—an "obsession" that, indeed, may be "personal" (given his own perceived deformity), but also derives from his association with Chaney. If obsessed with anything, Browning is obsessed with the 'exotic' in all its melodramatic possibilities: exoticism of place ('foreign' settings appear in at least 19 of his films, including five that use the circus or carnival as background); unconventional family relationships (bizarre father-daughter relationships, for example, appear in at least six films); human deformity (various 'grotesques' people at least 12 of his films); and 'aberrant' sexuality (vampirism, relationships between 'normal' and 'abnormal' characters, sexual phobias, and transvestism show up in at least ten films).

Browning's films also reveal, however, his deep concern for realism. Accepting both the excesses and confines of melodrama, Browning begins from the most incredible premises and proceeds to create a credible world. Indeed, what makes Browning's films truly unique is the tension created between flights of Expressionism, Surrealism, the baroque (call it what you will) and an almost documentary realism, the latter emerging through camera style and the casual acceptance of the 'bizarre' as 'normal'. This tension seems to be the one absolute that runs through Browning's work. His best films offer us a delicate balance between the bizarre and the real. Upon often incredible premises, the characters move about with a matter of factness that is, at times, overwhelmingly realistic, at times comic, at times eerie and chilling—but always quite amazing. Indeed, Browning's unique talent seems his ability to reconcile fantasy and realism without losing their respectively distinct qualities.

Just how much of this tension is conscious on Browning's part is impossible to determine, but there exist a few glimpses into his methods. Interviewed in 1928, Browning said:

> Mystery stories are tricky, for if they are too gruesome or horrible, if they exceed the average imagination by too much, the audience will laugh. *London After Midnight* is an example of how to get people to accept ghosts and other supernatural spirits by letting them turn out to be the machinations of a detective. Thereby the audience is not asked to believe the horrible impossible, but the horrible possible, and plausibility increased, rather than lessened, the thrills and chills.[49]

What Browning says here about mysteries indicates more about his own penchant for the "horrible possible" than it does for the audience's. Indeed, critics found the "plausible" endings of *London After Midnight* and *Mark of the Vampire* somewhat disappointing in their final refusal to accept the supernatural premises the films had set up. Browning's comments also explain to some extent why the epilogue of *Dracula* has a place in Browning's work. In relation to his work with Chaney, Browning also indicated that his story ideas did not begin with plot:

> This writes itself after I have conceived the characters. *The Unknown* came to me after I had the idea of a man without arms. I then asked myself what are the most amazing situations and actions in which a man thus reduced could be involved.... It was the same for *The Road to Mandalay*. The initial idea was simply that of a man so frightfully ugly that he is ashamed to reveal himself to his own daughter. In this way one can develop any story.[50]

As with *Freaks*, we see here a filmmaker who starts with the visual rather than narrative. What else we know of Browning's directorial vision must come from secondary sources. David Robinson writes that Browning was "a conscientious, painstaking craftsman at all times".[51] Browning's close friend, Mrs William S Hart Sr, reports that the scale of *The Devil Doll* interiors involving the film's miniaturised humans weren't built exactly to Browning's meticulous calculations, and when rushes showed that the scenes in question looked preposterous, he had the sets struck and completely rebuilt.[52] The

only other commentary on Browning's method comes from the director
Edgar G Ulmer, who indicates that before 1925 Browning was already expert
in trick cinematography and bizarre makeup—and that "until the end of his
career, Browning tried to avoid using dialogue; he wanted to obtain visual
effects".[53]

We might also ask to what extent others influenced Browning's work.
Chaney immediately comes to mind, but there are, as well, the two studios
—Universal and MGM—for which he made most of his films; screenwriter
Waldemar Young; and, in addition to Chaney, performer Priscilla Dean. Certainly,
Browning's best work was for MGM. This may be because, with the exception
of three 1930s works—the sound version of *Outside the Law*, *The Iron Man*, and
Dracula—all his films for Universal were made before 1924 and his maturity as a
filmmaker. Furthermore, a number of the Universal films were remakes of his
earlier work. At MGM, Browning did not repeat himself. Some credit must surely
go to Irving Thalberg who, a vice-president at Universal while Browning was
there, left in 1925 to join the newly-formed MGM. According to Ulmer,
Thalberg "had been so fascinated by the results of Browning's imagination that
he took him with him".[54] Thalberg also admired Chaney and put him under
long-term contract. What Thalberg said of Chaney may illuminate, as well, his
fascination with Browning: "He [Chaney] was great, not only because of his God-
given talent, but because he used that talent to illuminate certain dark corners
of the human spirit. He showed the world the souls of people born different
from the rest."[55] In regard to the triumvirate of Thalberg, Browning, and Chaney,
there are contradictory stories about *The Unholy Three*—the first film at
MGM for both Browning and Chaney. One suggests that Chaney convinced
Thalberg to sign Browning to direct the film.[56] The other supports Ulmer's
description of Thalberg's relationship with Browning. Browning had been
drinking heavily for two years prior to coming to MGM, and, during that time,
had directed only a few films for independent production companies.
Apparently, after listening "to Browning's woes and to his description of the
story of *The Unholy Three*… Thalberg wired New York to buy it. Everybody said
it was too bad Browning had selected such an impossible story for his
comeback."[57] The film was, of course, a huge success. Thalberg also came to
Browning's defence in relation to *Freaks*. Clarens notes: "That *Freaks* was
made at all is extraordinary. That it was made at Metro, the glamour factory…
seems hard to believe. It appears that Irving Thalberg backed Browning against
mass opposition."[58]

Browning was involved with writing the scenarios for most of his
films. Thus, only one screenwriter, Waldemar Young, figures prominently in
Browning's career, and this was primarily as Browning's collaborator. Young is
credited on 12 of Browning's films: three in 1919 at Universal, and nine at
MGM between 1925 and 1929. Not much is known about him. It's possible
that Thalberg brought him from Universal at the same time as Browning and
Chaney, and their first film for MGM was also his: *The Unholy Three*. He alone
was credited with the script, but, as noted, Browning had possibly pushed
the story to Thalberg. Young is also solely credited as scenarist for *The Show*,

suggested by Charles Jackson's novel, *The Day of Souls*, but one can speculate that, as an avid reader of gothic literature, Browning found the novel. Whatever the case, Young was clearly compatible with Browning: after *The Unholy Three*, he wrote the scenario for *The Mystic* but the story was Browning's; the same is the case with *The Blackbird*; *The Unknown* reverses the credits, with story attributed to Young and script to Browning; *London After Midnight* came from a story by Browning called "The Hypnotist" and both men wrote the scenario as they also did for *The Big City*; Browning is credited as co-scenarist for *Where East is East*, but Young adapted it. Nonetheless, Young's 'influence' is belied not only by the fact that the majority of their work was collaborative, but also because Browning often wrote completely on his own or with other one-time collaborators. Indeed, Browning is officially credited with the stories and/or scenarios of 20 of his films (five of them before 1920). Indeed, it is difficult to imagine that Browning who, early in his career, worked in the story department of Majestic Pictures, was not involved with all the scripts he directed. Ulmer suggests as much: "I've always had the impression, although I'm not certain, that the final shooting script was Browning's rather than the scenarist's…. I have this impression because, in spite of his using numerous writers, each of his films was always representative of his own peculiar style."[59]

The first major star with whom Browning worked regularly was Priscilla Dean, Universal's 'leading lady', known for playing 'tough girls'.[60] She starred in nine Browning films (four before 1920), two with Chaney (in 1919 and 1920), and three with Wallace Beery as the villain (in the 1920s). Most were exotic melodramas, but her generic influence is negligible as Browning continued making such melodramas long after he left Universal and Dean behind for MGM. Then, of course, there was Chaney, whose influence on Browning seems considerable. His first major role for Browning was (with Dean) in *The Wicked Darling*, 1919, and he later starred in Browning's 1921 crook melodrama, *Outside the Law*—both Universal films. Their significant collaboration really began at MGM and with *The Unholy Three*.

Browning, like Thalberg, was fascinated by Chaney's talent—and also by his life. Mrs Hart reports that Browning was not only curious about Chaney's life as the son of deaf-mute parents but also loved to hear the story about how Chaney met and married his second wife. Apparently, Chaney discovered her behind a newspaper and tobacco concession; her husband, the proprietor, was a man with no legs, who wheeled around on a little dolly-like platform. After he died, Chaney then married the widow.[61] There was an obvious sympathy between Browning and Chaney. Both men led extremely private lives off the set and were extremely reticent about their families. Both also died of throat cancer. Both, however, also enjoyed very different lifestyles, for Chaney lived so simply that the more up-scale Browning referred to him as "the star who lived like a clerk".[62] At Chaney's funeral, Browning was among the honorary pallbearers, who included Louis B Mayer, Nicholas Scheck, Irving Thalberg, and Lionel Barrymore (who appeared in four of Browning's films). Browning said of Chaney: "He was the hardest working person in the studio."[64]

One can view Chaney's connection with Browning as, at the very least, catalytic. With Thalberg supporting their imaginative freedom, Chaney's ability and unique presence fanned the flames of Browning's passion for the extraordinary. In one sense, Chaney showed Browning how far he could go. Thus, after Chaney's death in 1930, Browning continued their imaginative leaps with *Freaks* and *The Devil Doll*—both films heavily influenced, perhaps, by his former association with Chaney. Nonetheless, in the end (as in the beginning of his career), Browning exercised a great deal of personal control over his films—Mrs Hart mentions that he was always fighting to get what he wanted, and usually got it in the long run.[65] In this regard, it should be emphasised that most of Browning's films—until *Freaks*—made money.[66]

Who was Tod Browning? Ulmer remarks that Browning was, perhaps, the first in Hollywood to have seen the Expressionist fantasies made in Germany and Sweden (Victor Sjöstrom became a good friend) and was greatly influenced by them. Nonetheless, Ulmer suggests:

> Browning, who knew the work of Wiene on *Caligari*, began
> to move away from the expressionism of the time in order to
> draw nearer to a conception which has been pejoratively called
> baroque. [He] was a man of more widespread and infinite
> culture than most people. He was an expert on literature and a
> specialist, not only of Edgar Poe, but of all 'black' literature written
> in English.[67]

Indeed, Sadoul mentions that Browning was sometimes called "the Edgar Allan Poe of the cinema", and was "a 'dark angel' whose phantasmagoric creations were much admired around 1925 by the surrealists".[68] Browning's was, of course, a commercial cinema as well. The films suggest a man of humour and compassion who had a dark and melancholic fascination with physical deformity and with the exotic and extraordinary, and yet who also observed the oddities of life and place with unprejudiced objectivity and some delight. A Southerner who ran away with the circus; a former Vaudevillian, jockey, and magician who traveled the world before he became a filmmaker; an aesthete and a beer drinker; and above all a storyteller, Browning was both a poet and a pragmatist. After *Miracles for Sale*, 1939, he retired. In 1948, Browning was awarded a life membership in the Directors' Guild of America—an honour afforded to only four other individuals by the time of Browning's death from cancer in 1962.[69]

⋈ NOTES

1. Sarris, Andrew, *The American Cinema*, New York: EP Dutton, 1968, p. 36.

2. Faulkner actually worked with Browning in 1933 on a film for MGM that was never completed: "an opus alternatively entitled Louisana Lou and Bride of the Bayou".

3. The Internet Movies Data Base also lists 15 short films that Browning supposedly directed between 1914 and 1916. In his earliest film career, Browning acted, was an assistant director, and wrote many scenarios.

4. Geltzer, George, "Tod Browning", *Films in Review*, no. 4, October 1953, p. 411. The *AFI Catalog of Feature Films 1911–1920* suggests the film cost $500,000.

Review of The Virgin of Stamboul, *The New York Times*, 28 March, 1920, in *The New York Times Film Reviews 1913–1970*, 7 vols., New York: Arno Press, 1970–1971.

5. Review of *Under Two Flags*, The New York Times, 25 September, 1922.

6. Review of *Drifting*, The New York Times, 20 August, 1923.

7. Hall, Mordaunt, review of *The Road to Mandalay*, The New York Times, 28 June, 1926.

8. Hall, Mordaunt, review of *West of Zanzibar*, The New York Times, 31 December, 1928.

9. Braff, Richard E, "A Lon Chaney Index", *Films in Review*, no. 21, April 1970, p. 228.

10. *Motion Picture News*, 25 December, 1920.

11. Bodeen, DeWitt, "Lon Chaney, Man of a Thousand Faces", *Focus on Film*, no. 3, May–August, 1970, p. 26.

12. Hall, Mordaunt, review of *The Mystic*, The New York Times, 31 August, 1925.

13. Hall, Mordaunt, review of *The Black Bird*, The New York Times, 1 February, 1928.

14. Hall, Mordaunt, review of *The Big City*, The New York Times, 26 March, 1928.

15. Bodeen, "Lon Chaney", p. 29.

16. Hall, Mordaunt, review of *Outside the Law*, The New York Times, 1 September, 1930.

17. Gifford, Denis, *A Pictorial History of Horror Movies*, London: Hamlyn, 1973, p. 68.

18. Hall, Mordaunt, review of *The Unholy Three*, The New York Times, 4 August, 1925.

19. Sadoul, Georges, *Dictionary of Film Makers*, Peter Norris trans. and ed., Berkeley, California: University of California Press, 1972, p. 395.

20. Hall, *The Unholy Three*.

21. Hall, Mordaunt, review of *The Show*, The New York Times, 14 May, 1927.

22. Geltzer, "Tod Browning", p. 415.

23. Gilson, Paul, quoted in Jean-Claude Romer, "Tod Browning", *Bizarre*, nos. 24–25, 1962, p. 4. My translation from the French.

24. Bodeen, "Lon Chaney", p. 28.

25. Hall, Mordaunt, review of *The Unknown*, The New York Times, 13 June, 1927.

26. Gifford, *A Pictorial History of Horror Movies*, p. 95.

27. Thomas, John, "Gobble, Gobble… One of Us!", in *Focus on the Horror Film*, Roy Huss and TJ Ross eds., Trenton, NJ: Prentice-Hall, 1972, pp. 136–137.

28. Thomas, "Gobble, Gobble", p. 137.

29. Thomas, "Gobble, Gobble", pp. 137–138.

30. Clarens, Carlos, *Horror Movies: An Illustrated Survey*, London: Panther Books, 1971, p. 108.

31. Harrison's Reports, 16 July, 1931, cited in the 1930s volume of the *AFI Catalog*.

32. *Motion Picture Herald*, 23 July, 1932, p. 48, cited in the 1930s volume of the *AFI Catalog*.

33. Review of *Freaks*, *Daily Variety*, 12 July, 1932.

34. Nugent, Frank S, review of *The Devil Doll*, *The New York Times*, 8 August, 1936.

35. Baxter, John, *Hollywood in the Thirties*, New York: Paperback Library, 1970, p. 101.

36. Butler, Ivan, *Horror in the Cinema*, New York: Paperback Library, 1971, p. 71.

37. Huss, Roy, "Vampire's Progress", in *Focus on the Horror Film*, pp. 50–52.

38. Gifford, *A Pictorial History of Horror Movies*, p. 82.

39. Huss, "Vampire's Progress", p. 56.

40. Huss, "Vampire's Progress", p. 53.

41. Huss, "Vampire's Progress", p. 51.

42. Butler, *Horror in the Cinema*, p. 44.

43. Gifford, *A Pictorial History of Horror Movies*, p. 68.

44. Butler, *Horror in the Cinema*, pp. 35–36.

45. Cited from Bela Lugosi's autobiography by the *AFI Catalog of Feature Films 1921–1930*.

46. Nugent, Frank S, review of *Miracles for Sale*, *The New York Times*, 10 August, 1939.

47. According to close family friend Mrs William S Hart Sr (widow of the silent cowboy star), because of his scars from the 1917 accident, Browning refused to appear in public wearing shorts or a bathing suit. Interview in Los Angeles, May 1974.

48. Sarris, *The American Cinema*, p. 229.

49. Browning, Tod, quoted in "Motion Picture Classic", March 1928, in Gifford, *A Pictorial History of Horror Movies*, p. 71.

50. Browning, Tod, quoted in Sadoul, *Dictionary of Film Makers*, p. 32; and in Romer, "Tod Browning", p. 4.

51. Robinson, David, *Hollywood in the Twenties*, New York: Paperback Library, 1970, p. 125.

52. Mrs William S Hart Sr. Interview in Los Angeles, May 1974.

53. Ulmer, Edgar G, "Karloff, Lugosi, Browning et Whale", in *Le Cinema Fantastique*, René Predal ed., Paris: Éditions Seghers, 1970, pp. 266–267. My translation from the French.

54. Ulmer, "Karloff, Lugosi, Browning et Whale", p. 266.

55. Thalberg, Irving, quoted in Gifford, *A Pictorial History of Horror Movies*, p. 78.

56. Shipman, David, *The Great Movie Stars: The Golden Years*, New York: Crown, 1970, p. 99.

57. Geltzer, "Tod Browning", p. 412.

58. Clarens, *Horror Movies*, p. 106.

59. Ulmer, "Karloff, Lugosi, Browning et Whale", p. 267.

60. Romer, "Tod Browning", p. 6.

61. Mrs William S Hart Sr. Interview in Los Angeles, May 1974.

62. Locan, Clarence A, "The Lon Chaney I Knew", *Photoplay*, November 1930, p. 60.

63. "Lon Chaney Obituary", *The New York Times*, 26 August, 1930.

64. Shipman, *The Great Movie Stars*, p. 100.

65. Mrs William S Hart, Sr. Interview in Los Angeles, May 1974.

66. Geltzer, "Tod Browning", pp. 410–416.

67. Ulmer, "Karloff, Lugosi, Browning et Whale", pp. 266–267.

68. Sadoul, Dictionary of Film Makers, p. 32.

69. "Tod Browning Obituary", *Daily Variety*, 10 October, 1962.

TOD BROWNING
AND THE SLAPSTICK GENRE

Boris Henry

Before becoming a film director, Tod Browning acted in at least 50 short slapstick movies, working with actors whom he would later direct, his past as a slapstick actor thus becoming incorporated into his career as a filmmaker. Amongst these actors, Edward Dillon was the author of most of Browning's short films; he himself acted in half of them, and later played the character of Jeff in Browning's own *Iron Man*, 1931. Max Davidson also acted in several of the short films: as the police superintendant in Dillon's *Casey's Vendetta*, 1914, then as the libidinous police officer, with rolling eyes and exaggerated facial expressions, in Dillon's *Bill Joins the WWWs*, 1914. He is also the sinister fortune teller in Dillon's *Sunshine Dad*, 1916—sinister to the point of caricature. In the movies directed by Tod Browning, he plays Scaramouche in *Puppets*, 1916, and the role of Ferdinand Brandeis in *No Woman Knows*, 1921. In the latter melodrama, Davidson plays the role of a Jewish businessman who ruins his health trying to keep his business from floundering. Here, Davidson brings drama to the screen by accentuated looks and facial expressions, an evocative echo of the technique he used in some of his slapstick movies.

Like most Hollywood actors in the 1910s to the 1930s, some of those who play in Tod Browning's movies have a slapstick background, in particular those who acted in Mack Sennet's Keystone films: Wallace Beery, Ford Sterling, Polly Moran, Wheeler Oakman, Raymond Griffith, Kalla Pasha, Mae Busch, Wallace MacDonald, and Laura La Varnie, to name a few.[1] If most of the time Browning casts these actors in dramatic roles, some aspects of their acting reveal that they had started out as comic performers—Wallace Beery's villains in *The Virgin of Stamboul*, 1920, *White Tiger*, 1923, and *Drifting*, 1923 are each a case in point. Similarly, in his turn as Roy Donovan in *White Tiger*, Raymond Griffith integrates a clumsiness that is typically burlesque. Polly Moran, too, as a flower girl in *The Blackbird*, 1926, and a maid in *London After Midnight*, 1927, is irresistibly comic; while Kalla Pasha as the Strong Man behind the bar in *The Wicked Darling*, 1919, and the lost soul Babe, with a teddy bear at his side, in *West of Zanzibar*, 1928, also recalls earlier slapstick routines.

Moreover, Browning authored screenplays for slapstick films such as Dillon's *Sunshine Dad* and John Emerson's *The Mystery of the Leaping Fish*, 1916.[2] He continued to work with other authors of the slapstick tradition, such as Al Boasberg, a gagman who worked on Buster Keaton's movies and who with Edgar Allan Woolf wrote the additional dialogues in *Freaks*, 1932, softening the original script by Willis Goldbeck and Leon Gordon with a comic touch.

Stills from (top) *The Mystery of the Leaping Fish* and (bottom) *Sunshine Dad*, for which Tod Browning wrote the screenplays.

Although Browning's films may on the surface have little in common with the slapstick genre, aside fom the actors who reappeared in them, several elements are apparent in his work as a director and writer that recall directly either the short films in which he acted, or other movies in the slapstick genre. In *The Unholy Three*, 1925, for example, when a fight occurs in the side-show, a spectator shows her support for Hercules by beating herself, directly recalling a similar scene in *Bill Manages a Prizefighter*, which Edward Dillon made with Browning in 1914. Likewise, the last shot of *The Show*, 1927, with its play around a fake beard that gets in the way of a closing kiss between the two main characters, is similar to a gag in *The Mystery of the Leaping Fish*, for which he wrote the screenplay. In *The Blackbird*, it would not be surprising if the fights that Lon Chaney as Dan Tate mimes between his two characters (The Blackbird and The Bishop) were inspired by Max Linder's performance in *Be My Wife*, 1921. In the latter film, Linder similarly mimes a struggle between two roles played by the same character—snatching his own cap and trying to strangle himself, pulling down curtains and throwing lamps to the floor in the process. In an interesting reversal of this relationship, George Jeske's 1923 film *Under Two Jags*, with Stan Laurel, is very likely a parody of the film *Under Two Flags*, directed by Browning a year earlier.

On a broader view, some scenes in Tod Browning's films are archetypical of burlesque cinema: a barman kicks a customer out of his establishment in *The Wicked Darling*; tramps row amongst themselves; a drunk totters unsteadily, notices suddenly that he is going the wrong way and turns on his heels in *The Blackbird*. In the same film, the simpering West End Bertie, a fake gentleman, makes clumsy and exaggeratedly seductive gestures, constantly gesticulating— his hands combing through his hair, stretching out, pointing his fingers, in a gestural language typical of slapstick performance.

Max Linder in *Be My Wife*, 1921, which inspired Lon Chaney's fights with himself in Tod Browning's *The Blackbird*.

Another obviously borrowed technique consists in the deployment of one or several characters whose principle function is to make the audience laugh; in Browning's work, their presence serves to relieve tension. The comedy they bring to the scene is dependent largely upon their physicality; their characteristic clothes, their behaviour, their unusual gestures, and especially the faces they pull. More often than not, this comic character is clumsy, ill at ease and shy—yet lucid. They are just passing by—a drunk, a servant, a porter, a spectator—or otherwise, they are often a secondary character, such as Herr Bauer, the violin teacher in *No Woman Knows*; Martin, the sanatorium keeper in *Dracula*, 1931; Roscoe, the stammerer in *Freaks*; Pinky, the workman in *Fast Workers*, 1933; or Quinn, the policeman in *Miracles for Sale*, 1939. They might be part of a duo—like "Daddy" Moffat, Paul Porter's partner in *The Man Under Cover*, 1922—or it might be the interaction between two characters that provides the comic element, for example Dr Doskil and Jan, the butler, in *Mark of The Vampire*, 1935, or Inspector Gavigan and Dad Morgan in *Miracles for Sale*.[3] In pure slapstick tradition, it is often the members of an institution whose role is to provoke laughter—above all policemen, characterised as 'cops', the absurdity of the characters making the authority they represent ridiculous in turn. These policemen hurry but achieve little, turning in inefficient circles—literally in *The Mystery of the Leaping Fish*, symbolically in later films. They are entirely ineffectual in their fight against crime, sometimes even communicating with the villains without realising their identity. *The Devil Doll*, as a typical example of this comic device, can be seen as a hymn to the ridiculousness of the police force.

Seen from a broader perspective, whether it comes from his past as a slapstick actor or not, some of the main figures, procedures and themes of Tod Browning's movies recall those of the slapstick genre: a rapid tempo for the action; the taste for repetition; the double and the notion of duality; the importance of gesture; bodily transformation, disguise, the diminutive, miniaturisation; the main character's loneliness and inability to fit into society; a ferocious antagonism towards the establishment....[4] Furthermore, Browning incorporates elements of slapstick without necessarily using them to comic effect, such as unexpected gestures, or the confrontation of opposite elements; two attitudes, two different concepts of the body create discrepancies, double meanings and confusions.[5] Browning's work, then, uses these devices for their potentially comic effect at times, but moves beyond a purely humourous intent.

The irony in these films arises from the intentional discrepancy between what is obviously suggested or announced—by an intertitle, a dialogue or a plan—and what is seen on the screen, or between what the character says and what he or she does. These discrepancies create a voluntary *mismatching* in the role played by the character and/or in the account.[6] At other times, and against all expectations, language and visual representation are conflated, so that metaphor is literalised—such as in *The Mystery of the Leaping Fish*, where the gangster described as "the gentleman rolling in wealth" is seen sleeping and covered with a mountain of banknotes.

More simply, Browning visibly used slapstick movies' often melodramatic frameworks, and the exaggeration of situations through exaggerated gesture and physicality. In Edward Dillon's *Casey's Vendetta*, Casey the Policeman walks by a fruit stand and proceeds to taste the wares, biting into them and throwing them away without paying, while the fruit seller Pedro (played by Browning) is distracted by Nina, who runs the fruit stand beside his own. When Pedro realises what Casey is doing, he approaches to confront him, leaving the path clear for Casey to flirt with Nina in turn—prompting a murderous Pedro to kidnap him. Is it not a similar situation—laughable, but pushed to its extreme—which incites Alonzo to cut off his own arms for love of Nanon and then to try to kill Malabar in *The Unknown*, or which leads Phroso to bring up Maizie in a dump because he thinks she is the daughter his wife had by her lover, in *West of Zanzibar*? If, as Petr Král writes, "the 'subversion' [of the burlesque] consisted in reminding us that in spite of decorum the body existed", the subversion of Browning's films follow a similar logic, the body being in both of these cases at the centre of the show.[7]

Perhaps it is because he began his career in the cinema in slapstick or, hypothetically, in variety shows and the circus, that Tod Browning considers the body and gesture so important, studying them and emphasising one or several characteristics. Perhaps it is also from slapstick that he develops the way he structures certain films—particularly those he made with Lon Chaney—starting from the characterisation of a body and its actions. Similarly, as Petr Král remarks: "Many old farces were first 'written' by the protagonists' bodies; it is with their flesh itself, in a way, that they create the space for an exchange between imaginary and reality."[8] Although humour about the body can be expressed verbally, it is more often expressed immediately, physically. It becomes the object of a play on the nature of the body itself, on its size and its movements. Movement expresses the nature or the state of the body, even its culture. The latter commands and organises them and is a source of comedy; the body might be perceived as an excessively programmed machine, like that of Dad Morgan in *Miracles for Sale*; or, conversely, like a machine out of control, moving like a disjointed puppet, such as the staccato jumping and twisting of the drunken Doc in *West of Zanzibar*.

The play of transforming the body also produces comic effects, often using make-up and costume—equally important to the burlesque and to Browning—as a starting point. Just as Browning himself played roles in which he was dressed up as a woman, in the films he directed Echo in *The Unholy Three*, Paul Lavond in *The Devil Doll*, and Roscoe in *Freaks* do the same. In these films, Browning sketches the comic effects of such costumes but doesn't exploit them fully, rather conferring upon them a quality that goes from the fantastic to the burlesque. Another typically burlesque motif is the symbolic or imitative handicapping of a body by the removal of some of its parts.[9] In Browning's movies, those transformations are frequent—such as the clown's new act in *Freaks*, in which his head disappears by being pounded down with a mallet. Here, we encounter "the fantastic spirit of the slapstick" described by Jean-Loup Bourget, which he particularly observes in Charlie Chaplin's *Behind The Screen*, 1916, as well as in Charles H Rogers' *Them Thar Hills*, 1934. In those movies, characters are transformed into grotesque monsters through the use of chairs, a helmet, feathers, hair and a plumber's bell. In a similar fashion, in *The Wicked Darling*, a man is covered with objects that follow the form of his body, lending him a weirdly voluminous appearance.[10] In Browning's movies, as in the burlesque, "it will be the body that receives the reward or the punishment, that will be the way of the Law".[11] Thus, in the comedy of assimilation pushed to its extreme, as is the case in cartoons, "the victims of violent blows [take] the contours of objects that have fallen upon them and have modelled them under their weight".[12] It is the same process in Browning's movies; the physical shocks, or more often emotional shocks to which characters are subject take on corporal form, so that characters are literally transformed—because Nanon cannot stand men's arms, Alonzo gets definitively rid of his in *The Unknown*; Cleopatra marries the dwarf Hans for money but refuses to integrate herself among the freaks and become "one of us", and ends up being transformed by them into a monster.

In both slapstick and Tod Browning's movies we also see the importance of animality and the presence of animals. Petr Král notes: "In general, when animals' intervention occurs it marks the final and culminating peak of the catastrophe where the comic engulfs its surrounding world and destroys its 'established order'."[13] The lion's presence in Edward Dillon's *Sunshine Dad* seems to exemplify this, as does the gorilla in *The Unholy Three* when he finally kills Hercules after the latter strangles Tweedledee.[14]

Just as the intrigues of many slapstick films are an excuse to showcase a succession of gags, are not the intrigues of Tod Browning's movies the pretext for sequences of bodily humour? But unlike the slapstick genre, where the gags that succeed each other can function independently of each other, in Browning's films, the physical gags form a unity, a thread leading to the intrigue.

The Unholy Three: Harry Earles as Tweedledee.

The use of the burlesque in Tod Browning's films can be seen to serve a utilitarian end. It helps introduce the arrival in a place, it brings bodies together—such as the gag involving the sugar bowls in *Miracles for Sale*—and it leads us to the main issues of the movie. While those elements of burlesque can be a source of laughter, serving to relieve tension, they are often also a tragic component. Along with other elements, they form an essential element of the 'Browningian Universe'.

Translated from the French by Catherine Gamonnet and Helen Bouvÿ; translation edited by Jennifer Panara.

⋈ NOTES

1. Mae Busch plays Rosie O'Grady in *The Unholy Three*, 1925, and a small part in *West of Zanzibar*, 1928. Later she joined the "Hal Roach Comedy All-Stars" and acted in numerous films with Stan Laurel and Oliver Hardy, sometimes playing Hardy's wife, in particular in *Unaccustomed As We Are*, 1929, *Sons of the Desert*, 1933 and *The Bohemian Girl*, 1936.

2. The burlesque is very likely introduced by the presence of a well-known comic actor (De Wolf Hopper in *Sunshine Dad* and Douglas Fairbanks in *The Mystery of the Leaping Fish*) rather than by Tod Browning's skills.

3. In physical appearance and performance style, this duo is somewhat a precursor to Laurel and Hardy's work in the mid-1920s. The famous duo is supposed to have been brought together by Leo McCarey, who was an assistant to Browning in nine films, from *Bonnie, Bonnie Lassie*, 1919 till *Drifting*, 1923, including *The Man Under Cover*.

4. As an actor, Browning plays with costume and make-up, and several of his characters dress as women (such as in *Ethel's Teacher* and *The Million Dollar Bride*, both 1914, Edward Dillon), or as a Hindu (as in Dillon's *The Mascot*, also 1914).

5. Upon recognising Phroso in *West of Zanzibar*, Crane, cracking a big laugh, slaps his thigh, enjoying the situation as a joke, whereas "Fingers" O'Dell, pleased to see the police coming to fetch him, waits for them at the front door to harangue them (*Outside the Law*, 1930).

6. For example, characters who steal or lie will criticise the same behaviour when they become the victims themselves (Echo in *The Unholy Three*, or Madame Rosalie La Grange in *The Thirteenth Chair*, 1929).

7. Král, Petr, *Le Burlesque ou Morale de la tarte à la crème*, Paris: Stock, 1984, p. 237.

8. Král, *Le Burlesque ou Morale de la tarte à la crème*, p. 63.

9. During the classy evening party when Roy Donovan brakes into the safe, he pretends to be deaf and mute and makes hand gestures to imitate sign language (*White Tiger*).

10. Bourget, Jean-Loup, *Hollywood, années 30—Du krach à Pearl Harbor*, Renens: 5 Continents/Hatier, 1986, p. 83.

11. Desbarats, Carole, "La vitesse burlesque et le chaos du monde", *Cahier de notes sur… 5 burlesques*, Paris: Les enfants de cinéma/Yellow Now, p. 4.

12. Mars, François "Autopsie du gag I", *Cahiers du cinéma*, no. 113, November 1960, p. 31.

13. Král, *Le Burlesque ou Morale de la tarte à la crème*, p. 115.

14. To escape the lion in *Sunshine Dad*, the widow Marrimore goes to the bathroom and hides in the bathtub. The lion, still on her heels, comes in and grabs the housecoat under which she was hiding, but doesn't do her any harm. The lion's owner then enters the bathroom and orders it out. The latter obeys…. The whole scene is quite hilarious. There is a similar scene in Howard Hawks' *Hatari*, 1962, when Sonia, the tamed cheetah, pays a visit to Anna Maria "Dallas" D'Allesandro, who is in the bathroom.

Staging Deception

Theatrical Illusionism
in Browning's Films of the 1920s

Matthew Solomon

⋈ BROWNING AND HOUDINI ⋈

In the November 1906 issue of the *Conjurers' Monthly Magazine*, the following item appeared in the column "Answers to Various Questions": "Browning. We do not know the present address of 'Milwaukee Rapp'. If you mean Augustavus Rapp, his permanent address is Hesperia, Mich."[1] The reply was written by the magazine's editor, none other than Harry Houdini, the famous Hungarian-American escape artist (born Ehrich Weiss) who published this magicians' monthly while performing in vaudeville theatres. Was Houdini's answer addressed to Charles Albert "Tod" Browning? Did Browning, like Houdini and Augustus (a.k.a. Augustavus) Rapp, identify as part of the magic fraternity?[2] Browning had been an itinerant entertainer for nearly a decade in 1906, stints that included (he would later claim) handcuff escapes in tent shows and as an assistant to several prominent theatrical magicians. According to biographers David Skal and Elias Savada, Browning was living in Louisville in 1906, having recently married, and may have been looking for work.[3] Was Browning trying to contact former acquaintances in the magic profession through the pages of the *Conjurers' Monthly Magazine*, perhaps with the intention of going on the road with another magic show? Another possibility is that Browning was seeking employment in several show business areas in which he had previous experience. As Robert Bogdan suggests, with respect to another show business periodical, "Most amusement industry workers were not committed exclusively to any specific type of show—they were simply in the amusement business, waiting for each week's *Billboard* to check out employment prospects and see where their itinerant friends were working."[4]

While it is not possible to confirm that Houdini's response was indeed meant for *Tod* Browning, it is interesting to note the parallels between their professional backgrounds, as both came of age as performers in an interconnected network of cheap amusements that included circuses, fairground shows, concert saloons, and dime museums at the turn of the century. After Browning went to work as a film comedian for another Louisville native, DW Griffith, at the Biograph

OUR FIRST

Tod Browning posing with a cutout used in *The Show*—one of the tamer illusions from his 1927 film. Courtesy of Elias Savada.

movie studios in New York, his beginnings in this carnival *milieu* were often highlighted—an association that would continue throughout his entire career as a film director. One of the first published biographical accounts of Browning —a brief article about Browning, the film comic, that appeared in a 1914 movie fan magazine—describes him not so much as a 'carnie', but as a sideshow escape artist:

> Under the big top he formed a partnership with a young man who did the handcuff act. From him he learned the art of freeing himself from manacles without using a key or breaking the handcuffs. It was this trick which first won him fame.... Browning and his friend... made a tremendous hit. Shortly after they left the circus and for two months throve on the proceeds of their handcuff exhibitions.[5]

This account provides another intriguing parallel—however fictionalised Browning's partner and their exploits may have been—with Houdini, whose most successful tricks were escapes from handcuffs and manacles. Later, when Houdini began a career in the movies, he and Browning would work more or less concurrently with the same producer, BA Rolfe, who produced the Houdini serial *The Master Mystery*, 1919, as well as several films that Browning directed for Metro, including *The Eyes of Mystery*, 1918.

⌨ ILLUSIONS AND ILLUSIONISTS ⌨

A number of Browning's films of the 1920s contain striking reproductions of theatrical—or quasi-theatrical—illusions that are staged not only for the spectators within the films, but also for the contemporaneous viewers of the films themselves. These films involve elaborate deceptions that take place at the level of *mise-en-scène*, and often centre on spectacular set-pieces. In *White Tiger*, 1923, it is the false chess-playing automaton which the protagonists use to gain entrance to—and ultimately, to burgle—high society homes. In *The Show*, 1927, it is the trick beheading that takes place as part of a sideshow magic sketch. In *The Unknown*, 1927, it is the tightly laced corset that a fugitive criminal uses to masquerade as an armless freak. In the lost film *London After Midnight*, 1927, it is the contrived haunted house in which a detective and his assistant, dressed in elaborate disguises, ensnare a murderer. In each case, the working of the trick is revealed to the spectators of the film, who are shown 'how it is done' while characters within the film are deceived.

Given Browning's penchant for detailed reconstructions of the mystifying spectacles of show culture, his "experience of the circus and of vaudeville would be decisive", Jacques Goimard specifies, "with respect to one class which is dear to him among all, that of magicians".[6] As Goimard implies, the magician is a recurrent figure in Browning's *ouevre*. In addition to *Miracles for Sale*, 1939, a murder mystery set in the realm of theatrical magic, magicians appear frequently in Browning's silent films. In *The Blackbird*, 1926, a stage magician is seen as part of a concert saloon variety show that takes place in a seedy London district. Having seemingly just made an object disappear, he displays both sides of the cloth—a trick that is met by apathetic stares from the beer-drinking spectators. In Browning's silent films, the prototypical figure of the stage magician is found most clearly in *West of Zanzibar*, 1928. It is worth noting that before being crippled in an accident, the music-hall illusionist Phroso (Lon Chaney) resembles not so much the archetypal Mephistophelian visage of Herrmann the Great, but rather—with his finely waxed moustache—looks much like Browning himself appeared in photographs of the late 1920s.

Here, I foreground the relationship between Browning and theatrical magic, noting that prior to his career as a director, Browning was himself a magician; but also that when he began writing and directing films, he had already forsaken magic for comedy. "When I quit a thing, I quit", Browning reportedly said after making his last film, "I wouldn't walk across the street to see a movie."[7] His break with magic seems no less decisive. Despite being touted in studio publicity of the early 1930s as "an enthusiastic amateur magician… one of the most adept prestidigitators in an industry which boasts many devotees of the art of magic", Browning appears not to have been linked with the Society of Magicians that flourished in Los Angeles.[8]

Browning's reclusiveness certainly prevented him from joining many organisations, but more to the point, his films explicitly violate the magician's professional code, which stipulates that the workings of stage illusions be concealed from the spectator. As Alain Garsault points out: "Browning is interested in the surprise caused by the exposition of a trick and the revelation of the mechanism of a trick."[9] In contrast with Houdini, who sought to suppress public exposures of magic in various media, Browning did not hesitate to expose the methods of magic tricks on screen. Browning's approach to the presentation of illusions has affinities with a more revelatory mode of performance represented by sideshow magician and contortionist Marvin Smith. Smith would plunge several large knives into a box containing a person who later emerged unharmed, and immediately afterward—for spectators who paid an additional fee—would remove the side of the box, exposing how the trick was done.[10]

The original eighteenth century chess automaton, which inspired both Edgar Allan Poe's *exposé* and Browning's *White Tiger*.

♜ INSIDE THE AUTOMATON ♜

In *White Tiger*, two different sequences expose the hidden workings of a chess-playing automaton, then detail the way in which its human operator is hidden from the view of onlookers. Though neither Wolfgang von Kempelen nor Johann Maelzel, who exhibited the original chess-playing automaton, respectively, during the late eighteenth and early nineteenth century, were magicians, the automaton has been of considerable interest to magicians as a piece of quasi-magical apparatus. The automaton chess-player is discussed in the memoirs of the French magician Jean-Eugène Robert-Houdin.[11] Robert-Houdin's apocryphal account of the figure's history formed the basis of the play *La Czarine*, for which the magician constructed a replica of the famous automaton.[12] Magic historian Henry Ridgely Evans claims that the automaton chess-player "belongs to the realm of modern magic… for many famous prestidigitators of the past included automaton figures in their entertainments—pseudo-androids like the chess-player".[13] Milbourne Christopher adds: "The Hungarian baron never claimed to be a conjurer, yet he invented the first great cabinet illusion; introduced revolutionary techniques of concealment and misdirection."[14]

In 1836, Edgar Allan Poe published an *exposé* of the faux-automaton, "Maelzel's Chess-Player", which was then being exhibited in the United States. Though Poe's essay seems to have been derived from previously published exposures rather than observations of the automaton, its clear argument that the figure was operated by a person is a definite precursor to the ratiocinative process of detection which the detective C Auguste Dupin exercises in such later Poe tales as "The Murders in the Rue Morgue" and "The Purloined Letter".[15] Neil Harris cites Poe's *exposé* of the chess-playing automaton as an example of the "operational aesthetic" that animated PT Barnum's "humbugs".[16] The "operational aesthetic", Harris explains, "was a form of intellectual exercise, stimulating even when literal truth could not be determined…. Barnum understood, that the opportunity… to discover how deception was practised, was more exciting than the discovery of fraud itself."[17] Like Barnum, Harris writes, "Poe… was both an exposer and deceiver. Common to both modes was the interest in problem-solving."[18]

In *White Tiger*, Sylvia Donovan (Priscilla Dean), who claims to be the daughter of criminal Count Donelli (Wallace Beery), is a pickpocket in a London wax museum where The Kid (Raymond Griffith) owns and operates the automaton chess-player that is one of its most popular attractions. Like the wax museum scene in Maurice Tourneur's *The Whip*, 1917, the film blurs the distinction between moving people and motionless wax figures. An early scene cleverly juxtaposes the stealthy pilfering of the pickpocket with the conspicuously unmoving paraffin policeman that stands guard in the room. Though the wax figures that line the museum and its Chamber of Horrors are deceptively life-like, the mechanical chess-player is but a crude imitation of a human figure, mounted on a large wheeled cabinet. Browning's use of a wax museum setting highlights the role of misdirection in the construction of the automaton chess-player that Poe so incisively identifies in his essay:

> The external appearance, and, especially, the deportment of the Turk, are, when we consider them as imitations of *life*, but very indifferent imitations. The countenance evinces no ingenuity, and is surpassed, in its resemblance to the human face, by the very commonest of wax-works. The arm, particularly, performs its operations in an exceedingly stiff, awkward, jerking, and rectangular manner…. What this design was it is not difficult to conceive. Were the Automaton life-like in its motions, the spectator would be more apt to attribute its operations to their true cause (that is, to human agency within), than he is now, when the awkward and rectangular manoeuvres convey the idea of pure and unaided mechanism.[19]

An intertitle in *White Tiger* informs the viewer: "Most baffling of all the exhibits—the mechanical chess-player."

White Tiger: The Kid operating the mechanical chess player from his hiding place within the automaton, and making his escape through the cabinet beneath the chess player.

Successive shots reveal the "mystifying mechanics" of the purported automaton, showing The Kid in close-up working a lever that causes the arm of the figure to point to the appropriate piece on the board. After defeating his opponent, The Kid crawls through a panel in the side of the figure and into an adjacent room through a trapdoor. Unlike Robert-Houdin, who said that the original automaton was operated by a man whose legs had been amputated, Browning's representation of the chess-player follows Poe's contention that the automaton could in fact conceal a normal-sized person. One of the lynchpins of Poe's argument is the suspicious presence of candles on the chessboard, from which he concludes, "so strong a light is requisite to enable the man within to see through the transparent material (probably fine gauze) of which the breast of the Turk is composed".[20] In the *mise-en-scène* of the film, placement of several candles on the chessboard nicely dovetails with Poe's argument while providing the diegetic motivation for a shimmering point of view shot through the translucent fabric of the figure's chest. Years earlier, Browning claimed: "Light should come from natural sources and should not, as if by magic, appear

The Kid's view from within the automaton and Fifth Avenue high society celebrating the chess-player.

for no reason at all."[21] A surviving reel of *The Exquisite Thief*, 1919, suggests that Browning had previously used candlelight as a means of achieving sophisticated lighting effects.

A subsequent scene of *White Tiger* has the clearest correspondences with Poe's published exposé of Maelzel's chess-player. Count Donelli, his daughter, and The Kid (who is introduced as Donelli's secretary) take the automaton to the United States, where it is a hit with Fifth Avenue society. The automaton allows them to gain entrance to a mansion while The Kid lies cramped inside. As Donelli shows the automaton to his wealthy hosts, he alliteratively offers "to expose to… view the marvelous mechanism of this mystifying mechanical automaton". Donelli opens a panel on the base of the figure, revealing a mass of clockwork that purportedly animates the machine, which he then sets in motion. Poe, in order to explain how a normal person could be concealed inside the automaton, fixes on "the routine adopted by the exhibitor in disclosing the interior of the box", pointing out that the exhibitor never showed the entire inside of the cabinet at any one time.[22] From the arrangement of several doors on the box, Poe deduces the solution of the enigma of the chess-player, identifying the way in which its operator could escape detection: "His body is situated behind the dense machinery… which machinery is so contrived as to slip *en masse*, from the main compartment… as occasion may require."[23] Correspondingly, as Donelli closes the panel, a close-up shows The Kid crawling across a dark narrow space, and sliding the still whirring clockwork into the place he had formerly occupied. Donelli then opens an adjacent panel, revealing a mass of gears (the same arrangement of clockwork seen previously through the other panel). The Kid then sits up into the torso of the figure, ready to operate the chess-player.

Of all Browning's films, *White Tiger* is perhaps the most Poe-like of what one commentator described as the director's "decidedly Poe-like narratives".[24] Written by Browning and screenwriter Charles Kenyon, based on an original story by Browning, the film's second half distinctly echoes Poe's "The Tell-Tale Heart". While the three thieves hide out in a mountain cabin with the jewels they have stolen from their society patrons, mutually suspicious, they stash the jewels beneath a floorboard so that each is able to make sure that the others do not abscond with them. More than the choice of hiding-places, "between the scantlings", Browning borrows the maddening sense of being constantly watched which haunts the protagonist of Poe's famous story.[25] Browning protracts this sleepless tension and triangulates it cinematically between the three characters in the highly claustrophobic concluding scenes of *White Tiger*, which are confined entirely to the inside of the cabin. During his career as a director, Browning was compared to Poe because, as one often-cited account states, "The murky, the grotesque, the gruesome, the mystifying, is his stock in trade."[26] In a studio biographical survey from the late 1930s, Browning listed Poe as his "favorite classical author".[27] Just as Poe's work evidences a dialectical relationship between deception and detection, Browning's films counterbalance mystification with exposure. Browning's cinema is characterised by the "operational aesthetic" not simply because it illuminates the material processes used to deceive and to mystify, but because it is consistent with what Harris describes as "an approach to experience that equated beauty with information and technique, accepting guile because it was more complicated than candor".[28]

⋈ THE MAGIC OF DISGUISE ⋈

With its careful attention to concealment and misdirection, the *exposé* of the automaton chess-player in *White Tiger* is as much the revelation of an illusion as it is the unmasking of a disguise. Disguise is one aspect of the structural dichotomy between reality and appearance that Stuart Rosenthal identifies in Browning's films.[29] Like the automaton Q in *The Master Mystery*, which is unmasked to reveal a person inside, the automaton chess-player is a human being disguised as a machine. As a film performer, Browning himself was described in 1914 as having "a genius for make-up… there is virtually no limit to the number and variety of weird absurdities which he is capable of putting over when the opportunity offers".[30] Chaney, whose career as a film actor began at the same time as Browning's, was similarly characterised in a 1917 account as a magician of make-up, capable of assuming nearly any imaginable guise:

> You've heard of the magician Merlin, who could change himself
> into any form he chose? Well, Chaney is the Merlin of the
> Movies, and he doesn't have to depend on any cabalistic signs
> or mystic fireworks either…. That funny little old dusty, musty
> dressing room of his at Universal City, with its myriad make-up
> appurtenances, is a veritable conjurer's castle. Here he mixes
> his magic concoctions and dolls up in his magic rags.[31]

Browning made two films with Chaney at Universal, *The Wicked Darling*, 1919, and *Outside the Law*, 1920.

In a number of Browning's later films with Chaney, performed transformations lay bare the deceptive process of disguise. Unlike Wallace Worsley's *The Penalty*, 1920, in which Chaney plays the role of a man whose legs have been amputated, or Browning's *Outside the Law*, in which he plays a double role as two entirely different individuals, Browning films like *The Blackbird* and *The Unknown* place the act of masquerade onscreen, explicitly revealing the visual deception to the viewer. In *The Blackbird*, criminal Dan

The Blackbird: Lon Chaney playing the titular character playing The Bishop. Courtesy of the Lilly Library, Indiana University, Bloomington, Indiana.

Tate (Chaney), The Blackbird, periodically assumes the persona of The Bishop, who hobbles about on a crutch, in order to elude the police. While other characters in the film, of course, never see the two purported brothers together, the viewer is given immediate access to the acts of quick-change through which The Blackbird transforms himself into the cripple The Bishop behind closed doors.

The Unknown begins in the centre of the ring of a Madrid gypsy circus with a spectacular exhibition of marksmanship and knife-throwing executed by the armless Alonzo (Chaney), entirely with his feet. But, when Alonzo retires to his wagon for the evening—after repelling an attack by the whip-wielding manager of the circus—it is revealed to the viewer that Alonzo's arms are actually bound to his sides by a tightly laced corset, which his dwarf friend Cojo (John George) helps him to remove. Alonzo pretends not to have arms in order to conceal a supernumerary thumb that identifies him as a wanted criminal. Although characters within the diegesis of Browning's films are often fooled by an inability to see or to recognise something or someone concealed or disguised, the deception is almost always revealed to the spectator of the film. Citing *The Unknown* and *The Blackbird*, Joël Magny argues: "To trick, to deceive, to make others believe that one is something one is not, that is the profound obsession of the characters of Tod Browning. That is the essence of his *mise-en-scène*: a *mise-en-scène* which the camera uncovers little by little as such, the function of which is to reveal what has been hidden."[32] Browning's films of the 1920s place more emphasis on revealing the processes of physical deception than on foregrounding the sheer displays of the body that punctuate *Freaks*. Unlike the armless woman (Frances O'Connor) in the latter film, Alonzo in *The Unknown* is concealing something that can be exposed through Browning's *mise-en-scène* of revelation. In Browning's silent films, physiologically anomalous performers like John George played comparatively minor roles. Instead it was so-called "gaffed freaks" like "the armless wonder whose arms are tucked under a tight fitting shirt" that were the focus of Browning's stories.[33]

In *London After Midnight*—written by Browning and Waldemar Young from Browning's original story "The Hypnotist"—stage magic and disguise are exposed as parallel means of tricking appearances. Unlike Browning's *Dracula*, 1931, which uses largely cinematic special effects to ultimately present vampirism as scientifically verified 'reality', *London After Midnight* presents apparently supernatural phenomena as the work of stage magic. According to one surviving account of the film:

> The uncanny scenes of the flying 'bat woman', and materialisation of ghosts and vampires were staged by using famous stage illusions adapted to the screen and filming them as they were performed. In no case was trick photography used, the camera filming the 'spirit' illusions just as the eye saw them. Spirit secrets of Houdini, Keller [sic], and other famous magicians went into the making of these uncanny details of the story, Browning being aided in this work by Harry Sharrock, his assistant, and formerly a famous mystifier on the stage.[34]

Created through an elaborate *mise-en-scène* of spirit theatre, the paranormal occurrences seen in the film are staged by police inspector Burke (Chaney) to catch a killer. After he is apprehended, the deceptions are revealed to the viewer as such. Luna (Edna Tichenor), the Bat Girl, turns out to be a variety attraction hired by Burke to perform a series of stunts; as her partner exclaims in an intertitle, "We got more for doing this than we'd earn in a month at the theatre."[35] As Charles Tesson points out, "all is but theatre, palpable matter, a place where the artifice of scenic illusion always ends up giving way to its own unbending reality".[36]

Browning himself explains, with respect to *London After Midnight*, as follows: "Now, nobody believes in ghosts…. But, people *would* believe in your ghost if they found out later he was a detective solving a murder crime. The… audience is not asked to believe the horrible *impossible*, but the horror *possible*."[37] According to a review of the film, Chaney "even lets the audience into secrets of his make-up when, as the detective, he applies a disguise before the eyes of the audience".[38] This highly self-conscious approach to disguise has definite parallels with sensational fiction, as Browning suggests in a 1928 interview:

> Mystery stories appeal to me for the same reason they appeal to the little boy who sits on the back fence reading the harrowing experiences of *Nick Carter*…. They are colorful and exciting, and, with all the camera magic at hand, they are particularly adapted to pictures. I'm particularly lucky in carrying out my ideas by having an artist like Lon to take on guises and disguises of the most grotesque nature.[39]

The Show: Tod Browning posing with his actors in their more conventional personas (left to right) Renée Adorée, Tod Browning, John Gilbert and Lionel Barrymore. Courtesy of Elias Savada.

Much like Victorin Jasset's early film for Éclair, *Nick Carter: Le Guet-Apens*, 1908, in which dime novel detective Nick Carter is seen disguising himself before a mirror in a single shot, donning a wig and fake beard to assume the guise of an old man, Browning stresses the "operational aesthetic" of disguise.

Although Browning may have found "camera magic" useful for other aspects of his sensational stories, it is the camera's power to record Chaney taking on "guises and disguises" which is relevant here. It was not only Chaney's versatility, but also his ability to make quick changes onscreen, Magny specifies, that made him so invaluable for Browning's films:

> If the association between Lon Chaney and Tod Browning has been so fruitful and crowned with success, it is because the actor offered a marvelous subject for the director's *mise-en-scène*: a formidable malleability of the body as well as the face, but also an extraordinary rapidity in changing expression. In a single shot of scarcely several seconds, Chaney is capable of running through an astonishing gamut of contradictory emotions.[40]

In *London After Midnight*, Chaney plays the role of the role-player who personifies deception; but in many Browning films of the 1920s that foreground impersonation, Chaney also resembles the detective of dime novel fiction described by Michael Denning: "The detective, the master of disguise… can be anyone… there is a strong sense that the detective is merely an effect of his different disguises."[41]

⚏ THE POETICS OF REVELATION ⚏

Chaney's onscreen disguises point to the importance of revelation as a fundamental aesthetic principle for Browning that is not specific to his films with Chaney. In *The Show*, Cock Robin (John Gilbert) presides over the Palace of Illusions in a Budapest sideshow. For spectators on the midway, Robin assists a man dressed in oriental garb and a fez in performing an aerial suspension illusion, and then helps holds up a cloth as the woman vanishes from the platform. After a group of people place their coins in the disembodied hand of Cleo and enter the Palace of Illusions, Robin leads them past a series of optical illusions, drawing the curtains on several different cabinets containing different persons: Zela (Zalla Zarana), the Half Lady, a woman who appears to have no body below the waist atop a table; Arachnida (Tichenor), the Human Spider, a large replica of a spider's body on a web, from which protrudes a woman's head; and Neptuna (Betty Boyd), the Queen of the Mermaids, a woman with the tail of a fish apparently underwater. The film does not detail the exact methods of these carnival illusions—which were made by the Thayer Manufacturing Company, a Los Angeles producer of magical apparatus.[42] Subsequent shots showing Zela, Arachnida, and Neptuna cavorting backstage reveal that each illusion contains a fully formed woman.

Exhibits in *The Show*'s Palace of Illusions: (clockwise from top left) the hand of Cleo; Cock Robin and Zela, the half lady; Neptuna the queen of the mermaids; and Arachnida, the human spider. Their 'true forms' are later revealed to the film's audience.

The centerpiece of "The Show" is a magic playlet loosely based on Oscar Wilde's *Salomé* in which Robin plays the role of Jokanaan. Through a carefully choreographed stage illusion, Robin is apparently beheaded, and his severed head placed on a charger. Unlike Charles Bryant's film *Salome*, 1923, in which the beheading of Jokanaan takes place off-screen and the kiss of Salome is shielded from direct view, *The Show* reframes Wilde's play as stage magic. Where set design, costume, and dance (by Alla Nazimova) are preeminent in the former, Browning emphasises the theatrical apparatus used in the process of decapitation and the illusionistic interaction between Salomé (Renée Adorée) and the severed head, which blinks and speaks. The stage illusion involves the use of a mechanical piece of magic apparatus, a number of trick implements, a specially built mirror table, multiple trapdoors, and a series of carefully choreographed substitutions.

The Show exposes the illusionary beheading by aligning the viewer of the film primarily with the view of a privileged backstage observer rather than with the view of a spectator watching "The Show" from the front of the platform. As such, the display of Salome's belly dance is interrupted by shots of Robin backstage, donning a false beard and robe as he prepares to go onstage. As the trick is performed, the illusion is mediated by two onlookers in the wings, one of whom explains to the other how the trick is being accomplished. After cutting a block of wood in two to demonstrate the sharpness of the sword, the executioner deftly substitutes one sword for another while Jokanaan moves the wood out of the way. Although a large chest prevents spectators of "The Show" from seeing the deft exchange, the viewer of *The Show* sees the substitution in close-up. The next shot shows two men watching from the wings, one of whom says to the other, "You see... now he's got the fake sword." Recognising what he

The Show: Renée Adorée and Tod Browning in front of the Palace of Illusions set.

has just seen, the man nods in understanding, while the mass of spectators seen in the next shot, by contrast, looks on as if nothing has yet happened. After Herod gives the order, Jokanaan kneels at the executioner's block, and a basket is placed in front of the block. The film then cuts from the view of the show's spectator to a shot of the two men watching from the wings. Successive close-up shots from this lateral point of view show the foot of the executioner depressing a pedal, which retracts a part of the executioner's block, allowing Jokanaan to adjust his position. The illusionary decapitation is then seen from the point-of-view of the audience. They collectively recoil in horror as Jokanaan's head apparently tumbles into the basket. The executioner covers the body with a sheet, and the film again cuts to the two men in the wings. A shot from their shared point of view reveals Jokanaan crouched beneath the outstretched sheet, placing a fake head in the basket (which has a cutout side) and disappearing through a trapdoor. The audience again draws back in shock as the head is placed on a charger and carried across the stage. The film dissolves to a medium shot of the back of the executioner, who moves aside, revealing the head of Jokanaan on a charger atop a small table facing the kneeling Salomé. Jokanaan closes his eyes and reopens them in close-up.

The illusion of the beheading is further reinforced for spectators of "The Show" and viewers of *The Show* when Jokanaan speaks, saying, "Salomé, thou art a wicked woman" in an intertitle as Salomé embraces his head and the curtain is drawn to the applause of the audience. But, as the spectators move on to watch a snake show beginning on an adjacent platform, the film returns to the scene of the beheading, allowing its viewer to see the deceptive means, which enabled the second part of the stage illusion. A backstage view shows Jokanaan standing up with a cutout 'charger' fastened about his neck, which Salomé helps him to remove. The corner of the table has been cut away, while a carefully placed mirror between its legs makes it appear as if nothing is beneath it. Unlike the audience of spectators in the film, who realise that they have been deceived but do not entirely know how, the viewer of the film sees fully how the trick is done.

◄ BROWNING'S "ARTFUL DECEPTIONS" ►

The turn of the century show culture from which Browning emerged was steeped in a number of different spectacular forms of illusion, some of which no doubt inspired his later films. Studies of Browning tend to identify him simply with the circus sideshow, but his largely unexplored pre-cinematic career in stage magic points to an entirely different context for his work, that illuminates key moments in the director's films of the 1920s.[43] During the nineteenth century, James Cook argues, American mass entertainment was defined in part by what he terms "arts of deception", one of which was stage magic. But Cook stresses that practitioners of "artful deception"—PT Barnum most notable among them— were careful to complement entertaining deceptions with revealing information that hinted at (if not exposed outright) how the deceptions had been constructed:

> First, it seems clear that artful deception… routinely involved a calculated intermixing of the genuine and the fake, enchantment and disenchantment, energetic public *exposé* and momentary suspension of belief…. Second, as Barnum often noted in his own self-defense, no producers of such entertainment who wanted to stay in business for long simply fooled their viewers without also drawing attention to the act of fooling—or at least the possibility thereof…. And third, none of the tricksters in Barnum's milieu simply peddled deception as an end in itself.[44]

This self-conscious and thoroughly modern approach to deception was epitomised by Barnum's presentation of curiosities, whereby he sought not just to dupe spectators but also to excite doubt and debate by revealing seemingly compromising information about it. Barnum stirred up interest in the mysteries he proffered to the public through a process that included both secrecy and exposure.

A similar dialectic, Cook contends, was at play in Maelzel's chess-playing automaton and the performances of stage magicians, who set their work apart from predecessors and contemporaries claiming recourse to supernatural means by revealing the workings of certain conjuring tricks (however circumspectly or indirectly). Cook points out that Maelzel, "the one and only show business mentor Barnum mentioned in his 1855 autobiography", was responsible not only for publicising public showings of the automaton but also for orchestrating the publication of several different explanations of the automaton in the popular

Tod Browning examining one of *The Show*'s more complex illusions, the denunciation of Renée Adorée's Salomé by the decapitated head of Jokanaan.

press, a technique which Barnum readily applied to his own exhibitions.[45] Additionally, Cook argues, "explaining behind-the-scenes workings of one's magical performance was becoming as important and as central to the professional magician's craft as the more conventional work of designing and performing tricks".[46] This corresponds to the story about an unnamed magician with which Barnum begins his 1865 book *The Humbugs of the World*: "I once travelled through the Southern States in company with a magician. The first day in each town he astonished his auditors with his deceptions. He then announced that on the following day he would show how the trick was performed, and how every man might become his own magician."[47]

Although magicians had begun to uniformly eschew exposures of magic as they professionalised during the twentieth century, burlesque magicians visibly continued to offset deception with revelation, making exposures a mainstay of their acts. Vaudeville theatre manager Samuel Hodgdon noted in 1903, "There is always something about the exposure of magic tricks that seem to appeal to an audience as being funny."[48] Fred Siegel suggests that "the burlesque magician is more clown than conjurer", pointing to a circus tradition in which the clown plays the role of a magician who is unable to successfully execute tricks, instead exposing them.[49] Magicians objected vocally to burlesque magic, which they regarded as vandalism, but it thrived at the very time when Browning was a magic assistant and vaudeville comedian. Browning himself may have performed burlesque magic, but in a larger sense, this particular category of performance provides a historical link between the nineteenth century traditions discussed by Cook and the exposures seen in Browning's films decades later. Burlesque magicians staged deceptions but revealed the secrets of tricks in order to create laughter or some equally strong response. It is the figure of the burlesque magician—who irreverently mocks and undercuts the deceptions of contemporaries in the theatre—that resonates most clearly with Browning's treatment of magic and illusion. Yet, Browning's films of the 1920s were not so much a break with the codes of twentieth century magic as the displacement of iconic components of the tradition of "artful deception" from the 'Age of Barnum', to what Walter Benjamin termed the "Age of Mechanical Reproduction".

Renée Adorée and John Gilbert pose in another of *The Show*'s cutouts.

⋈ NOTES

1. "Answers to Various Questions", *Conjurers' Monthly Magazine*, 15 November, 1906, p. 87.

2. Rapp, Augustus, *The Life and Times of Augustus Rapp: The Small Town Showman*, Glenwood, IL: Meyerbooks, 1991, p. 166. Houdini and Rapp were boyhood friends.

3. Skal, David J, and Elias Savada, *Dark Carnival: The Secret World of Tod Browning, Hollywood's Master of the Macabre*, New York: Anchor Books, 1995, pp. 30–32.

4. Bogdan, Robert, *Freak Show: Presenting Human Oddities for Amusement and Profit*, Chicago: University of Chicago Press, 1988, p. 74.

5. The Biographer, "The Personal Side of the Pictures", *Reel Life*, 25 July, 1914, p. 19.

6. Goimard, Jacques, "Le jour où les maudits prirent la parole", *L'Avant-scène du cinéma*, no. 264, 15 March, 1981, p. 6. All translations are the author's unless otherwise noted.

7. Guy, Rory, "Horror: The Browning Version", *Cinema*, June 1963, quoted in Skal and Savada, *Dark Carnival*, p. 5.

8. "*Dracula* is Crowning Success of Director Browning's Career", quoted in Larry Edwards, *Bela Lugosi: Master of the Macabre*, Bradenton, FL: McGuinn and McGuire, 1997, p. 52.

9. Garsault, Alain, "Tod Browning: à la recherche de la réalité", *Positif*, no. 208–209, July–August 1978, p. 43.

10. Permanent exhibit, Hertzberg Circus Museum, San Antonio, Texas, USA.

11. Robert-Houdin, Jean-Eugène, *Memoirs of Robert-Houdin, King of the Conjurers*, Lascelles Wraxall trans., New York: Dover Publications, 1964, pp. 106–114.

12. Standage, Tom, *The Turk: The Life and Times of the Famous Eighteenth-Century Chess-Playing Machine*, New York: Walker and Company, 2002, pp. 91–96.

13. Evans, Henry Ridgely, *Edgar Allan Poe and Baron von Kempelen's Chess-Playing Automaton*, Kenton, OH: International Brotherhood of Magicians, 1939, p. 9.

14. Christopher, Milbourne, *The Illustrated History of Magic*, New York: Thomas Y Crowell, 1973, p. 47.

15. Wimsatt Jr, WK, "Poe and the Chess Automaton", *American Literature* vol. 11, no. 2, 1939, pp. 138–151.

16. Harris, Neil, *Humbug: The Art of PT Barnum*, Chicago: University of Chicago Press, 1973, pp. 61–89.

17. Harris, *Humbug*, pp. 75, 77.

18. Harris, *Humbug*, p. 87.

19. Poe, Edgar Allan, "Maelzel's Chess-Player", *The Complete Tales and Poems of Edgar Allan Poe*, New York: Vintage Books, 1975, p. 434.

20. Poe, "Maelzel's Chess-Player", p. 437.

21. "Tod Browning Discusses Lighting", *Moving Picture World*, 23 June, 1917, p. 1966.

22. Poe, "Maelzel's Chess-Player", p. 430.

23. Poe, "Maelzel's Chess-Player", p. 430.

24. Watts Jr, Richard, "The Directorial Stylist—Has He Passed from the Picture?", *Motion Picture Herald*, 28 March, 1931, p. 95.

25. Poe, "The Tell-Tale Heart", *The Complete Tales*, p. 305.

26. Dickey, Joan, "A Maker of Mystery: Tod Browning Is a Specialist in Building Thrills and Chills", *Motion Picture Classic*, March 1928, p. 33.

27. Browning, Tod, Metro-Goldwyn-Mayer biographical questionnaire, biography files, Margaret Herrick Library of the Academy of Motion Picture Arts and Sciences, Beverly Hills, California, USA.

28. Harris, *Humbug*, p. 57.

29. Rosenthal, Stuart, "Tod Browning", *The Hollywood Professionals*, vol. 4, London: Tantivy Press, 1975, pp. 23–25.

30. The Biographer, "The Personal Side of the Pictures", p. 19.

31. "Rich Man, Poor Man, Beggar Man, Thief—Lon Chaney", *Photo-Play Journal*, November 1917, p. 37.

32. Magny, Joël, "Tod Browning inconnu", *Cahiers du cinéma*, no. 436, October 1990, p. 77.

33. Bogdan, *Freak Show*, p. 8.

34. "Lon Chaney Becomes a Sherlock: In 'London After Midnight' He Became a Detective and Hypnotist", *Wichita Beacon*, 18 December, 1927, clipping, Metro-Goldwyn-Mayer Films and Personalities Scrapbooks, Billy Rose Theatre Collection, New York Public Library for the Performing Arts. Sharrock, a former vaudeville magician and mind-reader, also worked with Browning on *The Devil Doll*, 1936.

35. Riley, Philip J, *London After Midnight*, New York: Cornwall Books, 1985, p. 171. See also the 2002 reconstruction by Rick Schmidlin.

36. Tesson, Charles, "Le monstrueux sentiment de l'espèce humaine", *Trafic*, no. 8, Autumn 1993, p. 58.

37. Dickey, "A Maker of Mystery", p. 80.

38. "Screens Best Known Trio Triumphs Again: Chaney and Browning, Helped Greatly by Waldemar Young, Produce Still Another Brilliant Mystery Story for the Screen", quoted in Riley, *London After Midnight*, p. 177.

39. Dickey, "A Maker of Mystery", p. 80.

40. Magny, "Tod Browning inconnu", p. 77.

41. Denning, Michael, *Mechanic Accents: Dime Novels and Working-Class Culture in America*, London: Verso, 1987, p. 147.

42. McIlhany, Bill, "Side Show: The Magical Cinema of Tod Browning", *Magic*, August 1996, p. 66.

43. Solomon, Matthew, "Reframing a Biographical Legend: Style, European Filmmakers, and the Sideshow Cinema of Tod Browning", *Authorship and Film*, David Gerstner and Janet Staiger eds, New York: Routledge, 2003, pp. 235–246.

44. Cook, James W, *The Arts of Deception: Playing with Fraud in the Age of Barnum*, Cambridge, MA: Harvard University Press, 2001, p. 17.

45. Cook, *The Arts of Deception*, p. 70.

46. Cook, *The Arts of Deception*, p. 178.

47. Barnum, PT, *The Humbugs of the World*, Detroit: Singing Tree Press, 1970, p. vii.

48. Hodgdon, SK, "New York Show, Week of May 25th", unpublished "Managers' Report Books", vol. 0, p. 271, Keith/Albee Collection, Special Collections, University of Iowa Library, Iowa City.

49. Siegel, Fred, "The Vaudeville Conjuring Act", unpublished PhD dissertation, New York University, 1993, p. 109.

THE SPECTATOR'S SPECTACLE
TOD BROWNING'S THEATRE

Stefanie Diekmann
Ekkehard Knörer

The world's a stage in Tod Browning's films, but it is not the stage of traditional theatre. The return of and the return to the stage in so many of Browning's films is rather an attempt to return to popular forms of entertainment, prior to or beyond the conventional theatre of play-acting. The Browning universe presents itself very much as a world of spectacles. The director's interest in the circus (*The Unknown*, 1927), the sideshow (*The Unholy Three*, 1925; *Freaks*, 1932), fake séances, mediums and ghosts (*The Mystic*, 1925; *The Thirteenth Chair*, 1935) and the variety theatre (*The Show*, 1927; *Miracles for Sale*, 1939) is well-documented and well-known, as is his love for all kinds of acts (*London after Midnight*, 1927) and trickery (*The Thirteenth Chair*, 1929). Very often, shows and artistic performances will provide the setting for an entire film or at least a film's essential scenes, and those works which do not deal explicitly with circus and vaudeville still betray Browning's preference for the supposedly lower forms of spectacle and theatrical performance.

There is always a streak of Grand Guignol in the plots of these films, with their severed arms and heads and other horrors of mutilation, with criminal intrigues and jealous crooks turning nasty in the most graphic ways. Therefore, we will first turn to the history and the essential elements of Grand Guignol theatre in Paris that flourished from the beginning of the twentieth century well into the 1920s, when it started its decline from a genuinely sensational theatre of fear to a relic that was out-spectacled by, among other things, the horror films of the 1930s.

We will, however, go on to discuss the ways in which Browning's films are also essentially different from the nature of the Grand Guignol, in the sense that they are focused on the spectator in a manner that predates the immobilisation of the audience in front of the traditional stage or the cinema screen. These films are at once 'pre-theatrical' and 'meta-theatrical' as they re-stage the stage as a means of multiplying plots and glances, of starting, unfolding and finishing all kinds of intrigue, tricks, sleights of hand and double-crossing. Browning returns time and again to the lower forms of vaudeville and to the kind of stage that is not yet closely separated from the space of the spectator. It happens again and again that the spectator turns into an actor, becoming part of a spectacle which he thereby reframes. It is, we argue, this kind of meta-theatrical and at the same time paradoxically anti-cinematic impulse that lies at the core of Browning's cinematic *mise-en-scène*.

A poster for the Grand Guignol—the macabre predecessor to Browning's world.

⋈ THE HISTORY OF GRAND GUIGNOL ⋈

The term Grand Guignol has had the most astonishing career, developing from the name of a historic theatre into a generic adjective denoting "dramatic entertainment featuring the gruesome or horrible" with a certain tendency—by dint exactly of its own impulse toward the extreme—of turning into farce.[1] Grand Guignol nowadays is regarded as no serious business, in more ways than one.

Historically, however, it actually was a serious—profitable—business, and a very successful one at that. The milieu from which Grand Guignol emerged was the naturalistic drama of late nineteenth century Paris, especially André Antoine's famous *Théâtre Libre*, founded in 1887. It was especially the so-called "*rosse*" ('crass', or 'rotten') plays that set the stage for its development. These *rosse* productions featured characters and plots from the Paris underworld of criminals, crooks, alcohol addicts and prostitutes. Most importantly—and in contrast with traditional melodrama using the same kind of *milieu*—it doggedly offended the ethics and values of its bourgeois audience, obviously with considerable success:

> All the bourgeois concepts of love and loyalty followed a new and skewed logic. Wrongdoers (that is, the criminals, sociopaths, and young hooligans: the *apaches*) were rarely punished or praised. Almost always, *apache* life with its anti-social, indigenous traditions and conventions continued unabated at the play's end.[2]

One of the masters of this theatre of underclass naturalism was the former secretary to the Police Commissioner of Paris and then tabloid writer Oscar Méténier, who became one of the most successful playwrights for Antoine's *Théâtre Libre*. His *apache* play *La Casserole (The Informer)* of 1889, for example, in its search for exploitative naturalism, featured real criminals in minor parts and also an actual circus Strong Man. When Méténier opened his own theatre in 1897, after the *Théâtre Libre*'s demise, in a hidden cul-de-sac of Montmartre, it was exactly this mixture of naturalism and crass depictions of Parisian low life based on the *fait divers* (true crime newspaper items) that became its trademark. He deliberately combined those, however, with short comedies and farces, mimicking the effect of '*la douche ecossaise*'—'hot and cold showers'. Méténier named his stage Grand Guignol after the popular Punch and Judy character, promising a kind of adult Punch and Judy show.

Méténier's successor Max Mauray, a man more interested in finance and public relations than in aesthetics, with his radicalisation of 'slice of life' Grand Guignol to 'slice of death' drama, catered to a very special kind of audience: "This clientele, in other times, flocked to country freak shows and wax museums that featured chambers of horror and sensational crime."[3] Ownership changed several times in the next decades, but the most important person in the history of Grand Guignol is probably dramatist André de Lorde, who between 1901 and 1926 wrote more than 100 plays for the stage of fear and horror. He liked to collaborate with what might be called specialists, for example his therapist Dr Alfred Binet, the director of the Psychological-Physiological Laboratory of the Sorbonne. Some of de Lorde's plays prove very effective to this day even when read on paper, and this is because he knew exactly how to prepare the audience for, to put it as paradoxically as it has to be put, the 'expected shocks' which then took them by horrible surprise. The famous special effects of Grand Guignol (severed hands and heads, faces disfigured by vitriol, etc.), as well as the dialogue sketching a hopeless situation, are used to set a mood of despair and violence, but they do not quite prepare for the final twists into child murder and insanity. De Lorde's theatre, one could say, despite its graphic effects, is a theatre of modulating emotions and expectations.

A typical murder scene from the Grand Guignol.

Grand Guignol drama as a whole has been described as a very powerful mixture of melodrama and naturalism—and it is not by accident that it was most successful in the years after the First World War. The naturalistic effects of death, torture, horror and disfiguration completely depended on an arsenal of props, tricks, gadgets, and sleights of hand executed by the actresses and actors, who at the same time were not allowed to miss a beat in their expressive presentation of bleeding to death, of being maimed, killed and raped.[4] It had to be considered a huge success that in 1921 the police commissioner intervened when a decapitation by the guillotine was presented on stage.[5] The art of Grand Guignol, in an important sense, was an art of mixture—in the combination of melodrama and naturalism, in the *douche écossaise* sequence of short pieces alternating between horror and farce. Alternation, however, did not mean ambivalence: the effects of violence and horror were neither to be mixed with elements of farce nor to be laughed at. The reaction which was intended, expected and almost always, it seems, elicited, was the screaming or even fainting of an audience overpowered by fear. The gadgetry and trickery were worthy of a contemporary magician's artistry, in which, to quote from Tod Browning's *Miracles For Sale*, "the hand has to be faster than the eye":

> Mirrors, facial masks, concealed rubber pieces for wounds and
> burns, fake heads and limbs, all the paraphernalia of magicians,
> when expertly used—during moments of darkness or out of the
> spectators' view—created an atmosphere of sickening and
> eerie realism.[6]

And, just as in a magician's presentation, the gruesome effects were never exposed nor presented in intentionally ironical or comedic ways. This is the point where Browning's meta-theatre, undoubtedly much indebted to the plots and principles of Grand Guignol, is decisively different. Its power arguably lies exactly in the exposition of effects and the reframing of spectatorship, both of which do not necessarily ease the horror but rather inscribe it into an endless circle of inescapable theatricality.

⋈ TOD BROWNING'S SPECTACLE ⋈

As far as plots are concerned, the proximity of Tod Browning's cinema to the theatre of Grand Guignol is evident, at least from the mid-1920s to the disastrous experience of *Freaks* in 1932. The scripts of a lot of Browning's films from this phase would have guaranteed smash success on the Grand Guignol stage, or so it seems. From the castrating mutilations of *The Unholy Three* to the sadistic cruelty and bestial brutality intermingled with the orientalising *chinoiserie* of *Where East is East*, 1929; from the horribly misdirected revenge plot of *West of Zanzibar*, 1928, to the no less horribly successful revenge plot of *Freaks*; from the double-crossing gunplay of *The Mystic* to the erotically charged twists and turns of *The Show*: on the level of plot alone, all these films are close in spirit and in explicitness to André de Lorde et al's theatre of fear and horror. This has been acknowledged by Mel Gordon in his instructive study on Grand Guignol:

> Both in the silent and sound eras, Todd [sic] Browning created the films that borrowed most heavily from the Theatre of the Grand Guignol. Especially in *The Unholy Three* (1925), *The Unknown* (1928), *Freaks* (1932), and *The Devil Doll* (1936), Browning established a particular, unhealthy atmosphere that closely resembled pure grandguignolesque. Lon Chaney, John Barrymore, Bela Lugosi, Peter Lorre, Boris Karloff, and Charles Laughton all personified the acting styles that Choisy and his troupe perfected in the twenties.[7]

There is no evidence, however, that Browning literally borrowed from Grand Guignol—or *vice versa*. Although some movies were actually adapted for the Grand Guignol stage (most famously Robert Wiene's *Cabinet of Dr Caligari*, 1920), there is no trace of adaptations from Browning's scripts. And although there were movies based on Grand Guignol plays, we lack any recognition by Browning that Grand Guignol was an inspiration for the stories, the atmosphere and the style of his own films. The only direct connection we could find between the worlds of Grand Guignol and Tod Browning is the actress Raffaela Ottiano who, after a distinguished career as a Grand Guignol actress went on to act in supporting roles in a number of Hollywood movies, Tod Browning's *The Devil Doll*, 1936, among them.

It has been argued that "what excited Grand Guignol most, were borders, thresholds, states of consciousness modified by drugs or hypnosis".[8] In this sense, Grand Guignol is a theatre of transgression, most interested in the shocking things that can be found behind and beyond doors and thresholds and all the normal states and events of bourgeois life. And doors and thresholds, hypnosis as well as intimations of the supernatural and the beyond, certainly play important roles in Browning's cinema. Transgression, however, is never the sole, and perhaps not even a very important, intention in his use of borders of any kind.

Browning's interest is better explained by the fact that moments of theatricality can be found everywhere in his films. Double play and make-believe are an essential part of many, and in some cases even the whole story will be re-presented as staged—as a spectacle which is not at all what it was supposed to be. Two examples: only in the last five minutes of *Mark of the Vampire*, 1935, the audience will learn that everything it has witnessed over the last 50 or 60 minutes was nothing but a set-up—a theatrical trap designed to lure a suspect into the re-enactment of a crime; and the same is true of *London after Midnight*, 1927, a film which employs a nearly identical plot. All in all, Browning's scenarios appear as a long series of tricks performed and explained (*The Thirteenth Chair*), of *double-entendre* (*The Show*, *Freaks*), of exposures, revelations, and other *coups de théâtre* which introduce a sense of duplicity into the world of cinematic representation.

Spectatorship in Browning is therefore a trying and rather uncanny experience—and at the same time, it is at the centre of the director's interest. Watching characters watching a scene or an intimate event, which then becomes a scene exactly in the moment of being watched, is a much-repeated constellation in his films. Browning also frequently depicts an audience being suddenly thrust into the show that they have hitherto been watching—they are included in or attacked by the show. The observer is pushed onto the stage. This happens in what may be one of the most emblematic moments of Browning's variations on spectatorship, in the film aptly titled *The Show*, when a poisonous reptile jumps from the stage and attacks the throat of a man in the audience.

The fragile border between action and observation collapses, the two spheres merge into one, the spectacle turns out to be infectious, and no spectator can ever withdraw into the passivity typical of more conventional forms of Western theatre. In Browning's universe of aggressive performance, even the 'director' of the performance may himself be killed and burned, after the failure of a trick which quickly turns the observers of a magician's show into the actors of a ritual slaughter (*West of Zanzibar*). The spectator can never be safe in his position—and it usually is a male spectator, as Browning intimates an analogy between the spectator's gaze and the lustful male gaze (most obviously in *The Show*). It follows from this argument that the spectator in Browning's films can never remain a voyeur; or rather, that he is never safe in his voyeuristic position. The situation of spectatorship in the movie theatre (and this is the basic movement of a Browning film) will always be re-addressed and reversed.

We never see a traditional theatre performance in Browning's films. He prefers the 'lower' forms of spectacle—not only, we would argue, because of their grandguignolesque plots and actions, but also because they have not yet managed to stabilise the dramatic illusion to the extent that an imaginary 'fourth wall' separates the scene on the stage from a completely passive audience.[9] Browning's theatre is in fact, in a sense, a constant attack against the fourth wall. And it is, of course, a rather quixotic attack, as it had to be acted out *on the screen*, in a situation when cinema, after its beginnings as a vaudeville form of

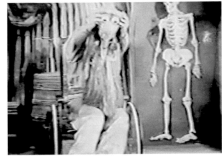

Tod Browning invites his audience to become participant as well as voyeur, as happens to the spectators within his films (clockwise from top left) *The Show, West of Zanzibar, The Mystic* and *West of Zanzibar.*

spectacle, had forever turned into a radical attenuation of traditional theatre in the late 1920s: an audience cloaked in darkness, their bodies immobilised and their eyes transfixed on a screen which frames a complete and unbroken illusion. In his attack on this closure, Browning never tired of staging events on the screen that turn against the spectator, so that they can remain passive only at risk of death; or otherwise, events are reframed and redefined by an observer who would sooner or later become an actor. This is true even in those cases which seem to be furthest removed from the *milieu* of vaudeville, theatre, magician's shows, and the like. The most important scenes in *Where East is East*, the sadistic melodrama of mismatched couplings, open the space to the scrutinising gaze of an observer even under the most confined circumstances: in a cabin on a ship. And in the next moment, arguably the signature moment of Browning's meta-theatre, this observer becomes an actor in the scene which is immediately reframed by his intrusion.

It would be interesting to rethink the famous narrative framing and closure of *Freaks* as a metaphor for a kind of show completely different from the spectacle of vaudeville. Not only does it—in a shocking fit of grandguignolesque mutilation and horrific vengeance—demonstrate the destruction of a beautiful body; perhaps the situation of the mutilated beauty in a box can also be seen as a final immobilisation which resembles nothing so much as that suffered and enjoyed by the modern cinema audience, wishing to be enraptured and transfixed by what happens on a screen completely severed from the space of the theatre. Grand Guignol, or so goes the story told in the historic overviews, suffered a decline into something like a parody of itself exactly at the moment when more effective kinds of horror found their way to the screen, with the beginning of the talkies.[10] Tod Browning's cinema of the spectator's spectacle was clearly démodé in the talkie era as well. His post-*Freaks* films were themselves close to parodies of what had made him one of the great directors of the 1920s. The one exception is his marvelous swan song, *Miracles For Sale*, which in the farcical form of a screwball comedy conjures up a world of traps and sleights of hand, of crookery and trickery—in short, the world of Tod Browning's theatre, one last time. His is a career that ended neither with a bang nor a whisper, but with a performance that makes fun of an audience that believes what it sees.

The unfortunate Cleopatra, turned into Chicken Woman at the revenge of the Freaks.

⊨ NOTES

1. Definition of "Grand Guignol", *Websters' New Collegiate Dictionary*, Springfield, MA: Merriam-Webster, 1981.

2. Gordon, Mel, *The Grand Guignol. Theater of Fear and Terror*, New York: Amok Press, 1988, p. 10.

3. Gordon, *Grand Guignol*, p. 18.

4. Paula Maxa, the biggest female star of Grand Guignol theatre, is reported to have been "murdered more than 10,000 times and in some 60 ways. A few examples: devoured by a ravenous puma, cut into 93 pieces and glued back together, smashed by a roller-compressor, burnt alive, cut open by a travelling salesman who wanted her intestines; she was also raped over 3,000 times under a dozen circumstances." Gordon, *Grand Guignol*, p. 26.

5. A story told in Kersten, Karin and Caroline Neubauer eds., *Das Vergnügen, tausend Tode zu sterben. Frankreichs blutiges Theater*, Berlin: Wagenbach, 1976, p. 69.

6. Gordon, *Grand Guignol*, p. 47.

7. Gordon, *Grand Guignol*, p. 42. The atmosphere and style of Grand Guignol was arguably revived by maverick director Alejandro Jodorowsky in all his films, from *El Topo*, 1969, to his emblematically titled *Santa Sangre*, 1989.

8. Pierron, Agnès, *Le Grand Guignol. Le Théâtre des peurs de la belle époque*, Paris: Robert Laffont, 1995, p. xxv.

9. Grand Guignol theatre was in an ambivalent position in this regard. It has been often reported that in the crammed room a first row spectator could easily have shaken hands with the performers. All the tricks and sleights of hand performed during the plays, however, depended on the illusion that what happened was—in the sense of the dramatic illusion—real. You were not supposed to applaud a virtuoso's ability to fool you in front of your very eyes—but to react with fear and horror to an illusion created by these tricks.

10. The Grand Guignol theatre actually closed its doors as late as 1963, but Hand and Wilson argue "that the Grand-Guignol [sic] became a victim of cinema". More specifically: "During the silent era the Grand-Guignol had enjoyed a fruitful relationship with the cinema, but the advent of talkies and a new genre of horror film in the 1930s, which made stars of Karloff and Lugosi, ushered in a new era…. [Cinema] entered a problematic relationship with the Grand-Guignol and one that was a mere foretaste of what lay in store." Hand, Richard J and Michael Wilson, *Grand Guignol. The French Theatre of Horror*, Exeter: University of Exeter Press, 2002, pp. 25 and 22.

DOUBLE IDENTITY

PRESENCE AND ABSENCE
IN THE FILMS OF TOD BROWNING

Alec Charles

There are a lot of odd things going on in the films of Tod Browning. There's a moment, for example, in *Dracula*, 1931, when Browning appears to have miscalculated the angle in the shot/reverse shot set-up, and Bela Lugosi, supposedly advancing menacingly towards his victim, appears to be heading 90 degrees in the wrong direction. Curiously, however, this only adds to the uncanny feel of the sequence: this apparently inadvertent alienating effect emphasises the otherworldliness of the vampire Count.

There are a couple of similarly disorienting moments in Tod Browning's original version of *Outside the Law*, 1920. In the first of these, the burgling hero Bill Ballard (Wheeler Oakman) has just cracked open a safe with his bare hands. He then wipes the safe of his prints, and exits the room removing a white glove (which, one presumes, is one of a pair) from his left hand, a glove that he hadn't been seen wearing in the previous shot. A naïve continuity error, no doubt, but one which, in this post-intentionalist age, opens a whole host of interpretations. Does the white left glove symbolise the *sinister* criminality that he is shortly to cast off? And, if so, does its ironic whiteness anticipate the anti-conventional use of colour symbolism (black for good, white for bad) to be employed nearly two decades later by Eisenstein in *Alexander Nevsky*, 1938)? Or are we perhaps reminded of the snake sloughing his skin, or of Pontius Pilate trying to wash his hands of his sin?

A more interesting discontinuity occurs when the film's heroine, Molly Madden (Priscilla Dean) opens the door of her apartment to a neighbor. As she does so, she drops her hand (which is holding a gun) so that it falls outside the frame of Browning's medium shot. Although invisible to the audience, the gun should be clearly visible to the neighbour within the scene's diegetic space. When the neighbour departs, Browning cuts to a long shot of Dean, once more revealing the gun in her hand.

For Browning here the cinematic world is the world in shot. That which falls outside the shot cannot be seen, even by those within it. It can be inferred by the viewer, but the protagonists remain in ignorance. When, in *Dracula*, the eponymous Count arrives at Lucy Weston's bedroom window and finds her apparently asleep, he is unaware that, just a moment earlier, she had been seen reading a book in bed. Neither Lugosi nor the audience has been privy to any intervening shots of Lucy (Frances Dade) discarding her book and settling down for the night: yet, through this discontinuity, the audience may interpret Lucy's somnolence as affected and therefore her surrender as the more wanton, or indeed the more seductive.

By openly acknowledging the camera's narrative mastery, Browning breaks the rules to bare the cinematic mechanism. Kaja Silverman writes that "a gaze within the fiction serves to conceal the controlling gaze outside the fiction.... [T]he subject of the speech passes itself off as the speaking subject."[1] In other words, the classical formula of shot/reverse shot, in which the characters never quite look straight at the camera (and thus never recognise it, or the audience's presence), persuades us that the presented viewpoint is part of the diegetic space; that is, we are seeing through the eyes of the character whose reaction we are about to see, not through the camera. This illusion lies at the heart of the suspension of disbelief, and therefore the processes of involvement and identification, upon which cinema's narrative structure is grounded.

Christian Metz argues that "it is essential... that the actor should behave as though he were not seen... as though he did not see his voyeur".[2] For the voyeuristic audience, the film is "something that *lets* itself be seen without *presenting* itself to be seen.... This is the origin... of that 'recipe' of the classical cinema which said that the actor should never look directly at the audience."[3]

Tod Browning implies the complicity of Lucy Weston (Frances Dade) in Dracula's attack on her.

This failure of an audience to see that it can be seen is played upon by that most self-consciously scopophiliac of filmmakers, Alfred Hitchcock, in his comedy of 1941, *Mr and Mrs Smith*. The protagonists, as played by Carole Lombard and Robert Montgomery, find themselves observed by a group of staring children while trying to enjoy an intimate candlelit supper *à deux*. Lombard suggests trying to stare them out: "That'll make them embarrassed." The couple stare directly at their audience: the children, the camera and the cinemagoers. The tactic however fails. The children (and the camera and the filmgoers) continue to stare, as if unaware that they are themselves the objects of their objects' gaze.

Voyeuristic pleasure depends upon its object's ignorance of the act of voyeurism. Film is an exhibitionist, but (like the masochist who conceals his or her pleasure in order to please the sadist), it pretends it's not. Like Browning's Lucy Weston, it poses as a virgin so naïve she doesn't even blush.

Hitchcock most famously breaks Metz's rule of classical cinema in *Psycho*, 1960, not only when Norman Bates stares directly into the eyes of the audience in the film's closing moments, but also when the detective Arbogast (as he's about to be murdered) looks into his killer's eyes and directly into the camera: thus not only putting the audience in the place of the victim, but also (in a uniquely disturbing way, commented upon by Slavoj Zizek) in the position of the monster, involving the viewer in "an identification with the 'impossible' gaze of the object-Thing itself".[4]

The first time we see Bela Lugosi in Tod Browning's *Dracula*, in a long shot which tracks into a close-up, he looks almost directly into the camera. This is the first of more than a dozen occasions in the film when Lugosi appears to take the audience into the confidence, threat or complicity of his gaze. When we see him next (when, disguised as the coachman, he is recognisable only by his eyes), he again looks almost directly at us. It's not until his servant-to-be, Renfield, sees him for the first time a few seconds later that Browning affords the audience the first of those famously intense and direct into-the-camera Lugosi looks, a style of gaze which would be duplicated time and again by the likes of Christopher Lee and Lugosi's lesser imitators. The whites of his eyes seem to glow as he looks down at his prospective victim from his coach. Browning leaves us in little doubt as to who's in the driving seat.

As Dracula travels by ship to England, we see, again from Renfield's point of view, those shining eyes staring directly at us while the rest of his face remains in shadow. When, once in England, he prepares to suck the blood of a flower girl on a London street, those glowing eyes once more look down directly into the lens. Browning cuts to the flower girl's reaction shot: she looks back up at Lugosi, but the point of view is only partial, she doesn't quite look straight at us. The meaning is clear: we are to identify with Dracula's victims, but (unlike in Hitchcock's *Psycho*) not with the monster himself.

Later, Lugosi's Dracula hypnotises a concert hall usherette, and, after that, tries the same trick on Mina's nurse. When he visits Renfield in his asylum, he communicates his commands to him with only a couple of meaningful looks. On each occasion he stares straight into the camera. Again, his victims do not.

When, however, he attempts (and fails) to hypnotise the stubborn Professor Van Helsing (Edward Van Sloan), he disdains that direct into-the-camera gaze; in this instance, perhaps, Lugosi's menace would be diminished, the failure of the direct gaze to hypnotise emphasising the strength of Van Helsing's will at the cost of the representation of Dracula's own power.

It is Dracula's hypnotic stare which affords him his power over his victims.

The only character other than the Count afforded a direct look into the camera in Browning's film is his servant Renfield, whose nature, when he's discovered aboard the wrecked and otherwise deserted ship, is recognised (by his unseen discoverers) by virtue of that gaze: "He's mad—look at his eyes." The influence of Dracula's gaze can be witnessed in that of his victims': "Your eyes", says the heroic John Harker to his beloved Mina, during her own process of conversion into one of the Count's undead minions: "They look at me so strangely."

At one point in the stage version of the story by John L Balderston and Hamilton Deane (upon which Browning's film is based), Dracula also "faces directly front".[5] Dracula's line at this point is charmingly threatening: he speaks of his love of London, a place so different from his native Transylvania, which he describes as a land of "so few people and so little opportunity".[6]

The only other character in the play to be accorded the same meta-diegetic privilege is the Count's nemesis, Van Helsing himself. This is perhaps unsurprising: Van Helsing is the only character encountered by Dracula in his vampiric mode whom the Count never seems interested in converting to his cause: almost as if the Professor were virtually already there. As Rosemary Jackson points out, "Dracula is the inverse side of... [Van Helsing's] legality."[7]

Van Helsing faces the audience at the end of the play to offer, in the form of an epilogue, "a word of reassurance".[8] He reminds the audience that, after they've returned to their homes, and perhaps are plagued by the nightmares that dwell in the dark, they should pull themselves together and "remember that after all *there are such things*".[9] In these direct addresses to the auditorium, both Dracula and Van Helsing combine quaint charm or homely reassurance with threats to the security of the audience's sense of homeliness.

In both the content and the ambiguously meta-diegetic natures of these two speeches (as the fantasy horror threatens to enter, and to reveal its origins in, the real world of its audience) the lines of demarcation between hero and villain, as between fiction and reality, are blurred. In the stage version this blurring is achieved by their modes of address; in Browning's film a similar blurring of moral positions is expressed (in a typically cinematic style) through the control of each character's gaze.

These refusals to suture over the cracks in the cinematic devices employed might to some extent answer Theodor Adorno, Max Horkheimer and Bertolt Brecht's laments as to the hypnotic and even soporific qualities of cinema: "sustained thought is out of the question if the spectator is not to miss the relentless rush of facts…. Those who are… absorbed by the world of the movie… do not have to dwell on particular points of its mechanics during a screening."[10] "What sinks in is the automatic succession of standardised operations…. No independent thinking must be expected from the audience."[11] "They look… as if in a trance…. These people seem relieved of activity and like men to whom something is being done."[12] It is ironic that the audience might only be sufficiently disturbed to break free from the hypnotic quality of the film itself by the direct hypnotic gaze of one of the film's characters; for it is only by foregrounding and acknowledging the illusory device that this mechanism becomes impotent.

In *Mark of the Vampire*, 1935, Browning demonstrates his penchant for the narratologically discontinuous when a pair of servants tell the tale of a bat transforming into Bela Lugosi's vampiric Count Mora, accompanied by an apparent flashback to this scene. It is, however, a false flashback: as we discover at the film's climax, Mora is no vampire at all, but an actor hired to scare the living daylights out of a murder suspect. Although, thanks to the visualised testimonies and hypotheses shown in Jerry Bruckheimer's various *CSI* series, among others, this mode of false flashback has become a commonplace of twenty-first century television, one mustn't forget the critical disapprobation it provoked as late as 1950, when Alfred Hitchcock experimented with it in order to provide an alibi for his murderer in *Stage Fright*. It may be that viewers find this technique disconcerting not merely because it is misleading, but because it is self-consciously misleading; because (like Lugosi's looks into the camera) it draws attention to the hypnotic and illusory nature of its medium, and in doing so it breaks the cinematic spell. Just as the Brechtian actor doesn't play a character so much as playing an actor playing a character, so Browning's story-telling method stresses the filmic/fictive nature of his narrative, and in doing so interrupts his own diegetic flow.

One might, of course, argue that these revelatory paradoxes, these aporia, are in fact nothing more than instances of directorial incompetence. Why, after all, does *Mark of the Vampire* fail to answer in any convincing way what it eventually announces as its central mystery: how the murderer managed to drain his victim of his blood without leaving so much as a stain on the carpet? And why, if the film's vampire theme is no more than a charade to catch a killer, do the conspirators (like a pack of method-acting obsessives unwilling ever to step out of character) continue this charade even when they're on their own? Is it that they know the camera's watching them? Is it that these dialogues are in fact as fake as the false flashback? Or is it that the truth behind the film, a truth which Browning refuses openly to acknowledge, is that, despite its happy "there-ain't-no-vampires-after-all" ending, there are in the film's world (as Van Helsing might say) really such things? And could this implication explain why, as we discover in the inquest scene earlier in the film, the murder on which the film focuses is not, it seems, the only suspiciously vampiric death to have affected the region in recent times? For, indeed, if the murderer were not himself a vampire, why should he be persuaded by the plot's cunning masquerade that his victim had become one?

Critics have relentlessly censured the happy ending tagged onto the final act of Robert Wiene's *The Cabinet of Dr Caligari*, 1920: its deeply disturbing socio-psychical horrors were all merely a madman's dream. And yet, just as Dorothy back from Oz sees the echoes of her dream in the faces that surround her, so Wiene's continued hints of insanely Expressionist set design back in the real world serve to call into question the comforting reality in which his film concludes. In a similar fashion, the reassuring perspective advanced at the close of *Mark of the Vampire* is somewhat undermined by the uncanny intimations of an ever-present but barely glimpsed underworld.

Franco Moretti draws out of the final moments of Bram Stoker's *Dracula* (which involve not the death of the Count himself, but that of the ostensibly heroic Quincey Morris) a similar set of questions, ones which, in ways rather more subtle (and therefore more uncannily effective) than Van Helsing's final line to the audience at the end of Balderston and Deane's (overly) theatrical version, begin to controvert the senses of stability and closure finally established by the text. As we shall see, Moretti is less interested in Stoker's intentions than in his text's effects, and one might offer a similar argument in defence of Browning's discontinuities.

Yet these semantic rifts, though rarely glaring, appear so consistent and so coherent (in that they tend towards similarly anxious sets of interpretations) that defence is perhaps less necessary or appropriate a critical strategy than sympathetically aligned semiotic analysis. Indeed, Browning's meta-diegetic (and thereby metatextual) moments, and his films' related discontinuities, invoke internal contradictions and even paradoxes which might bear comparison with those dialectical contrasts which characterise radical cinema from FW Murnau to Jean-Luc Godard, counterpoints which add a jarring quality to the montage, and thereby (as Robert Stam suggests) distinguish Eisenstein from advertising.[13]

There's a symbolic shot in *Battleship Potemkin*, 1925, which shows two rebellious sailors hanging by the neck from the yardarm of the ship's mast. The mast is presented as emblematic of a crucifix; but, rather than the two concrucifands (the two thieves) hanging, as might be expected, on either side of the cross, both hang on the one side. Eisenstein's message seems to be that those who step outside the system of Christian-imperialist orthodoxy face a more one-sided fate than the 50/50 odds of salvation clung to by the protagonists of Samuel Beckett's *Waiting for Godot*: "one of the two [thieves] was saved."[14] Like hanging Judas, they've already made their choice. You can't straddle the fence of the socio-economic dialectic: you can't hedge your historical-materialist bets.

Five years earlier than Eisenstein, Tod Browning had employed a similar piece of symbolism in *Outside the Law*. The heroine chooses to renounce her life of crime when she sees the shadow of a cross on the floor of her apartment. The hero draws the blind so that she doesn't notice (but in doing so makes the audience notice) that it is merely the shadow of a tattered, worthless and discarded icon, a child's broken kite. This is more complex and original an emblem than the heavy-handed imagery of the crosses which stand on the hillside and at the Volga Pass in the opening scenes of *Dracula*: images which are themselves no more interesting than the cross which tops the church near to the protagonists' hideout in *Outside the Law*. In the latter film, however, Browning's more sophisticated and problematic hints of Christian symbolism (in the form of the shattered kite) suggest that his film's own two thieves might, in a squalid, broken and unglamorous way, find their own salvation: no glorious and high-flying ascension into heaven, but at least (through repentance and risk) the chance to escape the fate to which the villainous Black Mike has threatened to consign them: "to crucify 'em both!".

It's hardly controversial to point out that Eisenstein's symbolism is rather more complex, subtle, ambiguous and sophisticated than Browning's. What is interesting, however, is the fact that one can advance any such aesthetic comparison between these two fundamentally different filmmakers. The possibility of this comparison to some extent authorises a reading of Browning's discontinuities as intentional; as anticipating Eisenstein rather than Ed Wood.

The discontinuities in *Outside the Law* reach a climax when, at the end of the film, in the chaotic final battle between the forces of good and evil, the combination of fast action, spasmodic cuts, long shots and remarkably similarly attired characters makes it extremely difficult to tell exactly who's fighting whom. This confusion is emphasised by the fact that Browning cast Lon Chaney in the dual roles of the villainous Black Mike and the mild-mannered Chinaman Ah Wing.

In the same film, Browning shows the radical transformation from thief to penitent undergone by his glamorous heroine Molly Madden, aka Silky Moll, as if physical beauty inspires moral perfection; while, conversely, in *Freaks*, 1932, the villainess's moral corruption is eventually manifested in her physical deformation, when the *femme fatale* once known as the Peacock of the Air becomes, or is exposed as, "the most amazing, the most astounding living monstrosity of all time"—half-woman, half-chicken.

The Siamese Twins, the half-woman/half-man, and the Bearded Lady of *Freaks* act as real living emblems of this ambivalence within the individual, as between fact and fiction itself. These real-life circus 'freaks' themselves actualise disturbing ambiguities that tend to have been long repressed: as the film's prologue argues, "the revulsion with which we view the abnormal, the malformed and the mutilated is the result of long conditioning by our forefathers". Browning's film attempts to reverse this conditioning, and in doing so reveals not only the humanity of the apparent monsters but also the monstrosity of those who seem to be human. This exposure of hidden, immanent horrors is what Sigmund Freud would have called uncanny.

Although the Freudian uncanny may classically be manifested by the physical *doppelgänger* or, like Joseph Conrad's Secret Sharer, the psychical alter ego, this duplicity may, in perhaps a more modern fashion, be internalised within the single individual: Dr Jekyll who is simultaneously Mr Hyde. This is the very revelation which underpins Alan Parker's *Angel Heart*, 1987, David Fincher's *Fight Club*, 1999, Christopher Nolan's *Memento*, 2000, James Mangold's *Identity*, 2003, and Alfred Hitchcock's *Psycho*. Indeed, it is in part the ambiguity as to whether he's dealing with a *doppelgänger* or disguised duplicity that underpins the uncanny nature of ETA Hoffmann's seminally uncanny tale of "The Sandman".

Sigmund Freud's essay "The Uncanny" focuses upon Hoffmann's nightmarish account of that "uncanny ghost… the terrible sandman".[15] There is a definite resemblance between the atmospheres conjured by Hoffmann and the story on which Tod Browning based his most celebrated film, *Dracula*. As Siegfried Kracauer points out (on the subject of FW Murnau's adaptation of *Dracula*, the first film version of Stoker's tale): "When speaking of *Nosferatu*, the critics… insisted upon bringing in ETA Hoffmann."[16]

The double-naturedness of the uncanny is evidenced in *Dracula*'s vampires who seem to be human, as well as in their polar opposites, the humans who seem to be vampires, of Browning's *Mark of the Vampire*. It is also witnessed in Lionel Barrymore's cross-dressing anti-hero, Paul Lavond, in *The Devil Doll*, 1936. There's a scene in that film in which Lavond delivers a threatening letter to one of his prospective victims by leaving it on the table in a restaurant where the victim is dining: Barrymore does so quite overtly, but his disguise (as an eccentric old woman) allows this act to pass virtually unnoticed.

In Edgar Allan Poe's tale of "The Purloined Letter" (a narrative beloved of Lacan and Lacanians) the detective Dupin discovers the eponymous epistle hidden in plain view: in a letter rack. Something similar happens in one of GK Chesterton's Father Brown stories: the murderer, who manages to approach and enter a watched house unseen, turns out to be that most trusted and homely of figures, the mailman. The letter or the mailman (the vessel or the vehicle of signification) passes through as unobtrusively as Roland Barthes' "natural sign".[17] The elaboration or exposure of this natural sign's true nature (as symbolically, ideologically, mythologically or diegetically loaded with secondary associations which lead from signifier to signifier, in an endless chain of signification or desire), its unveiling as a double sign, offers a moment of revelatory interpretation which Freud might have called uncanny.

In his study of the *Theory of the Film*, Béla Balázs announced that "the film camera has revealed new worlds… concealed from us… the souls of objects… the secret language of dumb things".[18] He proposes that the function of cinema, indeed of all art, is to make "old, familiar and therefore never seen things hit our eye with new impressions": to reveal "the hidden life of little things".[19]

One might recall, in this connection, a scene in Chaplin's *The Pilgrim*, 1923, in which the little fellow accidentally decorates a bowler hat as a cake.

The assembled company mounts a furious search for the missing hat, which in truth, though covered in cream, is plain for all to see, right at the centre of the tableau. The fact that the audience is aware of this leads to dramatic irony and suspense. However, a similar (but critically different) set-up in Browning's *Outside the Law* perhaps better fits Balázs' cinematic model, in that it relies upon surprise rather than suspense, upon a moment of revelation: the hidden jewels around which, like one of Hitchcock's MacGuffins (those empty grails), the film's plot has turned, have been concealed all the while (like the film's own protagonists) in plain view, under a pot plant that has sat in the middle of the room, and of most of the shots, for much of the central section of the movie. If cinema reveals to us brave, rich and strange new worlds, then they are worlds that we have already, unknowingly, known of old. It shows us the invisible things that surround us; it reveals the secrets that we've repressed and forgotten we know.

If seen from this perspective, the structure of cinema itself seems to resemble Freud's own depiction of the uncanny, the *unheimlich*:

> The German word '*unheimlich*' is obviously the opposite of
> '*heimlich*' ['homely'], '*heimisch*' ['native']—the opposite of what
> is familiar; and we are tempted to conclude that what is
> 'uncanny' is frightening precisely because it is not known
> and familiar.[20]

> In general we are reminded that the word '*heimlich*' is not
> unambiguous, but belongs to two sets of ideas, which, without
> being contradictory, are yet very different: on the one hand it
> means what is familiar and agreeable, and on the other, what is
> concealed and kept out of sight.... [E]verything is *unheimlich*
> that ought to have remained secret and hidden but has come
> to light.[21]

The uncanny is an intimation of the truly intimate. Its exposure of profound and dangerous secrecy represents an act of psychical dispossession. Bram Stoker's most famous novel terrifyingly reveals the violently repressed (and therefore violently resistant) unconscious sexuality and animality of Victorian Englishwomen, and, by extension, of their men—just as Freud unearthed the secrets of Dora and the Wolf Man.

Perhaps the most uncanny moment in Stoker's novel is a scene reminiscent of Browning's and Chesterton's invisible mailmen, when Dracula manages somehow, inexplicably, to slip into the Westenra home unnoticed while one of the novel's heroes, Quincey Morris, is supposed to be guarding it. Franco Moretti, in his book *Signs Taken for Wonders*, proposes that the reason for this apparent inconsistency in Stoker's narrative is the fact that Quincey himself "is a vampire".[22] (Although Christopher Frayling has argued, not unjustly, that one might "take too seriously Franco Moretti's suggestion that Quincey Morris is a vampire".)[23] Moretti himself has commented on the question of whether or not Stoker intended Morris' apparent vampirism:

Was it intentional? I doubt it (although Stoker was a curious fellow, you never know...). On the other hand, texts such as *Dracula* (fantastic, in Todorov's definition [cf. Tsvetan Todorov, *The Fantastic—A Structural Approach to a Literary Genre*]) have a structural grey area in them, where 'intention' is probably an empty category—the author may well be playing with possibilities in a rather inchoate way.[24]

Terence Fisher's 1958 movie version of Stoker's novel, *The Horror of Dracula*, solves the problem of how Dracula slips past the home's sentinel with a literalisation of Freud's idea of the *unheimlich*: the Count has his coffin delivered directly to his victim's cellar. The Englishman's home becomes *his* (that is, Dracula's) castle: and the hidden strangeness within the homely, the *heimlich*, is thus revealed. As Lionel Barrymore puts it in Browning's *Mark of the Vampire*, "the vampire… he is still somewhere within this house". The vampire is still here; that manifestation of our darkest fears and desires is always with us. Like the man engaged to one of a pair of conjoined twins in Browning's *Freaks*—the hapless fiancé who proclaims himself "the boss of [his] own home"—we find that, as the other twin tells him, we're just the boss of "half of it".

The homely becomes the site for self-discovery and self-revelation. As they hide out from the police, the protagonists of Browning's *Outside the Law* discover the truth in WH Auden's depiction of modern man as living in the "cell of himself".[25] These "two self-sentenced prisoners" find that in truth there's no escape from the law (there's only, after all, the constant conflict between the law of the father and the law of nature, between order and chaos, between the superego and the id): "a guy might as well be in jail in here…. I'm getting sick and tired of being caged up here, like a criminal!" Those anarchists who believe they have barricaded themselves against the imperatives of society find themselves already hemmed in and imprisoned by the agents of authority; while, conversely, those who feel protected by those very forces of patriarchy find themselves opening their hearts and their homes (and even their jugular veins) to the most disturbing and immanently alien (or strangely familiar) of influences.

In Tod Browning's version of *Dracula* (as in the stage play by Balderston and Deane) the Count is the charming neighbour and invited guest of his victims. This familiarity and homeliness synthesise not only a dramatic irony generated by the distance between the audience's and the protagonists' expectations of Lugosi's character, but also the uncanny thrill felt by Edward Van Sloan's Professor Van Helsing (and also shared vicariously, despite their foreknowledge of the Count's nature, by the audience) when the professor glimpses Dracula's lack of a reflection in a mirror. The homely, insidious signifier is exposed as being dangerously loaded, overdetermined, and ultimately empty.

In Browning's *The Devil Doll*, we witness something similar in the ease with which the escaped (and disguised) convict Paul Lavond hides himself out in the open: in front of the police, in front of the men who once betrayed him, and in front of his own daughter.

Lionel Barrymore in the *unheimlich* world of *The Devil Doll*.

Mark of the Vampire: Count Mora and his daughter condemned to Freud's "compulsion to repeat".

    Browning's *Outside the Law* similarly sees its heroine and hero, a pair of wanted criminals in hiding from the police, living in an apartment next door to a police officer, and befriending his child, hiding under the very nose of the law—just as the heroine's gun remains (as we have noted) both seen and unseen at the same time. This unconscious flaunting of their concealment at one point leads the heroine to suggest to the hero: "If you want the cops to know we're here, why don't you just blow a horn?!"

    Both *Outside the Law* and *The Devil Doll* concern young women who have lost their fathers to false imprisonment: just as Browning's *Mark of the Vampire* centres upon a woman whose father has been murdered. The loss of the patriarch (at once, the dissolution of the law of the father and of the quasi-Oedipal desire which this law prohibits) leads in each of these films (as most famously in Alfred Hitchcock's *Psycho*) towards a process of the frustration, confusion and substitution of these objects of signification and identification. In *Mark of the Vampire*, the lost father is uncannily and distressingly replaced by a look-alike; in *The Devil Doll*, he appears transgendered and unrecognised; in *Outside the Law*, the moral conflict taking place within the father, the choice as to whether to stand within or without the law and socially acceptable family relations, is enacted first by his daughter, but also by Lon Chaney in his two roles: that of the gangster villain and that of a mild-mannered Chinese manservant to a Confucian master, the figure of grace who finally dispatches the representative of inner evil.

Despite their moral and psychical experimentation, these films eventually reinstate the natural balance of patriarchal presence. Van Helsing defeats the usurping post-patriarch; the good Lon Chaney appears to vanquish his evil double; Paul Lavond experiences the moral triumph of a reconciliation with his daughter and a reassertion of his authority. Lavond's corruption is redeemed: evil is exposed as good. If the Freudian uncanny demonstrates the repressed desires which linger in the shadow of the superego, then the returns to legitimacy which conclude *The Devil Doll* and *Outside the Law* argue for precisely the opposite process. While the climax to *Dracula* re-establishes the patriarchal structures that the Count's contagion has sought to dissolve, then the revelations of the mundane on which *Mark of the Vampire* ends advance the proposal that, despite appearances, we have never in fact left the psychically and actually policed realm of the superego and of patriarchal authority.

And yet, advertently or not, these conclusions, in all their diegetic, thematic and tonal inconsistencies, are nowhere near as unproblematic as they purport to be. In his great meditation upon Poe's "Purloined Letter" Jacques Lacan announced that "a letter always arrives at its destination".[26] But it doesn't always arrive at the address to which it's been sent, nor does it invariably convey the meanings it had been intended to signify. The eventual emptiness and inconsistency of patriarchy's triumphant and transcendental signifier is mirrored in the absence and slippery ambiguity that underpins and undermines the sign of its hollow double, alter ego and opposite. This absence represents, far more than any presence, the uncannily uneraseable trace of unredeemable loss and impossible desire.

In *Mark of the Vampire*, one of the fake vampire-hunters, played by Lionel Atwill, points out that the false vampire's lair offers few clues as to its master's presence (apart, of course, from that odd menagerie which, in Browning's imagination, the vampire likes to maintain: cats, bats, rats, rubber spiders, and even opossums and armadillos): "not so much as a mark on the dust-covered floor". His co-conspirator Lionel Barrymore adds that "the dust lies thick and undisturbed. That's what makes it so difficult to find the vampire's hiding place."

These two heroes do their best to impose their own semiotic system, their own map of the world, upon the undead realm: when they eventually track down the Count, they decide "put a mark on that door so we'll know his hiding place". Yet this most slippery of signifiers continues to evade their grasp. The lights go out, and, when they come back on, Lugosi's gone: it seems he's just slipped away. Like Lewis Carroll's Cheshire Cat, indeed like Schrödinger's cat, the vampire is at once a symbol of presence and of absence, a symbol whose uncanny double identity reveals the similar duplicity of its diametrical (equal yet) opposite—the shadow's substance, the reality it mirrors: human being.

The vampire is here, in Browning's *Mark of the Vampire*, supposedly a pseudo-vampire, and yet, like the mere shadow of a shadow, it nevertheless leaves no prints in the dust. As such, it's even more of a vampire than an actual vampire is: "Did you watch me?" Lugosi asks at the end of the film. "I gave all of me. I was greater than any real vampire."

But perhaps then he really is a pseudo-pseudo-vampire, a doubly-disguised vampire, a vampire disguised as a man disguised as a vampire. Beneath these facades, this simulacrum has no real being, and, therefore, despite the film's title, leaves no substantial marks upon the world, apart from a pair of barely visible puncture wounds, signs not of presence but of absence and of loss, at its victims' throats. And thus its eventual vanquishing seems more like a vanishing, a submerging, a return to the underworld, the unconscious, the world of the dead, a domain whose doors are always open, the dark heart in each of our homes, the place from which that which we have temporarily repressed constantly struggles to return.

Patriarchy may, on the surface of things, and for the time being, have reasserted the balance and the distinction between life and death, but death shall in the end have its dominion. For, as Lionel Barrymore reminds us in *Mark of the Vampire*, "we all must die". And, as Jacques Derrida once proposed, the triumph of life (in French, *l'arrêt de mort*) is also "a sentence that condemns someone to death".[27]

The cunning plan upon which *Mark of the Vampire* hinges offers to restore justice and balance and life, and yet it requires the murder victim's daughter to play her part alongside an actor who uncannily and painfully resembles (a vampirised version of) her dead father. "To live through those moments again, to act as if you were my father", she laments, "…. Don't you see the horror of it?" In the end, as Freud says, this "compulsion to repeat" (this "urge inherent in organic life to restore an earlier state of things") isn't a manifestation of the will to life, but represents "the instinct to return to the inanimate state": the death-drive.[28]

For, as Alfred Hitchcock once asked François Truffaut, in a question whose deceptive simplicity encompasses the entire impossibility of eternal desire, the parasitic and vampiric inevitabilities of absence and emptiness that relentlessly frustrate our transcendental dreams of meaning and being: "If the dead were to come back, what would you do with them?"[29]

Or, as Lionel Atwill says towards the end of Browning's *Mark of the Vampire*, as patriarchy's plan appear to have gone awry: "We all thought our vampire scheme was so simple, so certain of success. We never thought we'd fail…."

⋈ NOTES

1. Silverman, Kaja, *The Subject of Semiotics*, Oxford: Oxford University Press, 1984, p. 204.

2. Metz, Christian, *The Imaginary Signifier*, Celia Briton et al trans., Bloomington: Indiana University Press, 1982, p. 96.

3. Metz, *The Imaginary Signifier*, p. 63.

4. Zizek, Slavoj, *Everything You Always Wanted to Know about Lacan (But Were Afraid to Ask Hitchcock)*, London: Verso, 1992, p. 249.

5. Balderston, John L, and Hamilton Deane, *Dracula*, London: Samuel French, 1933, p. 24.

6. Balderston and Deane, *Dracula*, p. 24.

7. Jackson, Rosemary, *Fantasy*, London: Methuen, 1981, p. 119.

8. Balderston and Deane, *Dracula*, p. 74.

9. Balderston and Deane, *Dracula*, p. 74.

10. Adorno, Theodor, and Max Horkheimer, *The Dialectic of Enlightenment*, John Cumming trans., London: Verso, 1986, p. 127.

11. Adorno and Horkheimer, *The Dialectic of Enlightenment*, p. 137.

12. Brecht, Bertolt, *Brecht on Theatre*, John Willett trans., London: Methuen, 1978, p. 187.

13. Stam, Robert, *Film Theory: An Introduction,* Oxford: Blackwell, 2000, p. 41.

14. Beckett, Samuel, *Waiting for Godot*, London: Faber, 1965, p. 13.

15. Hoffmann, ETA, *Tales of Hoffmann*, RJ Hollingdale trans., London: Penguin, 1982, pp. 88–89.

16. Kracauer, Siegfried, *From Caligari to Hitler*, Princeton: Princeton University Press, 1974, p. 79.

17. Barthes, Roland, *Mythologies*, A Lavers trans., London: Vintage, 1993, pp. 109–159.

18. Balázs, Béla, *Theory of the Film*, E Bone trans., New York: Dover, 1970, pp. 47, 93.

19. Balázs, *Theory of the Film*, p. 54.

20. Freud, Sigmund, Freud, Sigmund, "The Uncanny", *Art and Literature*, The Penguin Freud Library, vol. 14, London: Penguin, 1990, pp. 335–376, p. 341.

21. Freud, "The Uncanny", p. 345.

22. Moretti, Franco, *Signs Taken for Wonders*, S Fischer et al trans., London: Verso, 1997, p. 95.

23. Frayling, Christopher, personal correspondence with the author, 3 February, 1999. See Alec Charles, "Some Versions of Dracula", *Language Issues*, vol. 5, no. 1, March 1999, p. 148.

24. Moretti, Franco, personal correspondence with the author, 20 March, 1999. See Charles, "Some Versions of Dracula", p. 148.

25. Auden, WH, *Collected Shorter Poems* 1927–1957, London: Faber, 1966, p. 142.

26. Lacan, Jacques, "Seminar on The Purloined Letter", Jeffrey Mehlman trans., *The Purloined Poe*, J P Muller and W J Richardson eds., Baltimore: Johns Hopkins, 1988, p. 53.

27. Derrida, Jacques, "Living on—Border lines", James Hulbert trans., *Deconstruction and Criticism*, Harold Bloom et al eds., New York: Continuum, 1979, p. 110.

28. Freud, Sigmund, *On Metapsychology. The Theory of the Unconscious*, The Penguin Freud Library, vol. 11, London: Penguin, 1984, pp. 293, 308 and 311.

29. Truffaut, François, *Hitchcock*, New York: Simon & Schuster, 1985, p. 309.

BODY DREAMS

LON CHANEY AND TOD BROWNING – THESAURUS ANATOMICUS

Nicole Brenez

Tod Browning made 11 films with his main actor, Lon Chaney—or, as one could equally well put it, Lon Chaney made 11 films with his main director, Tod Browning. Both of them were among the most innovative creators of their time in the realm of the image—a powerful tandem. The aesthetic result of this fertile collaboration is the focus of this essay—as the other contributions in this volume deal directly with Browning and his films, we will take it from the perspective of Chaney's general body of work. The question of authorship will thus be equally shared between these two geniuses.

⋈ THE ANATOMICAL INVENTION OF APPEARANCES ⋈

The principle, and perhaps the challenge, of the work of Lon Chaney and Tod Browning, lies in thinking that one can portray the uncanny without depicting the so-called normality, in treating various forms of distortion without including integrity. When Chaney plays two characters at one time, his speciality as an actor, it isn't in order to build a paradigm between the same and its other; between the good guy and the bad guy, between what is normal and what is pathological. The point, instead, is to match two monstrous forms and let their resemblances proliferate. In a way, his rare straightforward roles speak of an even more violent desire for alienation that leaves tremendous symptoms in its wake: for example, in *Nomads of the North*, directed by David M Hartford in 1920, Chaney plays a Canadian trapper—the paradigm of health. At the beginning of the movie, we see him shave carefully, smiling into the camera, as if he were washing the smallest trace of make-up off his face. But as the shot widens, we discover that his companion is… a bear, a monstrous version of the faithful dog that immediately fits into the bestiary inhabiting Chaney's creations: the lion in Victor Sjöström's *He Who Gets Slapped*, 1924, the gorilla and the mute parrots in Browning's *The Unholy Three*, 1925, the chimpanzee and the swarming beasts in Browning's *West of Zanzibar*, 1928.

Tod Browning with Lon
Chaney on the set of
West of Zanzibar.
Courtesy of Laurent Preyale.

Lon Chaney's dual roles offer a way to dissolve what is One. This can occur, as in *Outside the Law*, 1926, when Lon Chaney as Ah Wing shoots Lon Chaney as Black Mike Sylva, though the characters are distinct despite the dual role; or, as in *The Blackbird*, 1926, this duality acts like a drill that perforates the character. Dan Tate, aka The Blackbird, a tough from London's underbelly, makes up a good brother for himself, The Bishop, who he uses as an alibi whenever he commits a crime. But The Bishop is the materialisation of The Blackbird: hunched over his crutches, a dead leg folded up under him, a preacher clad in black, he represents a wading bird, a crane, a hideous stork. This misshapen double embodies the bandit's name as if it were a dreadful slip of the tongue. At the end of the film, The Blackbird quickly turns into The Bishop to escape his punishment: a policeman opens the door, The Bishop falls and breaks his back: "I played it once too often… now I *am* a cripple!" His wife tells him to feign sleep so that he is not brought to the hospital. His spine broken, he bites his fist in pain, he hits his pillow—"Oh! God! The pain! The pain!" Driven mad by necessity, agony and the drive to playact ("I'm fooling them, I'm fooling them, I'm fooling them!"), he wills his features to relax, pretends to fall asleep… and dies. The creation of a double, such as the priest in *The Blackbird*, the vampire in *London After Midnight*, 1927, or the ape man in Wallace Worsley's *A Blind Bargain*, 1922, like Professor Echo's puppet in *The Unholy Three* or like Professor Paul Beaumont's transformation into a clown in *He Who Gets Slapped*, proves to be a process of sheer self-destruction. With Lon Chaney, phantasy crushes, destroys and lays to waste without leaving any possibility for redemption, self-recovery or peace.[1] On the contrary, to die as one's double means being deprived of oneself even in death: death, then, is no longer a beautiful vanishing but a terrible spiriting away.

Lon Chaney deals with everything that can go against self-preservation. His most famous creations portray scenarios of dismemberment and mutilation: no arms (*The Unknown*, 1927); no legs (*The Miracle Man*, George Loane Tucker, 1919; *Flesh and Blood*, Irving Cummings, 1922; *The Shock*, Lambert Hillyer, 1923; *The Penalty*, Wallace Worsley, 1920; *West of Zanzibar*); no eyes; no face (*The*

Phantom of the Opera, Rupert Julian, 1925); no reason (*The Scarlet Car*, Joseph de Grasse, 1917; *A Blind Bargain*, Wallace Worsley, 1922); no morality. The reason why he was so intent on playing Quasimodo, his first public success, was perhaps because he had comments to make on the character's deformity. *The Hunchback of Notre Dame*'s Quasimodo approximately visually recreates the creature imagined by Victor Hugo, but above all, Lon Chaney plays him as a being who does not know what he is, who is untroubled by this, and who constantly acts against his own vital interests. Quasimodo's great scene is not the one in which he rescues Esmeralda from death, nor even the scene of his own lynching; it is when, besieged in Notre Dame by beggars and thieves, he jumps for joy and pours scalding pitch onto people who had no feelings of enmity towards him and who could have saved him. In clinical discourse, one calls 'agnosia' the illness that consists in not being able to recognise a part of one's body, not having an image of it.[2] The character's physical deformity is interpreted by Chaney as total agnosia, and Quasimodo acts as a complement to the characters of disintegration: a figure that predates the self, a character for whom identity would not be an inevitable aim; a figure of the Unformed.

Mutilation scenarios scattered with nefarious doctors are therefore matched by fictions of loss and dispossession: Professor Beaumont suffers the loss of the fruit of his research and his wife; in *West of Zanzibar*, Phroso suffers the (physical) loss of his wife and the (moral) loss of his daughter; Alonzo, HE, Echo, all fail to win over the women they desire; and just about all of Chaney's characters lose their lives. Emotional loss immediately translates into physical mutation: Professor Beaumont, fragile and elated, becomes HE, a powerful, frenzied clown; Phroso represents the magic left in the civilised world and becomes Dead Legs, who embodies the hatred swarming in the very depths of nature. The love of disintegration is perhaps at its height in *West of Zanzibar*. Dead Legs crawls along the ground like the bugs and larvae in the primal mud; the jungle is filled with grotesque fetishes; a tribe spends nights burning corpses. In the beginning of his route through the Congo, Dead Legs swallows fire in a violent incorporation impulse, to ensure his power over the tribe; in the end, he is cooked and eaten by the cannibals, no longer impressed by his tricks.[3] Incorporation has devoured itself, the body is no more than human meat, and organic life is a sheer nightmare.

⋈ BEYOND THE CARCASS ⋈

"The face is pleasing. The carcass is hypnotic."
Henri Michaux, *Ordeals, Exorcisms*

So, in order to be able to bear life, must one imagine it without a body? "You will be free when your love for Erik's mind has overcome your fear." Erik, the Phantom of the Opera, is a sublime character, evoking a love that would forgo the body. Lon Chaney created three masks for Erik. First of all, there is the screen-mask.[4] As he first appears, after a lengthy prelude filled with shadows and outlines, Erik presents himself to Christine with a white, featureless mask, ending with a veil of gauze that moves to the whisper of his voice. What does it conceal? It is the mask of emptiness; the veil anticipates the hole, the void of the face. A blurry shot comments on this figurative event: the superimposition of mask and want, the transformation of the face into an enigma, and above all the loss of appearances. Later on, Christine rips off the phantom's screen-mask while he is playing the organ, unveiling the mask of the nonexistent face, a juxtaposition of gaps and strips of flesh that abolishes both the face and the skull, a hodgepodge of pulp and emptiness that Erik, without the slightest hesitation, invites Christine to partake of. "Feast your eyes, glut your soul on my accursed ugliness!" Lon Chaney plays Erik as the representation of the repugnance of the body; he is a figure of anguish that is broken down by its apparitions, that falls apart a little more each time it becomes visible. Finally, the third mask is the supreme mask of the Red Death: then the classic shape of the skull seems reassuring, well-established in a long iconographic history and made legitimate by ancient anatomical certainties. But one suddenly remembers that there is something hidden under this sumptuous skull; under Death, there is something worse, something really abject—"the loathsome beast", as Christine says: the disease of appearances, the intolerable phenomenon of having a visible body. Lon Chaney tackles negativity as if it were the actor's natural material, giving a definitive image of it in the contrast between, and the overlapping of, the three masks.

⋈ THE GREAT PUZZLE: FIGURATIVE CIRCULATION ⋈

"My little body is aweary of this great world."
William Shakespeare, *The Merchant of Venice*

> It seems as though thinking men, as yet at a low level of culture, were deeply impressed by two groups of biological problems. In the first place, what is it that makes the difference between the living body and the dead one? What causes waking, sleep, trance, disease, death? In the second place, what are those human shapes which appear in dreams and visions? Looking at these two groups of phenomena, the ancient savage philosophers probably made their first step to the obvious inference that every man has two things belonging to him, namely, his life and his phantom.[5]

In *He Who Gets Slapped*, Lon Chaney plays a scientist, Paul Beaumont, whose research has to do with the origin of humanity. He cries out: "My theories are irrefutable!" before having his brilliant work taken away from him by his patron, the vile Baron Reynard. Victor Sjöström's film thus pays tribute to the anthropological dimension of Lon Chaney's work, this systematic investigation of an imaginary wholly fantastic body, whose fantasy is neither capricious nor arbitrary: it is first characterised by a multiplicity of appearances structured by the intensity, accuracy and constancy of certain somatic scenarios, in which the Phantom (whatever his shape, be it an obscure and sacrificed double, a clown, a cripple, a criminal, a beast, a skeleton) always comes to experience life from the standpoint of its limits.

At the end of *The Penalty*, Blizzard, the protagonist, "that cripple from Hell", recovers both his wits and a sense of what is right. But this man, who had lived through all that is evil, through disability, voyeurism, sadism, criminal conspiracy, paranoia, the slavery of modern capitalism, hatred of humankind, does not survive this recovery: an old accomplice comes along and shoots him in the back. He dies after saying this to his fiancée, Barbara: "That is a great puzzle. Perhaps I am going to see it solved. Don't grieve, dear—death interests me." Lon Chaney's great somatic fictions are organised according to a simple movement of disintegration and of possible corporal redemption. Most often, the disintegration is complete, as in *The Phantom of the Opera*; *West of Zanzibar*; *The Hunchback of Notre Dame*; and Herbert Brenon's *Laugh, Clown, Laugh*, 1928, in which Chaney, as Tito, a clown shattered by love, invents an acrobatic suicide device, the Death Slide, thanks to which he slides along an oblique wire on his head in order to be able to crash onto the stage. But corporal redemption does not spare one from death; on the contrary, this can occur when recovery is sanctioned by murder, as in *The Penalty*; or it can occur, as in Lambert Hyllier's *The Shock*, 1923, when San Francisco's earthquake is necessary for the cripple to recover his legs; or it can occur, as in *The Unholy Three*, when the fact of relinquishing his woman's disguise represents for Echo

The Unknown: Lon Chaney in action as Alonzo the Armless.

the definitive loss of love. Reparation is therefore not restoration, as if falling apart physiologically were in fact the only way to survive and to resist death, which will take you at the very moment of recovery.

The corporal scenarios are therefore based less on a linear logic of resolution than they are on a dynamic and circular principle: the circulation of organs. This means, on the one hand, that organs and limbs endlessly circulate within the body, that the body becomes a pure organ circuit, upset by certain anatomical fetishes; and, on the other hand, it means that the selected organs are tampered with, contaminated, that their value lies elsewhere than in themselves, the pieces of the puzzle make up a final picture that does not add up at all to the sum of its parts.

This circulation first obeys a selective logic: it works on one organ or one limb only, whose shape spreads and proliferates throughout the entire body, or erases it entirely in favour of the sick part. In a classic mode, for example, this is the use made of the hand in Frank Lloyd's *Oliver Twist*, 1922. To play Fagin, the leader of the thieves, Lon Chaney chose to reduce the surface of his body and leave as much space for his hands as possible: he plays the character bent in half, hidden behind his beard and under his great cloak, and from this shapeless and senile mass emerge two enormous hands, trembling claws shaken by tics, set in motion by cupidity and fear. During his last appearance, Fagin is sitting in prison, in an empty cell, facing us, totally motionless, his big paws neatly placed on his knees, as if his body were but the display of the instruments of deceit. The display of the hands as a representation of the cause, and the clarity of Lon Chaney's posture, is an argument that transforms the shot into a conclusion.

But Lon Chaney's somatic scenarios combine a selectivity in the choice of organs with an emphasis on defects and excess. In *The Unknown*, the most drastic film in this regard, the body sometimes lacks arms, sometimes displays too many of them (since the legs act as arms and Alonzo mechanically wipes his face or lifts his glass with a foot), sometimes allows them to proliferate as unlikely growths (he has two thumbs on his left hand). In *The Penalty*, Blizzard, the cripple, enters Barbara's place, a sculptor who wishes to portray him as Satan, while she is working on women's legs: with her, Blizzard comes across everything he does not have but that he rejects deep down, since he dies as a result of recovering his integrity. In *The Hunchback of Notre Dame*, to portray Quasimodo, the creature that is deprived of everything, Lon Chaney only keeps that which is in excess: the proliferation of the additional body part, the hump, spreads throughout the body, a bump on the forehead, the *kyphosis* of the nose, prominent cheekbones that weigh down the rest of the face, eyelids as heavy as goitres, a rounded belly, knock knees; the creature is full of lumps, in a horrible excess lacking in all that is necessary. In *The Phantom of the Opera*, the face is wanting, which can be either a defect or an excess, as the first description of Erik by the ballet school pupils shows: "He did not have a nose!"—"Yes he did! It was huge!" And ultimately, the skull, the classic symbol of want, becomes a triumphant mask that does not lay bare; on the contrary, it protects from an even more dreadful lack of self. In *He Who Gets Slapped*, it is the heart that is at the centre of an intensive circulation: a small heart, a prop hidden in an enormous satin heart, is sown on the chest of the clown, HE, every evening by the horsewoman with whom he is in love; every evening the heart is ripped off by his partner who buries it in the sand of the arena and stomps on it; every evening HE unearths it after the show and, when he is about to die, he uses this crumpled heart to sponge the chest wound inflicted on him by the father of his beloved. One cannot avoid being reminded of the engravings that Cornelius Huyberts made for Frederic Ruysch's *Thesauraus anatomicus*, 1701, in which a small macrocephalic skeleton "lays his left hand in a romantic gesture on the area of the exposed thorax from which the heart has disappeared".[6]

The body seems to be made up only of a single limb that is replicated with slight variations and disseminated everywhere, even on other bodies. Lon Chaney's world is filled with figurines—dolls, puppets, statues, shadows, wax figures, masks, gargoyles, totems—which form a great many pieces that are projected outwards by the fragmenting of this problematic body. Chaney sometimes acts as a prop in this economy of figurines, but the result is even more pathetic and the crudeness of the phantasm even more violent. Thus the organ that circulates wildly in *Laugh, Clown, Laugh* is the foot: Tito's excessively large feet are the burlesque distortion of another set of unusual feet, those of his adopted daughter, Simonetta, a lost child that Tito found in a bush, her ankles caught in brambles. She will later hurt her feet again on the barbed wire she tries to cross to pick roses, although she is the most gifted tightrope walker in her father's circus. In both cases, the men who rescue her, Tito from the brambles and Count Ravelli from the barbed wire, fall madly in love with Simonetta of the swollen feet (really mad—these poor souls meet at the neurologist who treats them in turn): the representation of the Oedipus complex is absolutely literal. *Laugh, Clown, Laugh* catalogues forbidden love: that of the homosexual couple made up of the clowns Tito and Simon (under the names Flik and Flok); that of Tito for his daughter Simonetta, the make-believe child of this male couple; that of Simonetta for her father Tito, who commits suicide to avoid marrying her.

At the beginning of *Laugh, Clown, Laugh*, Tito tries to cheer up young Simonetta, who is in tears: he projects shadow puppets on the white screen made out of the skin of a drum, conjuring up chickens out of his head that peck at it, then turning into a giant monkey, and finally, collapsing as a rag doll between his daughter's knees. The body language created by Chaney to play Quasimodo in *The Hunchback of Notre Dame* sometimes alludes to a dog, to represent the fact that he is enslaved by love, sometimes to a sheep, to represent his historical status (he is the undisputed victim of history, more so than the *lumpenproletariat*), and sometimes to a chimpanzee, when he swings around the bells and over the cathedral's facade. "Man is a repetition, that is to say a summing up of his animal lineage."[7] When Echo flees from the police to a mountain refuge in *The Unholy Three*, what does he take with him? What is essential and imperative? He takes with him a cruel and lecherous dwarf, a German Hercules who is trying to kill him, a young girl in love with another man, an angry gorilla and a ventriloquist's puppet. That is the survival kit of a character played by Chaney; he has need of everything in the world that is implacably different from and hostile to him.

Thus, the multiple figurines are met by this highly colonised body. Chaney is always likely to change into something else, to bring forward some animal characteristic, a trace of otherness or a new form of want in his appearance through a gesture or a new twisting of the body. He is always likely to alter his shape, as illustrated for example by Quasimodo's telescopic physiology—sometimes stooping, bent towards the ground and almost crawling, sometimes straightened up with passionate energy, as when he strangles Jehan or when he captures Esmeralda. And he is always likely to welcome a little more disparity, as in *West of Zanzibar*, in which Dead Legs, in a state of deep melancholia, absent-mindedly strokes at first a monkey, then his daughter, and finally the incredible cardboard and straw mask of a dingo (which closely resembles the nightmarish creature bent over St Anthony in Salvatore Rosa's *Temptation*); this same gesture recurs throughout the film, referring the series of movements to their hallucinatory nature.

Lon Chaney's great somatic elaborations therefore pertain to an authentic disintegration, of which physical infirmity is only the most spectacular manifestation, because they abolish the disparity between the same and the other (in *The Unholy Three*, Chaney as Echo testifies at a trial disguised as an old woman: "The baby was asleep." "Was it a boy or a girl?" "Yes, sir"), between presence and absence ("He did not have a nose!"—"Yes he did! It was huge!"), between the one and the many (the colonised body), between the inside and the outside (the economy of figurines). And yet this set of suppressions are based on the vacillation of a deeper distinction between reality and phantasy.

⋈ THE MASTER OF IMAGES ⋈

"I'll send you postcards!"
Lon Chaney's last line in his last movie, the sound version of *The Unholy Three*, Jack Conway, 1930

Two of Chaney's films are based on the same figurative logic that juxtaposes an initial reality, a traumatic event, and the transposition of the initial situation on the level of phantasy: Victor Sjöström's *He Who Gets Slapped*, and Tod Browning's *West of Zanzibar*. One could probably add to these movies Victor Sjöström's 1925 lost film, *Tower of Lies*, in which Chaney's character invents the kingdom of Portugallia, which only his daughter and himself are able to see and to inhabit. As stated by Christian Viviani, the real native land of Lon Chaney, who has played so many Chinese, Russian, French, and other exotic monsters, is Never Neverland, the kingdom of fantasy.[8] Three masterpieces, two extremely skilled authors, one actor, the same producer (Irving Thalberg); two films structured around a *caesura* through the logic of trauma and the transcription of an event into a phantasy, the same scenario about the affective elaboration of images: Lon Chaney's art lies in opening up the doors of the dream world.

He Who Gets Slapped depicts the inner life of a scientist beset by a traumatic scene: during a session at the Academy of Science, his patron steals the fruit of his work and makes a mockery of it; that which was to be his hour of glory ends in disaster and, to make things worse, his wife leaves with his tormentor. Instead of rebelling, Paul Beaumont embraces humiliation, transposes it onto the stage of phantasy (he becomes HE, the slapped clown) and re-enacts the insult every evening in the arena of a circus. When one day, the baron attends the show, reality makes a comeback, and the dream-like nature of this transposition is made explicit by the dissolves and the change in props that associate the laughing audience in the arena, the audience at the Academy, and the clowns. One can then consider the clown version of the trauma as an actual biographical event within a dramatic duration (Paul Beaumont really had a life change, he really became a clown and the baron really returned) as well as the intensive display of a single affect, the way in which the protagonist experiences the session at the Academy. The clown version of the film is less an account than it is analytic montage, and the film is less of a melodrama than it is the detailed description of vertigo.

But what is the purpose of this transposition? Is the point of it only to explore an emotional collapse and depict a psychological fixation through images? That alone would already be a great accomplishment, but *He Who Gets Slapped* proves to be even richer. First of all, the transposition promotes a drastic inversion of the *persona*: the puny, obscure and individuated scientist turns into an athletic, famous and commonplace clown, as if Chaney could make any body emerge from any other body—as when he conjures chickens springing from his head—through a fantastic metamorphosis that does not simply obey a mechanical compensation principle (the weak becomes strong), but necessitates an overturning, be it minimal, of values and categories (here he is violent: a bad individuation, a good anonymity).

This transposition does more than simply reproduce the trauma, it also gives free reign to phantasy: an incestuous daydream takes the place of the initial tale of adultery; HE falls in love with a young horsewoman whom his rival, the sole element that hasn't changed in the transition from reality to fantasy, tries to seduce and then to buy off. At this point the scenario goes wild and takes a seemingly surreal turn: the horsewoman's father and the despicable baron, that is, the two other father figures, are devoured by a lion that HE lets out of its cage. The fiction of incest punished by the act of devouring—like the one, even more pure, in *West of Zanzibar*—hence describes that the preceding vertigo of humiliation is not the result of an external attack (the felony of the baron, the session at the Academy) but of a self-punitive delusion sanctioning the incestuous desire. The principle of the transposition of reality into phantasy can therefore not be reduced to a simple anamorphosis of the phenomena; it allows to bring to light the pathogenic source; the resurgence of the event on the level of phantasy has explanatory virtues.

Finally, the transposition takes place between two types of images. Paul Beaumont's heart is broken, HE lets his heart be ripped out every evening; HE falls in love with Consuelo who does not love him, the horsewoman sows an enormous heart onto the clown's costume and sticks her finger into it; Estrellita does not want to fall into a man's arms, Alonzo gets his arms cut off

(*The Unknown*); Phroso's life is wrecked when his wife leaves him, he falls and loses his legs (*West of Zanzibar*); Flick knows how to move his audience to the extent that they "laugh until they cry"—confronted with the same impossible love, Tito cries uncontrollably and his rival laughs hysterically, and both characters mechanically share the affects: "you can't control your laughter any more than I can my tears" (*Laugh, Clown, Laugh*). All in all, Lon Chaney's acting allows an immediate materialisation of verbal images, and provides a concrete iconography to an imaginary world of feelings as quaint as it is popular.

"No more Hercules, no more Tweedledee, no more Echo… we fade out." *The Unholy Three* also revolves around a *caesura* that juxtaposes, on one side, the life of the circus, and on the other, a life of crime in Mrs O'Grady's bird shop. There is an anamorphosis at work on three levels: on each body; between the characters; and between the group of criminals and the model that it sarcastically distorts, which is the bourgeois family. On two occasions, Chaney's Mrs O'Grady/Professor Echo and his accomplices deceitfully make up a touching family portrait, first for the benefit of Mrs O'Grady's son-in-law, then for the benefit of the police. In both cases, the picture is exactly the same, as if there was only one conceivable family portrait, rendering this distinguished image forever suspicious, a poor cliché become grotesque. An old grandmother, a father, a mother, and a baby playing with his little truck are sitting around a Christmas tree, in front of the crackling hearth. Who would not feel moved by this picture? But the grandmother is the head of a gang and a ventriloquist, the father a stupid Hercules, the mother a thief, the baby a libidinous, greedy dwarf, the pet that brightens up this household is an enormous gorilla (whose deliberately artificial appearance of an old, ill-fitting costume increases its

The Unholy Three: Tod Browning's subversion of the family portrait.

nightmarish look), while the outsider that threatens this unity is a weak, gentle, upright and hardworking person. In this family, the 'grandmother' has sex with the 'mother', the 'baby' commits infanticide at the first opportunity and the 'pet', perpetually locked up in a closet, terrorises the 'father' who would otherwise happily strangle the 'grandmother'. Together they plunder neighbouring aristocratic homes, by the unstoppable means of mute parrots. The sanctimonious ending of the second version (Echo surrenders to the police and hands his fiancée over to her decent suitor) does not succeed in softening the wild virulence that prevails in the figurative system: the harm is done, the images are destroyed. (It won't be until 1956, and Douglas Sirk's *There's Always Tomorrow*, before American cinema again produces such a harsh indictment of the family.)

Tod Browning and Lon
Chaney on the set of
The Unholy Three.
Courtesy of Laurent Preyale.

The distortion afflicting the bodies comes from an improper overlapping of appearances: certain props and certain movements are excessively superimposed on the silhouettes and reveal the overall duplicity of the bodies. The best example of this is the dwarf, disguised as a baby and dressed up as a fireman, who forgets to conceal his fat cigar; more generally, it is the way in which Lon Chaney activates and deactivates his old woman's costume. In *The Unholy Three*, Lon Chaney gives a brilliant demonstration of physical performance, working on the contrast between two appearances; sometimes he uses an "integral mask", such as when his Professor Echo look or his Mrs O'Grady costume dress him entirely like an flawless armour; sometimes he uses a 'semi-panoply', such as when, thanks to an emotional impulse or a surprise, he dismantles one character through another and degrades the mask to a simple outfit. This is the case when, furious with his *fiancée*, Rosie, he takes off his wig of wavy hair and his delicate glasses: there is nothing more imposing than this strange creature, clad in a dress with a lace collar, with a sinister-looking face and a harsh voice, whose convict-like shaved head seriously clashes with his earrings but who, threatened from all sides by ridicule, will not moderate his rage. When Tweedledee, in his pram, reaches for a ruby necklace, stammering with desire, childhood greed comes through as unbearable cupidity; when Mrs O'Grady, partly exposed as Echo, pours out a stream of abuse on Rosie, all of childhood's terrors toward parental figures, father and mother mixed up in the confusion due to fear, finally find a visual expression.

We see here that the acting frees itself from a one-dimensional approach based on the character; rather, it belongs to a set of dynamic configurations that can revert to the way in which the body symbolises and lends itself to symbolisation. For Lon Chaney, acting probably consists in giving credence to a character; but to him, this classic aim means creating clusters of acting that endlessly restructure the gestures, the repertoire of emotions, the outline of the body and the costume, into sequences, dividing them up and dismantling them with a technical virtuosity and figural intelligence that often prevails over narrative interest: in a way, the characters he plays are less individuals than they are corporal expressions. In *The Phantom of the Opera* for example, we see that investigating the corporal absence in visual terms outweighs narrative plausibility: during the underground fight against his rivals, Erik steps out of his lair, passes through a door and enters a lake area; the continuous action does not prevent him from changing masks, from one shot to the next he swaps the mask of nothingness for the mask of the destroyed skull—but this is because from one scene to the next, from the erotic scene to the death scene, he does not have the same relationship to the desire to see. Lon Chaney's artistry does not only appear in make-up techniques, it deals above all with the nature of images: the plasticity of appearances, the revival of verbal images through visual images, the relation between mental images and organic imagery—their mutual ability to lend more depth to each other, to criticise and to bring about anamorphosis, and the unsuspected properties of their circulation.

⋈ THE FORMS OF CORPORAL NEGATIVITY ⋈

"All he does is to undo his brother's work."
The Blackbird, Tod Browning, 1926

What is HE's act about, in which he incorporates the intellectual humiliation he suffered at the Academy? It consists of a string of forms of annihilation that are amongst the most violent ever shown in the cinema, because they are part of a logical succession that ascertains their implacable nature. There is a moral annihilation: HE enters the arena behind an army of little dancing clowns, perched on stilts that offer an extreme version of Lon Chaney's familiar crutches. "Gentlemen, tonight I will prove to you that the earth is round!" HE arouses everybody's hilarity, from the cruel audience in the tiers to the clowns in the ring. There is a physical annihilation: each clown slaps him in turn, and the more he gets slapped, the more successful his act; he falls to the ground under the many blows, the slapping continues while his hands are tied, he is lifted up and thrown to the ground like a bag, his partner Tricaud rips out the big cloth heart on his chest and then tears off the small heart inside it, buries it in the sand and stomps on it. The clowns then proceed to parody a burial: "Lay down! You are dead, you know!" HE is laid on a stretcher and covered under a pile of straw wreaths. But the stretcher does not hold, the corpse falls off, the procession goes on without the mortal remains it is commemorating, HE stays on the ground, alone, like a heap of hay, and all that is left of him is a vague, fragile and indistinct pile in the dust. HE finally emerges from it, bent over, walking backwards, still tied up and gagged, and disappears backstage.

And that's not the end of it. Fate has a third annihilation in store for this martyr of emotions: a formal annihilation, not of his feelings or even of his identity, but of what is left of a creature that has been totally disfigured, a complete destruction of this deserted, shapeless and deprived creature, who had nonetheless managed to preserve one ultimate thing: a link with the outside world through a minimal bond to the ground, the fact of being dust amidst the dust. After the show, HE unearths the trampled heart in the deserted ring. A stagehand puts out the lights. There is but a minute white speck on the screen, the trace of HE's face, lost in an immensity of darkness. The white dot lingers on for a long time, then goes out. HE then falls into nothingness, and Lon Chaney's work on the body reaches pure figural abstraction: it is no longer about disintegration or about disappearance, it is an attack on the very possibility of his existence.

If there were any doubts about the systematic nature of Lon Chaney's investigation, one need only to remember that this same figurative event occurred on a more narrative level in *The Phantom of the Opera*. Erik's rivals pursue him—down into the terrifying darkness of the Opera's caves; through many trapdoors; through traps and horrible memories of ancient massacres; down to the fourth, then the fifth cellar. Below the earth there is water; they come to a subterranean lake, they take a boat to cross it, but they cannot go down any further. Yet Erik does go down a little further. He takes a bamboo tube with him to be able to breathe and sinks slowly into the dark water, aiming to capsize the boat. He sinks lower and lower. Soon he is but a little white line, swaying as it floats away on the surface of darkness. The three masks of absence represent so many versions of the classic motif of the skeleton. Their abstract equivalent, which could be called modern by way of contrast, is outlined here; it is the body reduced to a simple line trembling in the dark, a remnant of what was visible.

Lon Chaney invented the most radical forms to treat corporal negativity, and he also invented a sublime syntax for them. These forms refer to something very deep and frightening in the usual experience of the body, but they are never obscure and hard to understand in themselves. Unlike Christopher Walken, for example, another great actor of negativity, who takes on the paradoxical forms of transparency (as in David Cronenberg's *Dead Zone*, 1983; James Foley's *At Close Range*, 1986; and Abel Ferrara's *King of New York*, 1990: the more the

light penetrates his pale eyes and his smooth face, the more he is mysterious),
Lon Chaney works in great clarity.

⋈ MENTAL MAKE-UP: THE SOMATIC CONJUGATION ⋈

"There are places in man's poor heart that do not yet exist
Where sorrow penetrates so that they may be."
Léon Bloy

At the end of *The Penalty*, Dr Ferris describes the operation he has just carried
out on Blizzard: while grafting on legs, "as long as I was operating", he says, "I
did the head as well". In Lon Chaney's world, there is no difference between a
surgeon and a neurologist, between a physical defect and a psychical weakness;
the obviousness of perfect somatic transparency reigns undisputed. There is
no mystery about the nature of the prejudice either: "Give me legs and I'll be
the perfect son-in-law", Blizzard tells his future father-in-law. The aesthetics of a
great physiological transparency legitimise the expressive style used by Lon
Chaney, but it also makes it problematic. Roberta E Pearson has shown how the
tradition of the Delsarte code, of which Chaney can be seen to be a part, passed
on from the theatre to the cinema at the end of the nineteenth century, deeply
shaping the conventions of silent movie performance.[9] The code provides a
configuration of gestures and facial expressions to portray any emotion
understandably. "Founding his system upon the observation of human behaviour,
[Delsarte] assumed that posture mirrors emotions, a different posture
corresponding to every shade of feeling."[10] This 'histrionic' code is based on an
old philosophical and iconographical tradition that dates back to Aristotle and
Quintilian, and whose emblematic moment is Charles Le Brun's 1698's *Lecture on
Expression*.[11] Centuries later, Tex Avery's cartoon in which a scarecrow father
teaches his scarecrow son the necessary poses to scare away crows with the help
of a "Scare Chart" (*I'd Love to Take Orders From You*, 1936) provides an
exemplary description of this code, and testifies to its endurance. Quasimodo,
chained to the wheel on Notre Dame's square, struggles against his heavy
chains, sticks out his tongue, raises his head, his mouth wide open, and howls to
the heavens: one suddenly recognises Le Brun's *Head of Heliodorus* in this face
distorted by pain. "When Satan fell from Paradise, he searched for power in
Hell!": Blizzard's face is distorted by a hateful grin, the exact replica of the one
formalised by Le Brun. "Do I look like Satan?": an expression of contempt, again
the same one established by Le Brun, appears on Blizzard's face. One could give
endless examples, take note of the facial expressions chosen to represent
despair, "astonishment and terror", anger, "scorn and hatred", aversion, "acute
pain", "mental pain", "when the heart feels some passion which heats and
hardens it", compare Lon's gestures to Delsarte's recommendations, and
discover many local analogies that signify the same thing: Chaney, a self-taught
actor, is the pre-eminent guardian of the classic tradition of the expressive
gesture, its last living manifestation. In that capacity, he displays a monumental

and heroic quality no matter what role he plays. He rediscovers its principles (clarity, diversity, depth) and he passes on the last of its splendour, since after him and because of him, classic expressiveness will only be parody. Why is this?

First of all, it should be noted that Lon Chaney was very fond of this tradition: not only did he use it as a natural resource, he also emphasised it, protected it, and, in a certain way, preserved it. In *The Penalty*, the point is precisely to preserve an expression, the one that the sculptor, Barbara, sees on Blizzard's satanic face, whose deep wrinkles form an emotional graph that Lon Chaney liked to sculpt upon his own face, and whose dark network can easily be superimposed over Le Brun's drawings. More generally, Chaney's acting, in several movies, functions as a repository of acting techniques: the clown films of course provide an opportunity to tackle one of the more stable repertoires, which any actor can turn to with nostalgia; but it is mainly the historical recreation movies that allow Lon to restage old acting styles. This is principally the case in two 'French' movies, *The Hunchback of Notre Dame* and *The Phantom of the Opera*: here, the remoteness of the geographical and historical setting require a gestural reconstruction that allows the revival of old techniques. In the scene of the attack on Notre Dame by the crowd of beggars, Quasimodo moves his body back and holds out a hand to show his dread, in a typical pose of the Delsarte code; he then proceeds to throw a gigantic beam on his assailants, depicting with his hand the act he is about to undertake and the way the beam will fall before going ahead with it. This device of announcing and explaining through gestures what is going to happen immediately relates back to the acting techniques of the early cinema—to Georges Méliès, and through him, to conjuring, to the circus and to the music-hall. Quasimodo's body language thus draws from numerous repertoires—animal movements, the Delsarte code, dazzling reminders of classic iconography, Victor Hugo's written and drawn prescriptions, gestures from the early days of cinema—in a great regressive tangle as untidy as the ugly mop of hair through which Lon Chaney manages to give credence to the existence of this archaic creature that predates identity. Conversely, Erik's body language in *The Phantom of the Opera* is an attempt at simplification. This character (remote in three respects: a Frenchman, a nineteenth century figure, and also a phantom), allows Chaney to work on the typical Delsartian poses—surprise, threat, terror, despair—accentuating them and sometimes slowing them down, sometimes almost taking them apart, as if the Phantom were haunted by a puppet or an automaton, a secret structure even more enigmatic than himself, acting hidden within this great impaired body. But in both cases, the acting's encyclopaedic and repetitive character furthers a formal expression of hallucination, as if its own organic archives endlessly resurface in the body.

And yet the somatic conjugations invented by Lon Chaney will put the "alphabet of passions" used with such historical intelligence by the actor back into perspective.[12] Although Chaney's style evolved throughout his career, following a path that leads more or less from frenzy to melancholia, he always subordinated his acting to Delsartism; but he also fitted his acting into a system in which what is at stake deals with psychical complexes, and not only with

Lon Chaney in
The Unknown with his
arms now on show.

passion; a system with a quite different relationship to disfigurement. Lon Chaney of course is not a contemporary of Descartes (from whom Le Brun drew his inspiration) but of Freud, and the physiological delusions that characterise the figures he elaborates manifest powers of disintegration that, far from any grammar, genuinely deal with the unspeakable. It is the debasement of having a body in *The Phantom of the Opera*; it is Dead Legs crawling in the mud of instinct in *West of Zanzibar*, in a land in which the body is only considered as human meat; it is the figure of absolute archaism that is Quasimodo; it is the family nightmare depicted in *The Unholy Three*; it is the incurable nature of all these characters and the fundamental dissimilarity of their nature.

They jump from the facades of cathedrals, they writhe on the ground like larvae, they are injured by their own gestures, they strain their legs dreadfully, they increase imbalance within their own disequilibrium (as in the case of Wilse Dilling as a cripple that everyone knocks about in *The Shock*), they die of pretending to be disabled, they are miraculously pieced back together (The Frog in *The Miracle Man*), they painfully haul themselves with their arms along hooks in the wall to reach a window to look at girls (Blizzard), and they fire off bursts of knives with their feet. The characters elaborated by Lon Chaney don't have an inkling of what could be called reason, their physiology is nothing more than a symbolic circuit enabling the appearance of crazy corporal situations, and their merest movements are a protest against uprightness. They are completely shattered by the law.

Two of Lon Chaney's remaining films proclaim their reactionary stance: *The Hunchback of Notre Dame* is a tale on the Russian Revolution, in which beggars attack Notre Dame as one would seize the Bastille or the Winter Palace, shouting "Cursed aristocrats! Down with the aristocrats!" Clopin and Quasimodo are its real protagonists: Clopin represents a failed part of the people, the *lumpenproletariat*, for whom he does not lead an economic revolution, but a political one: "My children, I wished to free you, let's fight!" The figurative handling of Quasimodo is then made clear: he is the raw creature, totally asocial and uncivil, in a state of nature, who instinctively refuses and repulses the revolt; it was necessary to show that nature does not want revolution. In *The Penalty*, Blizzard symbolises the Soviet economy: although he is legless, he runs a workshop with a rod of iron in which terrified dancers, probably kidnapped on the streets, manufacture straw hats day in and day out. Why hats? To cover the heads of the ten thousand men who will invade San Francisco. Who are these men? "Thousands of angry peasants." But the violence of Lon Chaney's work subverts, perhaps unknowingly, the reactionary nature of the fictions he acts in, and in which crime always results from perversion and never from destitution.[13] Indeed, Chaney never stopped questioning the accepted order of phenomena, he never stopped grappling with all that remains unformed, unstable in the human creature; all that destroys, threatens and scares. He never stopped outlining the idea of a man who would be different, a man who had crossed to the other side of the law and who would be twisted out of shape from that inhuman effort: a perpetually revolted body—and one that probably would not have a taste for happiness. By skilfully renewing figures, he showed how some very powerful forces stood in the way of the making up of identity and how anatomy could sustain and confirm phantasy. He invented the brilliant formal principle that destruction should not be thought and represented only in terms of breakdown and of absence, but also and especially, in terms of connections and even of sequences, of propagation, and of renewal. His most famous and most beautiful characters, Dead Legs, Alonzo, Quasimodo, Erik, Blizzard, HE, Echo, Tito, The Bishop, depict how the body assails the self; they tell us, each in turn and in their own way, of a terrifying event: how embodiment can only be disastrous.

All my thanks to Pierre-Jacques Brenez, Pierre Hecker and Stéphane du Mesnildot. Translated from the French by Briana de Berg de Marignac.

◄ NOTES

1. Translators note: in this text, the French word "fantasme" is translated as "phantasy", following the translation used by Donald Nicholson-Smith in J Laplanche and J-B Pontalis' *The Language of Psycho-Analysis*, New York: WW Norton and Company, 1973. It refers to the psychoanalytical sense of the word, defined as "a mental image or a series of mental images created in response to psychological need". The word "fantasy" will be used to refer to the following meaning: "a creation of the imaginative faculty whether expressed or merely conceived". Both definitions taken from *Merriam-Websters' Collegiate Dictionary*, Springfield, MA: Merriam-Webster, 1998.

2. Schilder, Paul, *The image and appearance of the human body: studies in the constructive energies of the psyche*, New York: International Universities Press, 1950, p. 29.

3. "Incorporation: process whereby the subject, more or less on the level of phantasy, has an object penetrate his body and keeps it 'inside' his body… it has a special relationship with the mouth and with the ingestion of food…. Incorporation provides the corporal model for introjection and identification." (Laplanche and Pontalis, *The Language of Psycho-Analysis*, p. 211.) Freud speaks of "cannibalism" to describe oral incorporation.

4. Translator's note: screen-mask is understood here as a mask that conceals and that shields what is below it at the same time. This translation follows the psychoanalytical meaning and is based on the French word "*souvenir-écran*", "screen-memory", defined as "a recollection of early childhood that may be falsely recalled or magnified in importance and that masks another memory of deep emotional significance" in *Merriam-Webster's Collegiate Dictionary*.

5. Tylor, EB, *Primitive Culture*, vol. 1, 1903, pp. 428–429, quoted in Schilder, *The image and appearance of the human body*, pp. 275–276.

6. Brion, Marcel, *L'art fantastique, Paris*: Marabout Université, 1968, p. 92.

7. Canguilhem, Georges, "L'homme et l'animal du point de vue psychologique selon Charles Darwin", in *Études d'histoire et de philosophie des sciences concernant les vivants et la vie*, Paris: Vrin, 1983, p. 116.

8. Viviani, Christian, "Lon Chaney ou la Politique de l'Acteur", *Positif* nos. 208–209, July–August 1978, p. 49.

9. Pearson, Roberta E, *Eloquent Gestures. The Transformation of Performance Style in the Griffith Biograph Films*, Berkeley, CA: University of California Press, 1992. See particularly Chapter Two, "The Theatrical Heritage".

10. Pearson, *Eloquent Gestures*, p. 22.

11. *Conférence sur l'expression générale et particulière*. For a scientific edition and a historical study of this text, see Jennifer Montagu, *The Expression of the Passions*, New Haven and London: Yale University Press, 1994.

12. This expression is based on the title of an article by Hubert Damisch on Le Brun's illustrations, "L'alphabet des masques", in *Nouvelle Revue de Psychanalyse*, no. 21, Spring 1980, pp. 123–131.

13. See for example the way in which Chinatown is introduced at the beginning of *The Shock*: "The neighbourhood of crime, fear, hatred and mystery."

FILMS

BETWEEN SILENCE AND SOUND

Robin Blyn

VENTRILOQUISM AND THE ADVENT
OF THE VOICE IN *THE UNHOLY THREE*

"That wasn't me talking. I didn't say a word." So Hector, a bookkeeper known derisively as "the Boob" in Tod Browning's 1925 silent film *The Unholy Three*, excitedly whispers to his lawyer as he descends from the stand in a trial that will seal his fate. "That wasn't me talking"—a verbal aside in a silent medium, a mute confession that speaks to the self-conscious condition of popular cinema as it meditates upon the possibility of recorded sound, and experiments with its consequences for the construction of the subject and object of perception. For, of course, Hector has not "said a word", if by 'speech' we refer to the convention of synchronous sound recording that came to dominate Hollywood cinema. Yet, even as he speaks, in the conventions of title cards and lip synch, the Boob remains unaware that he has served as the ventriloquist's dummy, and, as such, he has demonstrated a mode of sound production loosed from its anchor in the body of the speaker. When Hector says "That wasn't me talking. I didn't say a word", *The Unholy Three* admits the radical instability of the speaking subject in the years immediately preceding synchronous sound recording. Seen in the context of cinema history, films such as *The Unholy Three* thus make visible the extent to which popular film participates in a public debate about sound technology for the construction of the sensational subject. Who is the speaking subject? From whence does his voice emerge? What matter who is speaking?[1]

As the ventriloquist's dummy, Hector's courtroom aside is emblematic of the kind of self-reflexive performance that allows for a reevaluation of the strange body of Browning's work and of the interregnum period, roughly between 1925 and 1932, when cinema anticipates and responds to the emergence of the technology of recorded sound in its earliest deployments. Hector's aside draws attention to the film's own awareness of the artificiality of the cinematic medium, and to its own irreverent play with the conventions of realism standardised in the narrative cinema of the silent era—specifically to the conventions for representing the human voice.[2] Rather than paving the way for the synchronous sound recording and autonomous subject that were to become the signatures of the classical mode, films such as *The Unholy Three* convey the extent to which popular film served as a significant vernacular discourse about new conceptions of subjectivity—conceptions inspired by the prospect of sound recording. If, as James Lastra demonstrates in *Sound Technology and the American Cinema: Perception, Representation, Modernity*, such vernacular discourses shape both the technological development and the aesthetic history of the cinema, then popular films like *The Unholy Three* participate in a cultural conversation that both registers the multivalent potentials of sound technologies and actively informs the representational practices cinematic history has come to understand as the "advent of the voice".[3]

Like many films of the late silent era, *The Unholy Three* breaks with the predominant and long-established conventions of narrative cinema, and it does so by returning to the aesthetic of early cinema—an aesthetic that Tom Gunning has so influentially identified as a "cinema of attractions" and associated with the astonishment of the senses wrought by modernity. As Gunning writes, early cinema works as a "metonymy of curiosity" spawned by "the energy released between the shock caused by the illusion and the danger and delight in its pure illusion".[4] The films of George Méliès are a case in point, for Méliès came to cinema through the magic theatre and explicitly trafficked in illusion. In his 1898 *The Four Troublesome Heads*, for example, the screened magician pulls three heads from his shoulders in turn, performs a musical number with them, causes two of the heads to vanish with the swipe of his banjo, and returns the third to his own shoulders in 50 seconds flat. Flaunting the 'now you see it, now you don't' temporality of the cinema of attractions, *The Four Troublesome Heads* makes no pretence at realistic representation, celebrating instead a cinema of pure illusion. In fact, Gunning asserts that this cinema of attractions exemplified by Méliès is completely at odds with the narrative mode that would replace it, sharing more with the theatrical and fairground settings of its early exhibition, than with the realist aesthetic of narrative cinema: "Rather than being an involvement with narrative action or empathy with character psychology, the cinema of attractions solicits highly conscious awareness of the film image engaging the viewer's curiosity. The spectator does not get lost in a fictional world and its drama, but remains aware of the act of looking, the excitement of curiosity and its fulfillment."[5]

Inviting curiosity, rather than absorption, the cinema of attractions is at once the culmination of the spectacle culture of the nineteenth century, and a premonition of the avant-garde's deployment of shocks and attractions designed to undermine the bourgeois complacency that was encouraged by Hollywood's longstanding conventions of narrative realism. In this regard, Gunning references Sergei Eisenstein and the French Surrealists. By contrast, *The Unholy Three* represents a return to the cinema of attractions and an interrogation of the subject of Hollywood consumption, undertaken within the studio system itself. To follow Miriam Hanssen, films such as the *The Unholy Three* effectively deconstruct the opposition between Hollywood and the avant-garde, insisting that Hollywood cinema in the first decades of the twentieth century represents an active negotiation of modernity, an investigation into the subject and object of perception that is not so much the anti-thesis of the avant-garde as a vernacular enunciation of it.[6]

Framed by the sideshow, *The Unholy Three* represents its return to the cinema of attractions in 1925 as a return to an epistemological stance in which both the cinematic apparatus and the conventions of narrative realism are put on display as objects of curiosity. More specifically, *The Unholy Three* serves as a paradigmatic example of the "cinema of sound attractions" that thrives in the transitional years between silent and sound eras—a species of visual displays specifically associated with the representation of the voice.[7] Here, the *trompe l'oeil* (trick of the eye) of early cinema becomes inseparable from *trompe l'oreille* (trick of the ear). Revelling in the cinema of sound attractions, *The Unholy Three* bears witness to the myriad possibilities posed by the prospect of sound recording. At once, it challenges the integrated subject of narrative realism through its play with the representation of the voice, and it reveals the contest between regimes of spectacle embodied in its hybrid form. Taking its tale of moral conversion from the narrative mode and its construction of the subject-who-speaks from the cinema of sound attractions, it offers an

The Unholy Three: Strong Man (played by Victor McLagen) is caught in the act by a young girl in a scene that was eventually cut from the film. Courtesy of Elias Savada.

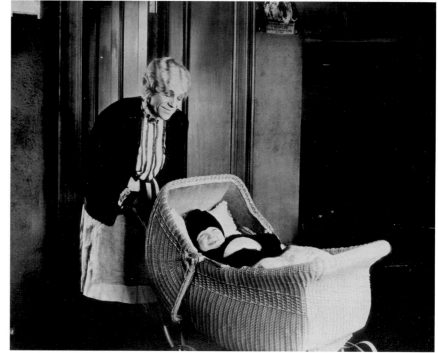

The Unholy Three: Lon
Chaney plans his next move
with partners in crime Harry
Earles and Victor McLagen.
Courtesy of Elias Savada.

Granny O'Grady (Lon
Chaney) and baby (Harry
Earles) prepare to
scope out the scene
of their next heist.
Courtesy of Elias Savada.

ambivalent allegory about the 'conversion' of cinema to synchronous sound recording.

The film's double allegiance to the cinema of sound attractions and to narrative cinema reveals itself in a conversion narrative starring silent film star Lon Chaney, the so-called "Man of a Thousand Faces". In *The Unholy Three*, Chaney plays Echo, a ventriloquist who leaves the sideshow with love interest Rosie (Mae Busch) and his pet chimpanzee, to team up with a dwarf (Harry Earles) and a Strong Man (Victor McLaglen) for a life of crime. As he leaves the sideshow, Echo changes from an explicit illusionist to a covert one. Dressed in drag, he poses as Granny O'Grady, proprietress of a bird shop specialising in parrots, which he ventriloquises to ensnare rich clientele. Harry Earles plays Granny's baby, Little Willie. When the parrot-purchasers return home to find that their parrots will not speak, Granny and Baby graciously pay a visit. While Granny attends to the parrot, Little Willie scopes out the potential booty that they can return to steal with the aid of the Strong Man.

The scam falters when the dwarf and the strong man murder one of the parrot owners in the midst of a theft and, simultaneously, Rosie falls for the sincere, if wholly uncharismatic, Hector (the Boob), the bookkeeper of the shop. Two birds are killed with one stone, so to speak, when the murder is pinned on the bookkeeper. In keeping with the narrative conventions of the melodrama, however, Echo proves vulnerable to sentimentality. Moved by Rosie's depth of feeling for the Boob, he saves the duped bookkeeper from the noose. His unreformed cohorts, however, meet their ends at the hands of Echo's chimpanzee, now filmed from low angle shots that transform it into a gorilla-sized menace. While the narrative thus meets the generic demands of the melodrama, it interrupts its progress toward moral conversion and the triumph of "true love" with a series of sound attractions.

From the very beginning, ventriloquism in *The Unholy Three* underscores the simulation of human speech as a scam, a means of ripping off a hopelessly naïve and novelty-loving class of consumers. Even as Echo ventriloquises his dummy before the crowd, the film shows Rosie picking the pockets of his spectators. The hoax goes beyond the sideshow audience represented in the film, however. It finds its double in the audience of the film. Just as the sideshow audience lose their wallets to a short and uninspired performance, the audience of the film pays their money to see a silent film about ventriloquism, a medium in which it is no trick at all. Rather, the lip sync that represents the dummy's speech is the same lip sync that represents human speech, a representational coincidence that registers the simulation of the voice as a condition of the medium. Moreover, ventriloquism, the very illusion that motivates the plot and registers the character's conversion at the end of the film, is completely unassimilable to the audience. It's rather like watching a disappearing act while wearing a blindfold. The cross-dressing of the ventriloquist is the way the film marks a hoax otherwise imperceptible in its medium of display. Throwing voices—speech unanchored in the body of the speaker—is figured as transvestism, emphasising the threat it poses to the autonomy of the integrated subject.

In *The Unholy Three*, ventriloquism becomes the occasion for the rehearsal of the conventions available for the representation of the voice. In other words, it is the need to simulate the voice in the enactment of ventriloquism that provokes the cinema of sound attractions that punctuate and often override the narrative. The result is, indeed, a metonymy of curiosity. For while the ventriloquised speech of the wooden dummy in Echo's sideshow act can be represented with the same conventions used to represent unventriloquised human speech, the 'speech' of Granny O'Grady's parrots appears on the screen in a whimsically alternative form. As the cross-dressing Echo ventriloquises their speech, their words are written in cartoon-like balloons that suddenly appear by the parrots' beaks. Apparently, the balloons represent the falsetto of Echo disguised as Granny O'Grady, although they never appear again—not for Granny's speech or for the 'speech' of the parrots. Rather, the choice appears to be entirely random. The balloons thus highlight the destabilisation of conventions of representation posed by the simulation of speech that sound technology would soon stake as its own terrain, fostering the illusion of the voice as the presence of an integrated and autonomous subject that ventriloquism so energetically here disturbs. It is thus entirely appropriate that when the wealthy customers discover that their

The dummy talks back in Lon Chaney's ventriloquism-without-sound from Tod Browning's silent era *The Unholy Three*. Courtesy of Elias Savada.

parrots won't speak, they offer their complaints to O'Grady's Bird Shop by way of the telephone, a technology that extracts speech from the corporeal, making it available without the physical presence of the speaker. Like ventriloquism, the telephone is a means of throwing voices and, as such, it links that traditional hoax to the more threatening simulations of human speech posed by technology.

Lon Chaney as the sinister Granny O'Grady.

If, in the form of throwing voices, ventriloquism threatens the autonomy of the subject who produces sound and troubles the integration of word (speech) and image (the visual representation of it) for its audience, then the ventriloquist's criminal activity is his threat to narrative cinema, which depends upon autonomy and integration. Echo's moral conversion at the end of the film thus represents a conversion from the cinema of sound attractions to the demands of realism as defined by narrative cinema in the silent era. This much can be seen in the courtroom climax to the film. At the behest of Rosie, Echo arrives in court to save Hector from the chair. He attempts to do so by instigating Hector's return to the stand and, then, by ventriloquising his speech once he gets there. As the Boob, Hector proves an adequate dummy; he proceeds to tell the court details he does not yet know: that Granny O'Grady is a man in league with a trio named "The Unholy Three". At this crucial moment in the narrative, ventriloquism does not fail the artist. Hence Hector can tell his lawyer, "That wasn't me talking. I didn't say a word." What fails, however, is narrative credibility itself. That is, the narrative provided by ventriloquism fails to save Hector because the jury and the general audience in the court fail to believe it. Echo's subsequent confession thus marks the impotence of the cinema of sound attractions and its sensational subject in the face of the law of realism.

Occurring as it does in a courtroom, Echo's conversion here represents one of the film's two final judgments on the conversion of the cinema of sound attractions to a sound-based narrative cinema disciplined to the demands of realism. Echo's decision to interrupt the proceedings and confess, rather than 'throwing voices' at the judge or the jury, conveys the extent to which the realist mode had become the reigning aesthetic law. Moreover, in refusing his illusionist gift, Echo relinquishes ventriloquism as an outmoded and ineffective art—which it is, of course, in the medium of silent film. The illusionism of the cinema of attractions, he implicitly conveys, will not suffice to further the narrative, to save the Boob. Thus, the contemporary demands of narrative realism clearly supersede the aesthetics of a cinema of attractions. Rather than providing the audience with the thrill of ventriloquism, Echo must come clean; he must not get away with murder. Finally, Echo's decision to confess and, hence, to reveal the finite location of his body to his voice, is an endorsement of the unified subject of speech and perception that sound technology would soon be disciplined by the industry to provide. Ultimately, the narrative of this film requires the integration of the senses and the autonomous subject that goes with it. By submitting itself to the demands of that narrative, *The Unholy Three* transforms the illusionist into a confessed criminal who loses his girl and the secret of his art in an act of self-sacrifice. From the perspective of the cinema of sound attractions, the sacrifice appears unnecessary, for why could themaster ventriloquist not simply ventriloquise the sentence delivered by the judge? From the perspective of the moral conversion required by the melodramatic narrative, however, the sacrifice is absolutely required. Hence, Echo's confession represents the conversion of one mode of spectacle into another as a triumph of justice purchased at the price of love.

Based on the climax in the court of law, it would seem that in 1925 *The Unholy Three* presages the interrelationship of sound cinema to narrative realism that the industry would accomplish largely in the next five years. In the midst of the court-ordered integration of the subject of sound and the narrative of moral conversion it serves, however, the film offers an irrepressible disruption, a spectacle that realism simply cannot contain. I am speaking here of Echo's chimpanzee. Of all of the strange elements in this film, the chimp is perhaps the most bizarre. As an attraction in the sideshow that Echo decides to take with him, the animal consistently references the sideshow and the logic of the hoax that sustains it. While he only makes his appearance in the latter half of the film, his presence is forecast in the monkey that appears, without explanation, scampering in a cage in O'Grady's bird shop. Neither Hector nor the customers question the place of such an animal in an establishment limited to selling birds. Like the monkey, the chimpanzee that later appears is a disturbance in the pretence of realism that no one seems to notice—at least until the ending of the film, when it transforms into a gorilla.

While sound attractions disappear from the film with Echo's confession, the artifice of narrative realism never fully recovers its power to contain the spectacular illusions and aesthetic of astonishment that challenge its jurisdiction throughout the film. As a marker of the sideshow and the cinema of attractions, the chimp turns out to be an instrument of justice that operates outside, and in excess of, the law of realism protected in the court. Thus we first view him threatening the police detective with a hearty growl. Moreover, while Echo walks away from the court a free man, rewarded for his goodness and honesty, and the bookkeeper gets his girl, the dwarf and the strongman get killed off by the chimp-turned-gorilla. Attacking the two unreformed criminals in their hideaway, it functions more as a premonition of *King Kong* than as part and parcel of melodramatic excess. In *The Unholy Three*, the ghastly murder of the dwarf and the strongman thus serves simultaneously as a gruesome alternative to justice meted out by the courts and as the irrepressible eruption of the cinema of attractions onto the screen. It is difficult to maintain, then, that *The Unholy Three* is an allegory of the capitulation to the realist mode of narrative cinema. Rather, juxtaposed to one another, the triumph of the cinema of attractions figured in the gorilla and the triumph of narrative cinema figured in Echo's conversion before the court, aptly produce the conflicting messages that make *The Unholy Three*, ultimately, a hybrid of contrary aesthetic modes. In its hybrid form, it imagines the location of the voice in the finite space of the individual body as but one of the possibilities latent in the technology of sound recording.

The vitality of the cinema of sound attractions even in the face of Echo's ostensible conversion can be seen in the return to the sideshow at the end of the film. In the end, Echo returns to the sideshow stage, completing the frame that surrounds the narrative of moral reformation and the triumph of love within the logic of the hoax. In fact, his sideshow act, as performed both at the beginning and the end of the film, presents the conventions of narrative cinema as a freak show hoax, an attraction equivalent to the conjoined twins, the fat lady, and the sword swallower. "That's all there is to life, friends", Professor Echo concludes, "A little laughter, a little tears...." On the freak show stage, Echo apparently comments not only upon his own sideshow art but on the tale of love and crime we have just seen. Thus, Echo's ventriloquist performance highlights not only the problem of the simulation of the voice, but the extent to which it destabilises the conventions of realism it both frames and disrupts.

The future life of *The Unholy Three* similarly evinces the resilience of the cinema of sound attraction in the years that follow its release. Given the narrative and the gimmick of ventriloquism that motivates the plot, it is not surprising that *The Unholy Three* was the first and only film Lon Chaney agreed to remake with sound. In the remake, he was commissioned to speak three parts and, in 1930, he signed a notarised affidavit swearing that all the voices were his. As the advance publicity indicated the "Man of a Thousand

Faces" was to "reveal the Voice of a Thousand Thrills".[8] Clearly the
unification of the subject was, as yet, a tentative affair, and the *trompe l'oreille*
of the cinema of sound attractions and its disassociation of the senses
continued to find their way onto the Hollywood screen even after 'the advent
of the voice'.

⌨ NOTES

1. A decade's worth of scholarship has confirmed Noel King's contention that silent
film was never a silent experience. See "The Sound of Silents", in *Silent Films*, Richard
Abel ed., New Brunswick: Rutgers University Press, 1996, pp. 31–44. For studies of
the myriad sound practices developed in the silent era, see especially Charles Musser's
The Emergence of Cinema I: The American Scene to 1907, New York: Scribners, 1991;
Noel Burch's *Life to Those Shadows*, Berkeley, California: University of California Press,
1990; and most recently, James Lastra's *Sound Technology and the American
Cinema: Perception, Representation, Modernity*, New York: Columbia University
Press, 2000.

2. I would suggest that this point has been largely absent in a critical conversation
primarily limited to ideological critique and psychoanalytic exegesis. From the perspective
of such critical paradigms, Browning's films retain their critical value merely as evidence of
historical manifestations of sexism, racism, and the vilification of the disabled, as well as
for their dramatisation of intrinsically ahistorical Freudian theory. Insightful as the resulting
studies have been, both ideological and psychoanalytic approaches share a tendency to
render the status of the film *as film* irrelevant. Martin Norden and Gayle Cahill are surely
correct in their assertion, for example, that the images of women in *Freaks* and
The Devil Doll "reinforce Hollywood's patterns of punishment of historically marginalised
women…", but their analysis could just as easily be focused on a novel or an
illustrated tabloid as it is on a film. So, too, David Skal and Elias Savada's reading of
The Unknown as a case study in the Freudian uncanny bases its interpretation so
thoroughly on narrative that the materiality of the cinematic medium becomes beside
the point. See Norden and Cahill, "Violence, Women, and Disability in Tod Browning's
Freaks and The Devil Doll", *Journal of Film and Television*, vol. 23, no. 2, Summer 1998,
pp. 86–94, p.92, and David J Skal and Elias Savada, *Dark Carnival: The Secret World of
Tod Browning, Hollywood's Master of the Macabre*, New York: Anchor Books, 1995,
pp. 110–111.

3. I am indebted here especially to Mary Ann Doane's "The Voice in the Cinema:
The Articulation of Body and Space", in *Film Theory and Criticism*, Leo Braudy
and Marshall Cohen eds., New York and Oxford: Oxford University Press, 1999,
pp. 363–375.

4. Gunning, Tom, "An Aesthetic of Astonishment: Early Film and the (In)credulous
Spectator", in *Viewing Positions*, Linda Williams ed., New Brunswick: Rutgers University
Press, 1997, pp. 126 and 129.

5. Gunning, "An Aesthetic of Astonishment", p. 121.

6. See Miriam Bratu Hanssen's "The Mass Production of the Senses: Classical Cinema as
Vernacular Modernism", *Modernism/Modernity*, vol. 6, no. 2, 1999, pp. 59–77.

7. As a "cinema of sound attractions", *The Unholy Three* keeps company with such
films as Rupert Julian's *The Phantom of the Opera*, 1925, James Cruze's *The Great
Gabbo*, 1929, Charlie Chaplin's *City Lights*, 1931, and Fritz's Lang's *The Testament of
Dr Mabuse*, 1932. My claims about the cinema of sound attractions that proliferate

in the transitional years between the silent era and the talkie are based both on my own research and on Michel Chion's groundbreaking *The Voice in Cinema*, Claudia Gorbman trans., New York: Columbia University Press, 1999. Here, Chion offers an extensive reading of Fritz Lang's *The Testament of Dr Mabuse* as an experiment with sound technologies, and, more generally, on experiments in the cinema that entail the dissociation of the human voice from the body of the speaker. Rob Spadoni has usefully drawn my attention to this dissociation in James Cruze's *The Great Gabbo*. I am grateful to him for allowing me access to his unpublished manuscript.

8. Crafton, Donald, *Talkies: American Cinema's Transition to Sound*, 1925–1931, Berkeley, California: University of California Press, 1999, p. 323.

White Bo(d)y in Wonderland

Stefan Brand

CULTURAL ALTERITY AND SEXUAL DESIRE IN *WHERE EAST IS EAST*

⋈ WHERE EAST IS EAST, AND WEST IS WEST ⋈

In its December 1889 issue, *Macmillan's Magazine* published a poem written under the pseudonym "Yussuf" that immediately caught the readers' attention. The poem, entitled "The Ballad of East and West," began and ended with the following quatrain:

> OH! East is East, and West is West, and never the twain shall meet, Till Earth and Sky stand presently at God's great Judgment Seat; But there is neither East nor West, Border, nor Breed, nor Birth, When two strong men stand face to face, tho' they come from the ends of the earth![1]

The author was, of course, Joseph Rudyard Kipling, who had slightly altered his first name to become Yussuf. Born and raised in Bombay, Kipling was known as an intellectual of multinational descent who tended to glorify British imperialism and heroism in India and Burma.[2] Interestingly enough, of the 96 lines of this poem, only one single line, "East is East, and West is West, and never the twain shall meet", has survived in the cultural imaginary.[3] The transformation of Kipling's phrase to a well-known parable of the Orient is not merely an example of misquotation, but also testifies to a common practice in Western discourse—that of reinforcing images which stress the homogeneity and internal consistency of 'the East'.[4]

Where East is East, 1929, the last co-production of director Tod Browning with Lon Chaney, playfully reenacts the symbolic dimension contained in Kipling's phrase. The expression not only re-emerges in the movie's title; the vision of the East that is negotiated and shown in all its absurdity here is very much akin to that associated with Kipling. The movie takes us to the picturesque scenery of 1920s Indo-China. Here, the main character Tiger Haynes (Lon Chaney) works as an animal trapper in the rainforest. After returning from a tiger hunt in the Northern part of Siam to his hometown in Vien-Tiane, Haynes finds his half-

Chinese daughter Toyo (played by Mexican-American actress Lupe Vélez) hopelessly in love with the cosmopolitan businessman Bobby (Lloyd Hughes), subsequently referred to as 'white boy'. Having been left by Toyo's mother when the girl was still a child, Haynes is tortured by uneasy feelings regarding his daughter's impending marriage. He finds his suspicion confirmed when Toyo's scheming mother, Madame de Sylva (Estelle Taylor) returns to steal her daughter's sweetheart away from her. While playing with the conventions of the romantic love comedy, the film also avails itself of the motifs of the classic melodrama. When the movie was released in May 1929, it was marketed by Metro Goldwyn Mayer as a colonial drama in the mould of British imperialist fiction. The official movie poster shows Lon Chaney in an Oriental setting, with Chinese letters appearing as a decoration in the upper right corner of the picture.

My aim in this essay is to situate *Where East is East* within the contemporaneous dialogue concerning the East, tracing both the film's treatment of ethnic issues and its complex aesthetics. As a highly ambivalent work of art, Browning's movie is caught in a strange predicament. While replicating some dominant images of the East and thus validating the ideology connected to them, the film also seeks to subvert and destabilise the authority of these myths. It oscillates between the recognition of the invented character of the Orient and a fascination with the magic emanating from it. The film's dilemma is epitomised by the figure of Bobby, the white boy, who finds himself torn between his fiancée Toyo (Browning's case in point that racial differences can be blurred) and her mother, Madame de Sylva, an oriental beauty whose villainous nature threatens to destroy the family. By situating the narrative in the borderland between Western civilisation and Eastern tradition ("a colourful spot of French rule and Chinese custom"), Browning's film hints at those "curious interrelationships between figures for sexual and racial Otherness" which have been described as key features of colonial discourse.[5] In my reading, the film capitalises upon the liminality of both scenery and character constitution, facilitating an intricate rhetoric of boundary transgression. Through its aesthetics of deconstruction, the film deactivates some of the mechanisms that commonly enable the development of 'fixity' in the ideological constitution of otherness.[6]

One of the underlying questions of this essay is how American cinema in the late 1920s behaved in its encounter with racial ideology and to what extent it succeeds in proposing an alternative concept of ethnic identity.[7] What is at stake here is not only the model of the Orient as a source of myths regarding the East, but also the legitimacy of the concept of whiteness, which still functions as an ideological point of identification in Western discourse. I will start with a brief discussion of the figures of colonial discourse in Browning's movie and then move on to an analysis of the movie's cinematic impetus, which I see marked by a complicated strategy of reinvention and deconstruction of ethnic stereotypes. For this purpose, I will utilise six categories of linguistic construction that Toni Morrison enumerates in her interpretation of imaginary models of race in American literature: "Economy of the stereotype", which "allows the writer a quick and easy image without the responsibility of specificity, accuracy, or even narratively useful description"; "Metonymic displacement", specifically the use

Where East is East: Vien-Tiane, borderland between Western civilisation and Eastern tradition.

of colour and physical traits to signify the ethnically different character; "Metaphysical condensation", that is, the collapsing of "persons into animals" in order to prevent human contact and exchange; "Fetishisation", a form of physical reduction that helps to evoke erotic anxieties and desires, thus establishing the notion of a fixed major difference "where difference does not exist or is minimal"; "Allegories of dehistoricisation", that is, symbolic formations that accentuate the vastness of difference through universal images; and finally "Patterns of explosive, disjointed, and repetitive language", namely cultural configurations such as "comic ethnicity" that serve to "indicate a loss of control in the text that is attributed to the objects of its attention rather than to the text's own dynamics".[8] These categories will be employed not so much as inflexible categories of measuring the film's ideological bias, but as analytic instruments. Using Morrison's framework for reference, I will argue that the visual aesthetics of Browning's movie is grounded on an ambivalent strategy: it reconstructs the established economy of ethnic stereotyping and simultaneously detaches it from its ideological framework.

⌦ THE FIGURES OF COLONIAL DISCOURSE ⌦

According to contemporary approaches in postcolonial studies and Afro-American literary criticism, Orientalism and Africanism must be regarded as the two most dominant ideological formations around which Western cultural hegemony is organised. Both Edward W Said in *Orientalism* and Toni Morrison in *Playing in the Dark* contend that hegemonic white cultures in Europe and the United States have constituted themselves in relation to an invented, subjugated, and eroticised Other.[9] Cultural alterity is deployed in colonial thinking as a means of essentialising and aggravating ethnic differences. In the ideologies of Orientalism and Africanism, these differences become signifiers for one fundamental distinction: that between Us and Them, Same and Other. The texts of colonial discourse, Homi K Bhabha argues, have produced "those terrifying stereotypes of savagery, cannibalism, lust and anarchy which are the signal points of identification and alienation, scenes of fear and desire".[10] For Bhabha, these images have a strong effect on both the practice of cultural self-fashioning and the rhetoric of exclusion. In the colonial rhetoric, the world is divided into symbolic regimes of lightness and darkness, control and chaos. While whiteness is associated with "order, rationality, [and] rigidity", blackness stands for "disorder, irrationality and looseness".[11]

Lloyd Hughes as Bobby ('white boy') the Western suitor of Lupe Vélez's character, Toyo.

In Browning's *Where East is East*, the binary logic of whiteness is symbolically suspended. Although the film does make use of a wide range of figures typical of colonial discourse, it never leaves these images uncommented. By portraying Madame de Sylva as the essential Eastern villain, the film toys with the stereotype of the duplicitous and mischievous Asian. However, this cliché does not come across unfiltered; the evil Madame is presented as a product of Bobby's imagination, more a hallucinatory apparition in the coloniser's twisted frame of mind than a 'real character'. Bobby Bailey, the film's paradigmatic 'white boy', is installed as the agent and creator of such fantasies gone berserk. Characterised as a noble businessman of British descent who finds himself entrapped in fantasies of the Orient, Bobby symbolises the qualities of innocence and Western naïveté as corrupted by the colonial imagination.

Significantly, Bobby wears, through most parts of the movie, a white shirt and a very light, almost white jacket. His father who has a circus in Singapore (a city that had been under British protection since 1819) stands for the adventurousness of the British imperialists. Bobby becomes an advocate of a dream hierarchy, in which the Orient functions as an empty screen for fantasies of Western imperialism and masculine endeavour in the East. By reconstructing the constitution of the myth of the Orient, from its genesis (Bobby's initial encounter with the Madame), to its symbolic eradication (Bobby's final recognition that not the Madame but her half-Chinese daughter is the right woman for him), *Where East is East* recreates the legend of the Orient as an incalculable narrative, in which the desiring white body is punished through an act of disillusionment.

This becomes clear in one of the final scenes of *Where East is East*, where Bobby, frustrated by his addictive obsession with the Madame, sits in a restaurant, visualising the evil woman everywhere around him. On the verge of a nervous breakdown, he tears his hair in desperation and violently looks about the room. At a nearby table, the duplicated image of Madame de Sylva appears to him. Sitting at the table with two native customers, she seems to stare at him from two sides at the same time. Bobby's daydream is contrasted with the reality of everyday life in the restaurant whose customers are visibly of European and Asian descent. In the midst of Bobby's fantasy, the film cuts to the image of a white couple at another table. "What's wrong with that man?" the woman asks her husband, "He's staring at everybody!" Both wife and husband are clad in suits that correspond to the image of British colonisers. They cast a blank look at poor Bobby, who is writhing in his chair in anguish. The husband's gesture (he points his finger at his head) suggests that both think that Bobby has gone insane. As if to make things worse, Bobby now envisions the image of his true love, Toyo, emerging as a superimposition between the duplicated mother figure. We sense that Bobby is still haunted by the memory of his "Oriental" experience with the seductive Madame although reality has already manifested itself before his eyes. The film here presents two contradictory reflections of the East: on the one hand, a stylish image of the 'essential' East, symbolised by the evil mother sitting at a table with other native customers; on the other hand, the concrete image of the mixed crowd in the restaurant. This second image is extended by the superimposed picture of Toyo, that character who functions throughout the movie as an icon of miscegenation (as the daughter of a European animal trapper and a local beauty). By putting these images next to each other, Browning creates a tension between myth and reality, through which the artificiality of Bobby's daydream fantasies becomes evident.

⋈ BROWNING'S ECONOMY OF STEREOTYPING ⋈

In the 1910s and 20s, Orientalism reached a high in American cultural practice.[12] The advertising business made use of Oriental imagery to sell products as diverse as tobacco (Fatima Turkish cigarettes) and electric light bulbs (Maxfield Parrish, *Lamp Seller of Baghdad*). Songs such as "My Turkish Opal from

Bobby is finally driven mad, caught between his obsession with Madame De Sylva and the pure love of Toyo.

Constantinople", 1912, and "In My Harem", 1913, topped the charts. Films like George Melford's *The Sheik*, 1921, and George Fitzmaurice's *The Son of the Sheik*, 1926, both with Rudolph Valentino in the lead role, grossed at the box office.[13] At first glance, Browning's *Where East is East* seems to deploy many of the well-known stereotypes concerning the Orient that were familiar from such productions—above all, in the notion of the East as fundamentally different and unique. At the same time, the concept of "East is East" is satirised through a staging of the Orient as an assortment of costumes and gestures. The conjunction "where" hints at the fictional dimension that the East accrued through Hollywood films. In Browning's ironic use of Kipling's phrase, it is, above all, this constructed world of cinematic fiction that harbours the myth of the East. Only in literature and film, Browning suggests, an imaginary space can come to existence, and it is *there* that "East is East".

In one of the film's most memorable scenes, Bobby and the evil Madame are stuck together on a boat on the Mekong River. Gazing at the "fading stars" and inhaling the "perfumed breeze" from "Lotus, Jasmin, and Moghra trees", Bobby sighs, looking at the Madame: "This is all like a poem of Kipling's." This statement, conveyed through an intertitle, raises the audience's expectations of a scene of romantic love. The following shot is thus rather sobering: framed in a two-shot with Bobby, the Madame immediately averts her gaze to look at some native passengers sleeping on the floor. These travellers are obviously too poor to afford a proper cabin and have to spend the night on the deck. This hardly romantic scenery is the catalyst for the next shot, in which the Madame, shown in a half-frontal take, moves her upper body towards Bobby's (who is now seen from the rear). The film cuts to a close-up of Bobby (the only close-up in the whole sequence). He looks skeptical, but curious; the use of the close-up suggests that we are to identify with Bobby, the innocent daydreamer. The whole setting is charged with clichés: "pale moon shadows through the Babul trees... Native song... weird, plaintive melodies". In one of the next two-shots, anticipating the final, cathartic kiss, we see Bobby sitting at the Madame's feet. She fondles his hair, looking down upon him from above. The way they are framed, Madame de Sylva appears less like a lover than a worshipped Goddess. The ensuing intertitle highlights the impression of treachery: "These nights of the East are strange and wayward things." Alluding to the proverbial connection between the images of Orient and Night, familiar to audiences from the Arabian Nights, the film once again emphasises the dimension of story-telling.[14] To the audience, it becomes evident that Bobby has lost himself in a fairytale, a myth that Madame de Sylva, the devious beauty, has helped to produce. We sense that Bobby is falling for a lie when the wicked Madame bends over him in expectation of a kiss. "My East will be your East", she tells him suggestively, "You will love it... I promise." Since we know how the promises of Oriental beauties usually end in fairytales, we tend to distrust her words. Alluding to the stereotypical image of lustrous harems and tempting beauties, the film seduces us into a strange, dream-like world. Browning here plays with the ambiguities involved in the common misreading of Kipling's poem, encouraging his American audience to question the existing patterns of colonial discourse and come to conclusions that lie beyond those modes of thinking. The romantic version of the Orient as a land of eternal mysticism is exposed here as a Eurocentric illusion that we must not fall prey to.[15] It is no coincidence that *Where East is East* was criticised by contemporary reviewers as being filmed "in the mood of a cheap magazine sex tale of the Orient".[16] The conspicuousness of Oriental imagery functions as part of the film's linguistic strategy of disclosure and deconstruction. It is precisely through this arrangement of flashy, lurid images of the East that we come to consider the nature of stereotyping itself.

Homi K Bhabha argues that one of the main features of the stereotype is its inherent ambivalence. "The stereotype... is a form of knowledge and identification that vacillates between what is always 'in place', already known, and something that must be anxiously repeated."[17] In *Where East is East*, it is not the stereotype's homogeneity that is foregrounded, but its hidden inconsistency.

By emphasising the staged character of the Orient, Browning's film invites us to put the opposition between East and West into question and follow a more complicated economy of identity. Kipling's phrase, "East is West, and West is West, and never the twain shall meet", is placed into a different context here. On various levels, East and West actually do meet, both within the film's fictional sphere and beyond it. First of all, we are asked, as Western moviegoers, to 'encounter' the East and to engage in a visual dialogue with a region unknown to us. Second, the film visually describes the merging of West and East—both in terms of intercultural marriage and in terms of the transgression of ethnic boundaries. The East depicted in Browning's film is visibly artificial; it is a site of escapist fantasies and unfulfilled desires rather than an actual geographic *topos*. In other words, we are brought to a position where we recognise Browning's East as a mere stage onto which those themes, already familiar from his other films, are transferred: sex and race.

Bobby is seduced by Madame De Sylva: "My East will be your East. You will love it… I promise."

⋈ METONYMIC DISPLACEMENT AND ETHNIC MASQUERADE ⋈

The metonymic displacement of 'ethnically different' characters can be regarded as a stable convention in American film and literature. Often a black character is displaced in the narrative through colour-coding and physical traits. These characteristics take the place of the character's actual persona, functioning as sole indicators of his or her nature. In *Where East is East*, the purity of such dislocations is systematically called into question. Right from the beginning, the film suggests that both land and people exist on a boundary. The establishing shot presents a highly ambivalent image—"the jungle of Laos… where Siam meets the border line of upper Indo-China". In the film's metaphoric language, Laos and Siam, which had been French Protectorates since the late nineteenth century, stand for unconquered nature and the prevalence of barbarism. Yet Laos, with its capital Vien-Tiane, also speaks of a notion of internationality. The emphasis on the city's liminal position between civilisation and savagery is not coincidental; the same motif is echoed in the constitution of the characters. Tiger Haynes, for example, is not portrayed as the typical white coloniser—physically distorted from his encounters with the jungle of Siam, he lives in Vien-Tiane together with a half-breed daughter and a non-European mother-in-law. The figure of Toyo also resists the logic of stereotyping; at various points in the film, we are reminded of her mixed ethnic origins, and her endeavour to cross the lines of those origins.

Even the wicked Madame does not entirely fill the stereotype. Marked as an Oriental character primarily through her appearance and *habitus*, her name, Madame de Sylva, however, also suggests a French influence. Her operatic gestures and excessive make-up point to performative behaviour, rather than to an innate 'Oriental' quality. Through the character of Madame de Sylva, we are also reminded of the Hollywood stereotype of the Eastern woman. "The discourse of Orientalism, its internal consistency and rigorous procedures", Edward W Said notes, "were all designed for readers and consumers in the metropolitan West."[18] *Where East is East* is aware of this interplay between myth-making (the Hollywood dream factory) and the level of reception (ticket-buying consumers). Not only does the film operate within the strategies of Orientalist discourse in its narrative structure, it also makes the genesis of this discourse and its potential deconstruction part of the plot. For this reason, Browning's film focuses not so much on skin colour and physical traits, but on performance and costumes. Notably, it is through markers of the surface (*habitus*, clothing, objects) that the film's characters are charged with 'Oriental' traits. In an early scene, Toyo is shown dancing along the Mekong River to welcome her father. In her left hand, she carries an umbrella decorated with Chinese signs and a landscape motif—the same type of umbrella that we later see in the hands of native girls walking on the streets.[19] An ethnically charged object, the umbrella is deployed here to identify Toyo as a local resident.[20] The picturesque scenery adds to this impression: there are native fishing boats and cargo ships on the water, elephants serve as vehicles of transportation, and a mixed crowd of Europeans and Asians strolls along the river. All these signifiers are used to endow Toyo with an external set of ethnic identities that does not necessarily

The joyful Toyo greets her father at the Mekong River: her Chinese umbrella identifies her as being from the East, as Bobby's white jacket identifies him as being from the West.

correspond with her inner identity. In the same fashion, the character of Madame de Sylva is introduced through an assemblage of ethnically coded images: she lies on a large sofa on the ship's deck, accompanied by what seems to be an entourage of willing servants. The scenery is enriched by a cascade of metaphors for the East in the intertitles. The vision of 'ethnic otherness' is demystified here as a Western construct. The markers of difference are so embellished that they serve to expose the performative character of ethnicity. In the case of Toyo, the various markers of ethnic difference are carefully kept in balance, making it impossible for the viewer to establish one clear-cut category.[21] The film, then, endorses a logic of ethnic masquerade—Toyo simply *plays* the Asian girl. Her true identity, we learn, extends far beyond the limitations of coded ethnicity.[22]

⋈ METAPHYSICAL CONDENSATION AND ANIMAL IMAGERY ⋈

The technique of metaphysical condensation allows an author, in Toni Morrison's words, "to transform social and historical differences into universal differences".[23] It implies the reduction of persons into beasts, or the identification of a person's nature with grunts or animal sounds. The differences between ethnic groups can thus be articulated through the underlying distinction between civilisation and savagery. Notably, in *Where East is East*, the technique of metaphysical condensation is applied mainly to the white lead character. Tiger Haynes, played by Lon Chaney, not only bears the conflation of man and beast in his name, he is also presented in a manner that underscores his savage nature. Make-up artists had prepared his face with nonflexible collodion to generate deep, hideous scars, indicating the character's previous fights with wild animals. Chaney, known to audiences from similar roles in which he had played beast-like and often physically crippled creatures, convincingly embodies the weather-beaten animal trapper here.[24] The analogy between the character and the beast is stressed in various scenes. Twice in the movie, we see Haynes actually imitating a tiger as he playfully fights with his daughter; in one scene, an exclusively Asian audience watches the performances of Haynes and Toyo from the background, visibly amused.

The animal trapper Tiger Haynes (played by Lon Chaney) imitating his namesake.

      This double discourse of performance is anticipated in the movie's very first scene. Here, we see a tiger sneaking through the wilderness of a tropical forest. Shown in an extreme long shot, the tiger is heading towards us slowly,

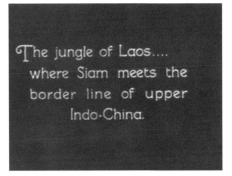

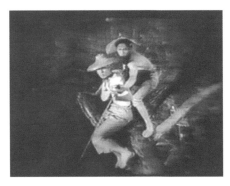

Tiger Haynes, at home in the jungle environment.

almost cautiously, with meandering movements, immediately conveying an impression of the animal's elegance and instinctive power. This creature is obviously the king of an exotic realm, a savage environment that embraces nature and yet involves its inhabitants in a continuous fight for survival. As the tiger's anxious movements suggest, it senses a lurking danger, but is nevertheless tempted (and perhaps driven by its animal instincts) to move forward. The ensuing shots familiarise us with the tiger hunt that provides the context of the story. Shot from a low angle, we see a white trapper hiding behind two thick branches of a tree, holding a rope that belongs to a giant net —from the outset, it is clear that this tough figure is the hero of the film. As we have already learned from the opening credits, this character is named "Tiger Haynes". The rhetoric of name-giving is highly important in the movie, establishing the Chaney character both as a tiger hunter and as the tiger himself, the true ruler of the jungle. Viewed from a low angle, he appears extremely large and dominant. His facial features are stern and determined, his whole body seems to merge with the setting of uninhibited nature, symbolised by the dim trees in the background. The environment is considerably reduced, as the character is placed against the blurred setting of the jungle. This concentration on the figure of Haynes is enhanced through a series of identification shots— starting with a full shot of Tiger Haynes sitting in the tree, we are carefully led towards him into a close-up, then again distanced with four medium shots, and two final long shots that show him climbing down from the tree to catch the tiger. Both the animal on the ground and the crew of Asian hunters in the trees who assist Haynes are shown in high angle shots that make them appear as subjects of this true 'king of the jungle'. The impression is, in a double sense, one of a battle for dominion in the wilderness. Framed by the colonial subtext of authority versus subjugation, Chaney becomes a figure of transgression. The border between Siam and upper Indo-China here functions as a metaphor for the character's movements across the lines of race and class. Hunting animals in the Asian jungle, Haynes also has a luxurious residence in Vien-Tiane where his daughter is waiting for him with her Chinese grandmother. While symbolically assuming the position of a coloniser (given his association with the trade in big game), Haynes has also assimilated to the colonial environment. Notably, he is clad in the same outfit as his fellow hunters. Moreover, he seems to cultivate a sense of closeness to nature. His *habitus* is raw and undigested, marked by impulsive gestures and spontaneous movements. This affiliation with nature is underscored by Haynes' deep connection with animals—he rides home to Vien-Tiane on the back of an elephant; at his home, he keeps a couple of tigers, a parrot and a female gorilla named Rangho.[25]

The establishing sequence foreshadows the film's idiosyncratic trajectory of an embodiment of colonial tropes. The identification of Tiger Haynes with an exotic animal that cannot be tamed sheds light on the character's own wildness and lack of control. Paradoxically, the same symbolic transfer takes place when the evil Madame appears on the stage to bewitch the innocent Bobby. "She is bad!" one of her maids tells Haynes, "White boy like sheep with tiger! Take him away!" Referring to the image from the first scene (the goat in the box waiting for the tiger), the film develops a double allegory, in which both the Madame and her counterpart, the animal trapper, are visualised as tigers.

The issue of race is negotiated in Browning's movie through codes of repressed and unleashed sexuality. In this context, ethnic difference is staged in the form of desiring, rebellious, and threatening bodies. Using the allegory of the tiger, which is a symbol of both bloodthirstiness and sexual emancipation, the film condenses its figural opposites (Tiger Haynes and Madame de Sylva) into one single image of unconstrained nature. The movie thus rejects the typical function of metaphysical condensation, namely that of rendering ethnic difference a universal category. Quite to the contrary, animal images are utilised to consolidate difference and evoke a notion of solidarity across racial boundaries.

☃ FETISHISATION OF THE ORIENT ☃

Fetishisation is commonly deployed in literary texts to evoke "erotic fears or desires" and establish "fixed and major difference where difference does not exist or is minimal".[26] Produced and shot in the late phase of the silent film era, Browning's movie relies heavily upon established 'Oriental' signifiers and metaphors, running the risk of reducing the East to a mere fetish, and creating images of a man-made Orient in almost every facet of its aesthetic structure. Far from simply reproducing the simplifications projected upon Kipling's poem, however, *Where East is East* engages in a thoughtful deconstruction of the authority of such myths. In utilising Kipling's phrase as a symbolic point of departure, the film explicitly calls attention to the romantic version of the East produced by literature of the colonial period. Yet, the conclusions the film wants us to draw are entirely different from those evoked by imperialist discourse. Whereas the portrayal of the Orient as a sexual fetish in colonial thinking invites us to participate in the production and distribution of a distinct ethnic mythology, Browning's film attempts to accomplish the opposite.

Madame's eyes are fetishised by Bobby, but they represent a surface illusion rather than her true nature.

The fetish of the Orient is recognisably a projection, a cultural construction that the white male gaze (and the white male body) falls prey to. As viewers, we witness the constitution of this fetish, and also its ensuing deconstruction, through the process of Bobby's disillusionment. The chief objects of fetishisation in the movie are the Madame's eyes. Tentatively looking into them, then averting his gaze, as if gripped by a sudden panic, Bobby tells her: "Doggone… you know there's something fascinating about your eyes." It is no coincidence that these eyes are the one part of her body that is most conspicuously disguised by make-up. What Bobby sees is not the Madame's actual self, but rather a beautiful masquerade. In his perspective, the whole landscape is transformed by this fetish: "Out there I stood looking at the stars… I couldn't see them… I saw only your eyes." The image of the Oriental night sky is metonymically replaced here by an image of the Madame's eyes, which equally promise the dream of uninhibited sexual fulfillment. This corporeal dimension is illustrated by the film's emphasis on sensual experience—the fetish of the Orient is not portrayed as a mere ornament but as an irresistible stimulus to the white body. "This is all so colourful", Bobby tells the Madame, "This country certainly gets under my skin." Significantly, it is not the true, inner nature of the land, but its "colourful" appearance that appeals to Bobby. The Madame's response underscores the performative dimension of this fascination: "That is the way of the East."

Browning's film clarifies that the fetishisation of the Orient is closely tied to a history of myth-making, which is also a history of cultural performance. Twice in the movie, we see native actors and actresses perform for a mixed audience in theatrical street performances. When we see the beautiful Madame staging her show for poor Bobby, we are reminded of these previous performances. The superficiality of the fetish thus becomes apparent. Finally, the Madame is no real Oriental beauty (as her name suggests), but rather a dream manifesting itself in the form of a fascinating, yet immaterial *fata morgana*. How volatile this fetish actually is becomes clear when Madame de Sylva asks Bobby to travel with her, "to Saigon... to Paris... to love". The fetish of the Orient is exposed here as an exchangeable signifier, pointing to either Saigon (the embodiment of the colonial dream) or Paris (an emblem for romantic love), the two tropes becoming conflated.

⋈ ALLEGORIES OF (DE-)HISTORICISATION ⋈

In colonial literature, allegories are often deployed to evoke a sense of dehistoricisation. Capitalising upon 'universal' themes, these tales often occlude social realities and historical background. *Where East is East* succinctly parodies this convention by choosing Kipling's phrase as its title. Yet Browning's film makes it unmistakably clear that the aspect of colonialism is an integral part of the story. We are familiarised with a topography that alludes to both French and British colonial rule. While Laos, Siam, and Indo-China were controlled by French colonisers, Singapore (the place where Bobby's father has his circus) had for a long time been a British post. *Where East is East* combines the recognition of this historical contiguity with a celebration of the possibilities for intercultural exchange emanating from these conditions. A key figure in this context is Ming (Mrs Wong Wing), the grandmother, who has retained her religion and faith despite colonial rule. Being a figure of reconciliation, Ming is both the guardian of Haynes's nubile daughter and the keeper of native, spiritual traditions. When the evil Madame enters the house, we see Ming praying to a huge statue of Buddha. "Ancestors! Ancestors!" she says, "Take care of this house! Evil has come into it!" After the viperish Madame has been destroyed by the gorilla in the film's gruesome finale, we see Ming again as she sits in front of the Buddhist altar, thanking the ancestors. Her granddaughter Toyo has obviously adopted the same ritual of exorcising evil spirits. Waiting for her father to arrive in Vien-Tiane, she tells her fiancé: "See Bobby! The sun kisses the great Buddha! It is time for wishing!" After her wish has been fulfilled, Toyo vows to "take a nice present to the great Buddha for bringing my father home safe". This positive portrayal of Buddha as a local deity is juxtaposed with allusions to Christianity, personified by the figure of the Padré (Louis Stern), a Roman Catholic priest who comforts Toyo in the moment of her greatest despair.[27]

The juxtaposition of cultures and religions in Vien-Tiane is exemplified by Toyo's grandmother praying to the "great Buddha" whilst she seeks comfort from the Padré.

The depiction of Christianity and Buddhism as equal forms of spirituality in 1920s Indo-China hints at the historical context of French colonial rule. Characterising Vien-Tiane as a "colourful spot of French rule and Chinese custom", Browning's film echoes the romantic vision of a peaceful idyll in the midst of colonial repression. The discourse of subjugation, however, is not omitted from this mode of representation; on the contrary, we are continually reminded of the ideological implications of the model. This becomes obvious when one of the servants, a character named Wong, speaks of Tiger Haynes as his "honorable master".[28] However, the same character turns into an active spectator just a few scenes later as he watches his master play with Toyo, crawling on the floor like an animal. Watching this spectacle together with Ming, the grandmother, and the female cook, he laughs out loud, moving his hands wildly in amusement. The ethnic characters, then, transform here into the bearers of the gaze, staring at their "honourable master" lying on the floor like a wounded animal.

Having said all this, we can ask: can the subaltern speak in *Where East is East*?[29] This question may seem simply rhetorical, given the fact that Browning's movie is not a talkie. Yet, Browning creates a number of powerful images and metaphors in his movie that actually position the colonised in the role of an agent who can speak on his or her own. The most informative scene in this context occurs in the first part of the film when Bobby, the British gentleman, stumbles over a Chinese child on a ship's deck. Bobby's rude behaviour evokes a strong response on the part of the mother, who immediately bombards him with unintelligible words, gesticulating wildly. The woman is shown from a high angle, corresponding to Bobby's condescending view. Yet her words are communicated to us in the form of an intertitle, consisting solely of Chinese ideograms, which interrupts the film's plot for 20 long seconds (the longest duration of any intertitle in the whole movie). Although the effect is intended to be comic, the scene carries strong connotations of protest through language. Interestingly, it is not Bobby but Madame de Sylva who manages to calm the infuriated woman. The Madame's answer, too, is given in a Chinese intertitle. The native woman's violent reaction points to a cultural phenomenon that Homi K Bhabha has described as "the traumatic impact of the return of the repressed".[30] By giving the colonised a voice and by including their native language in extensive intertitles, Browning attenuates the dominant rhetoric of the late 1920s, where imperialism is often justified "as a civilising mission".[31] Only one year before Browning's movie, Edward Thompson's novel *Suttee* appeared, condoning this version of the colonial myth. In contrast to Thompson's book, in which the

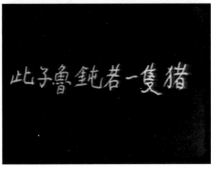

Bobby, the coloniser, finds himself (rather than the colonised) without a voice.

此子魯鈍若一隻豬

144

"construction of a continuous and homogeneous 'India'" is foregrounded, Browning's film rather accentuates the blank spots, inconsistencies, and untranslated spaces of the official image of the East.[32]

⋈ COMIC ETHNICITY AND EXPLOSIVE BODY LANGUAGE ⋈

Patterns of explosive, disjointed and cyclical language and behaviour are often used as a literary device to point to a loss of control, not so much of the text itself, but of the characters. *Where East is East* translates this technique to the performative medium, not only with regard to the main character, Tiger Haynes, who struggles for his countenance in almost every single scene, but also in the performances of the two female protagonists, Toyo and Madame de Sylva. The two characters were played by American actresses with notoriously extrovert personalities. Lupe Vélez, born and raised in Mexico, was labelled "the Mexican spitfire" by the American press and studio publicity. Taylor, who was married to the boxing legend Jack Dempsey at the time of the movie's release, had played exotic beauties in films such as Emmett J Flynn's *Monte Cristo*, 1922, and Herbert Brenon's *The Alaskan*, 1924. Both actresses were closely associated in cultural practice with performative adaptability and a tendency to cross boundaries. Displaying an inclination to throw temper tantrums in almost all of her films, Lupe Vélez was marketed in trailers as "a raging spectacle of comic ethnicity".[33]

Lupe Vélez's performance as Toyo reflects the actress's own masquerading to disguise her vulnerability.

In *Where East is East*, one of Vélez's early Hollywood films, the image of the Mexican spitfire is confirmed once again. The character of Toyo is marked by a wide range of emotional expressions, from deep sorrow to outward joy. She frolics, hops in her father's arms, and imitates other people. In one scene, she playfully struts through a gate, imitating a prostitute in search of customers. Followed by her father's critical gaze, she inhales from an imaginary cigarette and pretends to blow smoke into the air. This clownish behaviour is associated both with the character's cosmopolitan origins and with the actress' flamboyant screen persona. The character's performances in the film again function as signifiers for the masquerade-like nature of ethnic identity. This becomes obvious in one of the movie's final scenes where Toyo imitates an animal trapper, provoking her father, who plays the tiger, to show his claws. At one point in the performance, her hands, held before her face in a humourous gesture, suddenly become shields of protection, hiding her sad expression. We recognise in this scene that the character's happy-go-lucky attitude is also a mask, behind which a complicated and vulnerable persona is hidden.

The subaltern "speaks".

Where East is East, then, is a parable about the uses and abuses of stereotyping, in its more complex moments debunking the Orient as a cultural myth. Browning develops an ambivalent model of cinematic representation that engages the viewer in a dialogue concerning the validity of ethnic stereotypes. At first sight, *Where East is East* fits neatly into the clichés about the mysterious East so popular in 1920s cinema. At second glance, however, the film seems to debunk the essentialisms associated with this romantic image, raising consciousness in its audiences with regard to the artificial character of the Orient. By familiarising and at the same time defamiliarising his audience with the cultural stereotypes of race and ethnicity, Browning reveals the myth of the Orient as a cinematic invention that can only come into existence by attaching itself to certain codes and rules. Paradoxically, the film both essentialises the East as a universal and homogeneous entity ("Where East *is* East") and deconstructs it as a Western myth consisting of nothing but colourful male fantasies. It fluctuates between a reproduction of colonial myths and the attempt to alienate us from the dominant codes of colonialism. Continuously reminding us of the linguistic dimension of these conventions (like Kipling's romantic vision of the East), the film makes us aware of the shallowness and historical embeddedness of ethnic stereotypes. The film ends with a possible escape from the Orient. After releasing the gorilla that subsequently kills the Madame, Tiger Haynes is confined to a chair. Obviously, the gorilla has badly wounded him. Turning to the doctor, he expresses his wish that Toyo and her fiancé are taken away from this doomed place. Apparently, he fears that the curse brought to the house by Madame de Sylva is still hovering above it. "Soon as it's over, get them away on the boat... quick." This melodramatic ending raises more questions than it actually answers. Is the evil Madame still alive? Will Toyo and Bobby listen to Haynes and leave Vien-Tiane? Where will they go? To Singapore?... to Saigon?... to Paris? Precisely these alternatives have been intimated; however, they represent completely different choices, geographically and symbolically. Considering all these aspects, *Where East is East* remains a deeply ambivalent text; it opens the door to a fundamental demystification of Hollywood-based constructions of the East, while also indulging in the panorama of an Oriental fairytale—a tale of masculine jungle fighters, naïve British gentlemen, and tempting, sensual goddesses.

⋈ NOTES

1. Kipling, Rudyard, *The Sussex Edition of the Complete Works in Prose and Verse of Rudyard Kipling*, vol. XXXII, London: Macmillan, 1937–1939, p. 231.

2. From the mid-1880s on, Rudyard Kipling had travelled through the Indian Subcontinent as a correspondent for *The Pioneer*, a magazine published in Allahabad, Persia. Kipling's problematic attitude towards the question of race, displayed in his 1898 essay "White Man's Burden", has been widely documented. However, his narratives of the East are far from being one-dimensional. His novel *Kim*, 1901, centres around an Irish soldier's son who is born and raised in the streets of Lahore, where he is treated by everyone as a native. Kipling here dismantles the myth of ethnic essentiality, focusing on an identity constituted through the transgression of racial boundaries.

3. In a 1942 essay on Kipling, British novelist George Orwell claimed that "Kipling is the only English writer of our time who has added phrases to the language." As JK Buda observes, "East is East..." is not only "one of Kipling's most famous and memorable phrases, it is also one of the most misquoted and misunderstood". Kipling's biographer Charles Carrington adds that "no lines of Kipling's have been more freely quoted, and more often misquoted in exactly the opposite sense which Kipling gave them". Orwell, George, "Rudyard Kipling", *Collected Essays*, London: Mercury Books, 1961, p. 189; Buda, JK, "Rudyard Kipling's 'The Ballad of East and West'", 8 April, 2002, http://www.f.waseda.jp/buda/texts/ballad.html; Carrington, Charles, *Rudyard Kipling: His Life and Work*, London: Macmillan, 1955, p. 136.

4. As Edward W Said has convincingly shown in his seminal study, colonial ideology operates through images of fundamental difference rather than through hybridisation. Said, Edward W, *Orientalism*, New York: Vintage Books, 1978, p. 12.

5. Gates, Henry Luis Jr, "Writing 'Race' and the Difference it Makes", in *'Race', Writing, and Difference*, HL Gates Jr, ed., Chicago and London: The University of Chicago Press, 1985, p. 17.

6. Bhabha, Homi K, "The other question: The stereotype and colonial discourse", 1983, in *Visual Culture: A Reader*, Jessica Evans and Stuart Hall eds., London: Sage, 1999, p. 370.

7. Toni Morrison asks similar questions in her analysis of race and American literature. Morrison, Toni, *Playing in the Dark: Whiteness and the Literary Imagination*, Cambridge, Massachusetts: Harvard University Press, 1992, p. 16.

8. Morrison uses these categories from James A Snead's book on Faulkner, *Figures of Division*, from 1986. *Morrison, Playing in the Dark*, pp. 67–69.

9. Said, *Orientalism*, pp. 1–28; Morrison, *Playing in the Dark*, pp. 3–28.

10. Bhabha, "The other question", p. 373.

11. Dyer, Richard, *The Matter of Images: Essays on Representations*, New York: Routledge, 1993, p. 145.

12. The term "Orientalism" was coined in the middle of the nineteenth century. At the *fin de siècle*, Orientalism was widely accepted as an invention of writers like Nathaniel Hawthorne and Herman Melville, as well as painters such as Thomas Hicks and John Singer Sargent. The World's Columbian Exposition of 1893 marked a breakthrough in the depiction of American Orientalism. In the exhibition halls, visitors saw Eric Pape's painting *The Site of Ancient Memphis* and admired selected artifacts from Edward Moore's collection. In attractions such as "The Streets of Cairo", live belly dancers and 'Arab natives' taking care of donkeys and camels could be watched. See *Noble Dreams, Wicked Pleasures: Orientalism in America, 1870–1930*, an exhibition organised by the Clark Art Institute, 11 June–4 September, 2000, http://www.tfaoi.com/aa/1aa/1aa506.htm.

13. http://www.tfaoi.com/aa/1aa/1aa506.htm.

14. It is no coincidence that the movie uses images of darkness and opacity to convey the myth of the Orient. It is only "when the dusky dying light [leaves] the river dark and dim", as one of the intertitles has it, that the improvised nature of the East can come to a preliminary, shadowy existence.

15. Ironically enough, *Where East is East* not only refers to the notion of an essential East in contrast to the 'civilised' West. It also projects Western myths like the Biblical Fall of Mankind onto its Eastern setting. Just before Madame de Sylva and innocent Bobby meet on the ship, she drops an apple on the floor. Bobby picks up the fruit and walks towards the devious woman, not knowing this has been the first step to his doom. At this point, the film switches back to Eastern mythology, introducing the Islamic concept of *Kismet*, according to which human fate is always already predestined. When Bobby tells Madame de Sylva that he will sail from Saigon with the Formosa, she conjures up a common fate and future. "The Formosa? I, too, am sailing on the Formosa." Bobby instantly buys into the logic of *Kismet*, telling her, "It's funny… you've made me feel as though I've known you for years." By connecting Kipling's romantic adaptation of the East with other cultural constructions, the movie refrains from the usual claims to 'authentic' representation.

16. *New York Herald Tribune*, 27 May, 1929. Quoted in David J Skal and Elias Savada, *Dark Carnival: The Secret World of Tod Browning, Hollywood's Master of the Macabre*, New York: Anchor Books, 1995, p. 300.

17. Bhabha, "The other question", p. 370.

18. Said, Edward W, "East isn't East", *The Times Literary Supplement*, no. 4792, 3 February, 1995, pp. 3–6.

19. The fact that Toyo's father also carries the umbrella twice in the movie allows us to take the interpretation even further. Not only does this show that he has assimilated to local customs; there is also a notion of gender subversion involved, since, throughout the film, it is mostly women who are shown with this type of umbrella.

20. Likewise, Bobby is identified as a British gentleman by his top hat and his elegant European clothes, a fashionable jacket combined with a shirt and a tie.

21. The blurring of her ethnic identity into a heterogeneous mixture of Western and Eastern components anticipates the plot of Vélez's next movie, Monta Bell's *East Is West*, 1930, in which she plays a Chinese girl who is rescued by an American from an auction block and taken to San Francisco; there she discovers that she is not really Chinese, but was only raised by a Chinese family after her missionary parents were assassinated.

22. Toyo is linked to various positions of ethnic identification: her father, who lives and works in the area; her fiancé Bobby, who wants to carry her away from Vien-Tiane; and her mother Madame de Sylva, who stands for the mythic construction of the Orient.

23. Morrison, *Playing in the Dark*, p. 68.

24. In Wallace Worsley's *The Penalty*, 1920, Chaney played a criminal forced to walk on stumps after losing his legs in a botched operation. The actor's obsession with deformity reached its peak in Worsley's *The Hunchback of Notre-Dame*, 1923, where he performed in the role of a hideous animal creature. Two Browning movies ensued, *The Blackbird*, 1926, and *West of Zanzibar*, 1928, in which Chaney was seen as a crippled figure.

25. The equation of humans with animals runs through the whole movie, applied to the characters regardless of their ethnic affiliation. The rage of the gorilla that finally kills Madame de Sylva is associated with both Haynes' wrath against his former wife and with Toyo's understandable anger against her mother, who tries to steal her man. In another scene, Toyo and Bobby are called "parakeets".

26. Morrison, *Playing in the Dark*, p. 68.

27. In some scenes, the film plays upon a dichotomy between the Christian religion and other, 'heathen' religions. When he jumps at the Madame in rage, Haynes accuses her of using "heathen tricks" to break the hearts of men.

28. This echoes the words of Toyo, who calls Tiger in an earlier scene "my honourable father".

29. In her seminal essay by this title, Gayatri Chakravorty Spivak asks this question with respect to the representation of the colonised individual in colonial fiction. Basing her argument on Althusser's observations concerning the alliance of power networks and individual desires in hegemonic culture, Spivak contends that discourses of representation always rely upon "philosophies of denegation" that exclude rather than include the colonised as a subject. Spivak, Gayatri Chakravorty, "Can the Subaltern Speak?", in *Marxism and the Interpretation of Culture*, Cary Nelson and Lawrence Grossberg eds., Urbana and Chicago: University of Illinois Press, 1988, p. 271.

30. Bhabha, "The other question", p. 373.

31. Spivak, "Can the Subaltern Speak?", p. 305.

32. Spivak, "Can the Subaltern Speak?", p. 305.

33. Sturtevant, Victoria, "Spitfire: Lupe Vélez and the Ambivalent Pleasures of Ethnic Masquerade", *The Velvet Light Trap*, no. 55, Spring 2005, p. 31.

SPEAKING WITH EYES

TOD BROWNING'S *DRACULA* AND ITS PHANTOM CAMERA

Elisabeth Bronfen

⋈ A HUNGARIAN COUNT TRAVELS TO LONDON ⋈

In the opening sequence of Tod Browning's *Dracula* a coach drives along a rough mountain pass at dusk. The passengers include peasants from the region, a couple touring Eastern Europe with their daughter, and a solitary young man. While the coach races toward its destination, the young girl reads a passage out loud from her guidebook about enchanted castles from times past. Because the speed at which they are traveling has become uncomfortable, her father asks the coachman to drive more slowly, but immediately one of the peasants interjects. He claims that they must reach the village by sunset, explaining that it is Walpurgis Night, the night of evil, and ominously whispers the word "Nosferatu", only to be silenced by his wife, holding her hand to his mouth. Tod Browning then cuts to a folkloric mainstreet in a Hungarian village, where we see peasants covering their windows with wolfsbane before cautiously closing them. A few inhabitants have collected before the inn, clearly relieved at the arrival of the coach. Once the young solitary traveler, however, explains that his bags are to remain in the carriage because he must continue on to Borgo Pass, they show signs of alarm. Karl Freund's camera oscillates between the astonished gaze of Renfield (Dwight Frye) and the villagers, who are trying to warn him about Dracula and his wives. After the young British man reassures them that their worries are nothing but superstition, the shot cuts to a brief view of the setting sun, before returning once more to Renfield's face. He insists that he isn't afraid, since "it's a matter of business with me", and is about to mount the carriage, when one of the women approaches him holding a cross in her hand, meant to protect him on his nocturnal voyage.

Once more Browning cuts to the mountain pass before superimposing onto this scene, which resembles a landscape painting, the image of one of the enchanted castles the girl had read about. It is as though the guidebook, as well as the superstitions voiced by the villagers, have been transformed into a cinematic spectacle. As the film shifts its location to the dark vault inside the castle, Freund's camera moves toward a coffin, which has begun to open from

Dracula's inhospitable homeland.

within. A hand emerges from the dark slit beneath its lid, then a rat and other vermin. Finally a woman gets up from one of the coffins and is soon seen standing in a circle with two other women around a spider's web. At this point Count Dracula (Bela Lugosi) appears, presumably arisen from a coffin we were not shown, and stares hypnotically into the camera, before slowly mounting the stairs that lead to his chambers above. With the next scene we find him magically transferred to the front of his coach. Enveloped in his dark cape, he asks Renfield, who has duly been dropped off at the crossroads at midnight, to mount before proceeding back to the castle. At this point Browning employs one of the film's very few special effects; for a brief moment we are shown that the coach is now being driven by two bats.

Most critics have praised the opening sequences of *Dracula* for its convincing cinematic dramaturgy, attributing it primarily to Karl Freund, who had already become famous as Fritz Lang's cameraman (*Die Spinnen*, 1919; *Metropolis*, 1927) before going into exile. Indeed, reminiscent of the filmic language of Expressionism, Freund has Renfield, uncertain about what he is to expect, walk backwards into the vast space of the entrance hall, which is heavily lined with shadows, while Count Dracula slowly approaches him from behind with a candelabra in his right hand. Initially capturing the two characters from above, the camera moves to a close-up of Renfield, who turns around at precisely the moment when the Count greets him with what has become one of the signature lines from the film: "I am Dracula." The camera then draws back and we recognise, through a powerful visual metaphor, that Renfield has entered a fatal trap; behind him lies the over-sized shadow of a barred window, in front of him an enormous spider's web. Yet on the face of the clueless visitor we find a mixture of confusion and relief. Renfield still believes himself to be the master of his rational senses, even though he has watched his host simply slip through the spider's web, while he was forced to cut himself a passage with his walking stick. While the camera focuses on the spider at the heart of the web,

Dracula comments: "The spider spinning his web for the unwary fly. The blood is the life, Mr Renfield."

The young man has no other choice but to follow his host up the stairs to the upper level of the castle, where he finds a stately room lit with candles, a fire crackling in the fireplace, a table set with food and wine, and a bed prepared for his sleep. The camera repeatedly focuses on Dracula's hypnotic gaze, which along with his idiosyncratic articulation was to become his cinematic trademark. By pointing the spots of two flashlights into the eyes of the actor, Freund was able to produce the impression that these were illuminated from within.

The iconic image of Bela Lugosi as Dracula in the 1931 eponymous film.

After Renfield has presented the Count with all the papers necessary for his move to Carfax Abbey, a fatal seduction sets in, whose homoerotic subtext will structure the rest of the film. Renfield cuts his finger with a paper clip, upon which the film moves to Dracula's lustful gaze. As he approaches the young man, the peasant woman's cross falls in front of the finger on which Renfield has begun to suck. In order for the audience to savour the erotic game between the two characters, the bite, which will transform Renfield into a servant of the vampire, is deferred. Indeed, as Dracula turns away, having poured some of the wine into his guest's glass, the camera begins to drive around Renfield, as though it were spinning a web of its own. At its centre, a silent exchange of gazes takes place, with Dracula's desire reflected in Renfield's boyish smile. Suddenly the door opens and three female vampires enter, while Renfield, drunk with the heavy wine, moves to the balcony and opens a window. Once he has fallen into a stupor, Dracula re-enters what Browning clearly visualises as a stage. For as the three women open the door, we are shown that the space from which they enter is as decrepit as the vault containing the coffins. As the only furnished room this chamber exists exclusively as a stage for the fatal game of seduction, which is suggested but never explicitly shown. Having chased away the three women with a dramatic gesture of his hand, the Count bends over the body of Renfield, lying supine before him, even though the deadly bite itself takes place at the vanishing point of the camera's gaze.

Dracula's face is hidden in the shadows, which Tod Browning uses to highlight the power of his gaze.

A title introduces the next shift of setting, moving us from the enchanted castle to a ship caught in a storm. The Vesta is on her way to England. Renfield, who now calls Dracula his master, has helped him to emerge from his coffin, so that the latter can watch the deadly spectacle taking place on deck. As though he were the director of this disaster we see him standing next to a huge spotlight, while the crew and the captain, tied with ropes to his steering wheel, are shown only as shadows. The dramaturgic foreshortening of this scene is recognised by many critics as an implicit reference to Murnau's *Nosferatu*, 1922. Yet Lyndon Joslin has also discovered that, for financial reasons, the scenes depicting the Vesta's crossing were actually taken from stock material, from a silent film of which we no longer know the title. There can be no interaction between Dracula and the crew, because they actually exist in two separate film worlds.[1] The death of all the men on board, as well as Renfield's entrance to Dr Seward's clinic, bordering on Carfax Abbey, is shown only by way of newspaper headlines, just as Count Dracula's arrival in England is presented indexically, as a short notice in a newspaper describing his first victims. In the subsequent scene we initially see him at dusk, beckoning a flower girl to follow him into the shadow of an alley and feasting on her blood. He then enters The Royal Albert Hall while the police find the girl's corpse. Dracula as a character on the diegetic level of the film thus initially emerges only as an effect of interpretation, which presupposes a reader in the know. For all others the signs of his presence remain mysterious traces.

The dismissal of the Count's female vampires.

While Philip Glass produced a new score for *Dracula* in 1999, the original film had music only in two places—a theme from Tchaikovsky's *Swan Lake* during the title sequence, and short pieces from Wagner's *Meistersinger* and Schubert's *Unfinished Symphony* during Dracula's appearance in the theatre. In this scene the music was meant to support the theatricality of the Count's manner as he draws the attention of Dr Seward (Herbert Bunston) and his company away from the spectacle onstage onto himself. Indeed, as he enters Dr Seward's box, introducing himself as the new tenant of Carfax Abbey, he inaugurates a second spectacle, which will move well beyond the confines of The Royal Albert Hall. While Mina Seward (Helen Chandler) and Jonathan Harker (David Manners) take the Count to be a curious foreigner, their friend Lucy Weston (Frances Dade) finds herself immediately attracted to him. In the course of this very same night she will fall asleep, leaving her window wide open, allowing Dracula to enter and drink her blood. After her death and transformation into the spectral woman in white, he will turn his attention to the doctor's daughter Mina, while Dr Seward, suspicious about the strange bite marks on all the victims of the mysterious death wave that has suddenly befallen Whitby, calls Professor Abraham Van Helsing (Edward Van Sloan) in for advice.

The plot thus moves towards the battle of wills between two masters, the vampire and his hunter, who resemble each other not only in their foreign

accents, but also because of the way their gaze is staged. While Count Dracula's hypnotic power is visually foregrounded by virtue of the artificial lighting of his eyes, Van Helsing wears thick glasses with a transparent rim, which enlarge his eyes and make them appear to protrude from his face. Both recognise each other as enemies almost immediately, even while they also acknowledge each other as worthy combatants, since both believe in the superstition which British positivism, and rational discourse in general, refutes. The implicit cultural pessimism subtending Browning's *Dracula* is thus articulated in the fact that the infection which the vampire introduces to this community in the vicinity of London, can never be fully eradicated. Van Helsing's counter-attack—the ritual killing of the vampire before sunrise—simply represents an inoculation, itself working with the very poison of superstitious belief it seeks to undo. Indeed, Renfield, who surprisingly has unlimited access to the private rooms of the Seward family, repeatedly enters there to warn them of the danger Count Dracula represents for Mina, even while praising his master's omnipotence. He will prove to be right, given that the vampire's erotic charm will ultimately be more powerful than Van Helsing's prohibitions. Like Renfield and Lucy, Mina will also come to subordinate herself to Count Dracula's will, following him to Carfax Abbey on what is to be their wedding night, so that Jonathan Harker and Van Helsing can perform their rite of salvation.

As in the opening sequence, we find ourselves once more in a Gothic hall, which can be reached either by a stone staircase leading upstairs or a door on the ground floor. Because the Count has come to suspect that Renfield has unwittingly led his enemies to his hiding-place, he forces the young man to fall to his death from the staircase as he approaches his master. Dracula then carries the unconscious Mina to the vault; the vampire hunters have already cautiously approached the abbey and watched the fateful encounter between the two men from outside. Precipitated into action by Mina's cry, they break open the door and rush toward the coffins, only to find the Count but not his bride. For reasons unexplained by the dramaturgy of the scene, Mina has hidden herself in the rear part of the vault, watching as Van Helsing pierces the heart of the vampire with a piece of wood. Preserving the ambivalence of the scene, Browning does not allow us to witness the actual killing, only the traces it leaves on the body. Mina cringes in pain, as though it were her heart which was being penetrated, before waking from her trance, walking towards her fiancé and allowing him to embrace her as the first rays of sunlight fall on their ecstatic faces.

Critics have repeatedly faulted Browning for not having adequately used the filmic means available to him, by letting not only the vampire's fatal bites but also his own death occur off screen. Yet these ellipses can also be read as a critical gesture, meant to sustain an ideological ambivalence. After he has approached Count Dracula with his murderous tools, it is, significantly, Van Helsing who will not allow Mina to embrace him, as though he knew of his own contamination; analogous to an earlier scene, in which she forbade Jonathan to kiss her. Furthermore, while he encourages the two lovers to walk up the staircase, which is now flooded by sunlight, Van Helsing himself remains in the darkness of the vault.

Dracula's seduction of Mina.

As Uli Jung astutely notes, the curiously abrupt manner in which the film ends seems to be the result of a conscious decision. Because the destruction of the vampire is not shown and we can, therefore, not know for sure whether the sighs heard on the soundtrack really are emitted by the dying Count, the suspicion is sustained that Van Helsing might well have become part of the vampiric danger, rather than triumphing over it. Tod Browning's elision need not necessarily signify a lack of interest or talent. Rather, it can be read as a way of avoiding—on the visual level of his argument—the unequivocal triumph over evil, which the return of Mina to her bridegroom represents for the narrative. The alleged solution of the conflict, Jung concludes, leaves such a distinct sense of unease that any simple assuagement of fears is successfully prohibited.[2]

☙ THE FIRST TALKIE HORROR PICTURE ☙

As the first sound film of the horror genre and the most influential of all vampire films, endlessly cited by all subsequent film adaptations of Bram Stoker's novel, Tod Browning's *Dracula* came to inaugurate the beginning of the golden era of monster films, for which Universal Pictures was famous in the 1930s; it paved the way for such films as James Whale's *Frankenstein*, 1931, *Bride of Frankenstein*, 1935 and *The Invisible Man*, 1933, and Karl Freund's *The Mummy*, 1932, among others. After its opening night on 13 February 1931, at the Roxy Theater in New York City, it sold over 50,000 tickets within the first two days, bringing in a profit of $700,000 in the first year. As the most commercially successful film for Universal Pictures during the Depression, it ended up grossing a total of $1,012,189 worldwide within the first five years. Ironically, the production itself had taken place under extremely unfavourable circumstances. Bram Stoker's widow had successfully sued Prana Films, the company that had produced *Nosferatu*, demanding royalties or the destruction of all copies of the film. For this reason Carl Laemmle Jr had decided not to use the novel as a source for the screenplay, but rather the London stage version, written by Hamilton Dean. Rewritten in 1927 by John Balderston for an American production, it had been performed successfully on Broadway and the West coast, with the then unknown Hungarian actor Bela Ferenc Deszo Blasko in the main part, appearing under the stage name of Bela Lugosi. The Pulitzer Prize Winner Louis Bromfield had been engaged by Universal to insert scenes from the novel—such as the coach journey at the beginning—into the Dean/Balderston play script, even though while writing the screenplay he decided to remain as close as possible to the stage melodrama. The trip to the Carpathian Mountains with which Bram Stoker's novel ends was not re-included, while most of the action was limited to the clinic, Dr Seward's home and Carfax Abbey. At the same time, because he chose to reduce the story to Mina's salvation, all the sequences in the novel pertaining to Lucy Westenra—her seduction, her life as a vampire, and finally her highly eroticised killing—were left out of the screenplay.

Even though Browning's *Dracula* has become a cult film, assuming an unquestioned status in our cultural imaginary, film historians like David Skal accuse the director of sabotaging the possibilities of Bromfield's script, given his drastic cuts, his insistence on a static camera, and his decision to leave out special effects wherever possible. Skal takes particular issue with the way that the dialogue scenes that take place in Dr Seward's home only rarely have recourse to montage or shot/reverse shots, so that because these verbal exchanges are primarily filmed as medium shots, occasionally interspersed with close-ups, long stretches of *Dracula* look like filmed theatre. Other film historians have criticised the implausibility of the dialogue, as well as the incoherence of the narrative in general, given that it sometimes introduces plot elements that are not followed up; such as Renfield's biting one of Dr Seward's female servants, when no further mention will be made of this attack. Above all critics have complained that the uncanny events, seminal to all vampire stories, are almost exclusively narrated rather than visualised. According to his detractors, Tod Browning not only doesn't show a single vampire's bite—he also downplays the erotic charm of the vampire by not showing Mina drinking Dracula's blood. Finally, he avoids all cinematic horror by showing no transformation scenes, such as the Count turning into a werewolf or his victims turning into vampires.[3]

By way of explaining the alleged faults of this *Dracula*, film historians speculate that Browning, who had wanted to adapt Bram Stoker's novel for years, had lost interest in the project by the time he was able to do so. They like to cite Helen Chandler, who later claimed that during the shooting the director was usually standing somewhere on the periphery of the set, while she mainly received her instructions from Karl Freund, the cinematographer.[4] This shift in attitude is often attributed to the fact that Browning had not only wanted Lon Chaney, with whom he had successfully made several horror pictures (*The Unholy Three*, 1925; *London after Midnight*, 1927) for the part of the Count, but that the actor, who had turned down the part because of the progressive stage of his throat cancer, died during the shooting. Others, like Bela Lugosi himself, have pointed to the financial pressures imposed upon Browning by Universal Studios, who had categorically opposed any hefty additional production costs.[5] For this reason the director had been forced to shoot the film in sequence, even at that time not a common practice. The frugal use of special effects and the privileging of a static camera over complex travelling shots may well have been the result of these financial constraints. If, however, one considers how consistent *Dracula* is with the rest of Browning's *oeuvre*—particularly his fascination for and sympathy with monstrous and grotesque bodies—a different explanation comes to mind for his choice of privileging the spoken word over visual tricks. As in other films, such as *Freaks*, 1932, Browning's concern was always with the bizarre desires of those on the social and cultural margins. It is enough for him to render their fantasies as scenic fragments, which require neither a coherent, nor a sensational story line. Furthermore, the theatricality of his filmic rendition emphasises both the power of suggestion emanating from Dracula's hypnotic gaze and Van Helsing's will power, as well as the seduction transmitted precisely by foregrounding the voices of the marginal and the monstrous; notably the strangely lulling articulations of Bela Lugosi's vampire, the eloquence of Dwight Frye's Renfield, and finally the riveting transformation of Helen Chandler's Mina from the prim daughter of a doctor into a glamorous female vamp. Indeed, even the choice of a static camera seems logical, once one sees in it as attempt to savour the newly discovered possibilities of sound as a medium of seductive film horror.

Of course the notoriety of Browning's *Dracula* within film history resides above all else in the uncanny identification between Bela Lugosi and his role. The Hungarian expatriate, who had already played the alluring Count on Broadway, did everything to get this part and was even willing to have his wages reduced to $500 a week. He was to become famous over night, even though this celebrity would also prove to be a doom of sorts. The hypnotic effect of his acting was so convincing that the boundary between film illusion and reality became fluid. Universal Pictures used his Hungarian origins as advertisement for the film, so that for his audience Bela Lugosi became identical with the aristocratic Eastern European vampire. He had only one accent—the voice of Dracula—and the roles he was offered after his work with Tod Browning were almost all in horror pictures. Like Renfield, trapped in the Count's web, the actor found himself caught in the film persona he had always craved. In interviews he later confessed that he could have been angry with this vampire, but it had allowed him to make a living, even if it meant a form of dying at the same time. The strange vampirism by which the actor paid in blood for the celebrity he won found its acme during his burial at the Holy Cross Cemetery in 1956. As he had wanted it, Bela Lugosi was buried in the suit, cape and medal he had worn in his star role. Rumour has it that just before his death, so as to secure his artistic legacy, he gave Dracula's ring to Christopher Lee, who was in the process of re-interpreting the role under the direction of Roger Corman.[6]

Bela Lugosi never managed to escape his association with Dracula.

⋈ *DRACULA* – A MULTIFACETED TROPE ⋈

Any reading of *Dracula* must bear in mind that the world in which Tod Browning's vampire came to be born was a culturally precarious one. After the stock market crash in 1929, a cultural nostalgia for the vertiginous optimism of the Roaring Twenties was coupled with a desire to repress the stagnating economic situation. For this reason, the mass-market demanded more and more escapist fantasies. So as to draw the attention of the audience to the affective power of fantasy worlds, Van Helsing appeared on screen at the end of the original version of the film, in a sequence that was later cut. Standing against the proscenium of a motion picture theatre, and looking directly into the camera, he delivers the epilogue of the stage play:

> Just a moment, ladies and gentlemen! Just a word before you go. We hope the memories of Dracula and Renfield won't give you bad dreams, so just a word of reassurance. When you get home tonight and the lights have been turned out and you are afraid to look behind the curtains and you dread to see a face appear at the window—why, just pull yourself together and remember that after all *there are such things*.

Given that this cinematic rendition of *Dracula* declares itself to be a vampire, not only haunting its audience after the lights have gone on again in the theatre, but, owing to its performative power, also insisting on the reality of its revenants, David J Skal has succinctly called it "a lightning rod for prevailing social anxieties".[7]

Indeed, Browning's film is easily read as escapist cinema, because it seems to deflect the audience's gaze from the concrete social struggle of the 1930s (notably the economic bloodletting of the American public as a result of a breakdown of the economy), shifting its attention toward a different stage— namely one where a quasi-mythical battle against evil was being fought. At the same time, Bela Lugosi's elegant and courtly Eastern European Count also functions as a cipher for a cultural struggle. As the representative of a long lost world, he welds together in his monstrous body Bram Stoker's late Victorian culture with the post-First World War America of Tod Browning. Ronald R Thomas thus reads the displaced aristocrat—who on the diegetic level of the film emigrates to England to find fresh blood, while on the level of the film's production he moves to Hollywood to reinvigorate his life as an actor—as an embodiment of "the modern belief that the forces of the past drain the life from the present even as they sustain it".[8] Given that this embodiment of a past devouring the present was also connected to notions of an old European belief in superstition, rebelling against a Western European rationality and positivism, one might well read the battle between the two masters Count Dracula and Van Helsing along the lines Friedrich Nietzsche proposes in his discussion of the emergence of morality as the result of a battle between interpretations. Dracula thus functions not only as a cipher for the economic bloodletting of modern man, but also for an anti-enlightened attack on the West. As Thomas explains, it appeals most to those young Westerners whose desire for transgression poses a weak link in the cultural system of modernity. Only because they are either literally or figuratively willing to transgress the boundaries of the safe grounds of the West—Renfield as a tourist in Hungary, Lucy and Mina in the fantasies that lead them away from bourgeois notions of marriage—Dracula is able to subject them to his will to power. It is this ambivalence among young Victorians that is rendered visible, both in the novel and in the film, by virtue of the fact that the vampire can only come to those who open their window to him.

The shortening of Lucy's family name from Stoker's Westenra to Weston in the Dean/Balderston play text is read by Uli Jung as an indication of the fact that she, in turn, embodies the cultural crisis endemic to Anglo-American modernism. In the film's narrative a threat from outside, pitting Eastern aristocracy against Western bourgeoisie, invokes the longing for a leader typical of the 1930s, resulting in a battle against evil ultimately fought under the auspices of a loss of rationality. Thus, in Dracula, the struggle for supremacy with which modern Europe comes to reassert itself against the onslaught of an anti-enlightened interpretation of the world contains a seminal *aporia*. Evil can only be fought with the weapons of this very same evil. Dr Seward and his friends only have a false choice. They can either fall prey to Count Dracula or blindly follow Van Helsing, even while both gestures entail a subjugation of sorts. At stake is, then, not only the fact that neither Dr Seward's science nor Van Helsing's anti-enlightened superstition is able to triumph over the power of the vampire. What also becomes visible is the manner in which the Count and the vampire hunter ultimately resemble each other in their authoritarian fantasies of omnipotence, as well as in the violence they have recourse to so as to assert their will to power. Uli Jung concludes that the chase and destruction of the monstrous body should not be read as a gesture of civilisation but rather as an atavistic gesture of suppression, with which the dominant ideological discourse seeks to assure its *status quo*.[9]

The public success of Tod Browning's *Dracula* can, indeed, be compared to a cultural lightning rod for the diverse economic and cultural anxieties of the 1930s. One must, however, not overlook the fact that the ideological values of the West triumph over the vampire in the end because they are defended by a small band of men who believe unconditionally in both the means and the ends of this cultural struggle. Given that his sympathies were always with those whom a given dominant culture declares to be monsters, Tod Browning himself, however, decisively warns against such unquestioned subjugation. If some critics are right to accuse David Manners of never having fully stepped into the role of Mina's fiancée, this may well have been intentional on the part of the director. In Browning's version, Jonathan Harker, who would indeed more readily fit into a Lubitsch comedy, initially refuses to be part of the mass hysteria revolving around the hunting and killing of a vampire. At the beginning of the night of the showdown between the vampire and his adversaries, he actually disobeys Van Helsing's orders and tries to convince Mina to leave her father's home and drive with him to London. The fact that he fails in disassociating himself and his bride from the madness Van Helsing orchestrates, could thus be read as a further indication for how difficult it is to escape from any anti-enlightened gesture once it has actually taken hold of the modern Western mind.

If we are willing to read the vampire as a cipher for repressed, forbidden or past knowledge, which can never fully be eradicated but only transferred to the periphery of cultural consciousness, then Horkheimer and Adorno's notion of a dialectic of enlightenment can help focus the relationship between modernity and its mythical Other that emerges in Browning's *Dracula*. The West produces the vampire as its toxic counterpart, deploying the destruction of this monstrous freak body, so as to reestablish a claim to power, which had fallen into crisis. At stake isn't simply the fact that the infection can never fully be cured, but also that culture's monstrous Other be understood as the embodiment of a rotten kernel at the heart of the West. This dialectic becomes most poignant in the attack on the figure, who not only contains the West in her name but also represents its most marginal member. For in Tod Browning's Lucy Weston we find embodied the financially independent young woman, attracted to a world of morbidity, who, in contrast to the heroine of Stoker's novel with her three suitors, has no fiancé and instead determines her own sexual desire. After all, once she has spoken to Count Dracula in Dr Seward's box at The Royal Albert Hall, she begins to dream about a life as Countess in Transylvania. The same night she will open her window before going to bed. In a sequence of shot/reverse shots Browning shows us Dracula standing on the sidewalk below, and Lucy looking out of her window into the dark night, before going to bed with a book. She doesn't read for long, because the Count has already approached her window in the shape of a bat. In a close up we see that just before falling asleep she looks up from her reading, so that Dracula, who appears only a few seconds later next to her bed, is thus staged by Browning as the materialisation of her reading. If opening the window was an indication of her unconscious desire, this now assumes a concrete object in the shape of the Count, who after hovering over her body, begins to feast on it. As though she had called him in fantasy, his bite fulfills her fascination with the life of the Transylvanian aristocracy of past times.

Lucy Weston, already under Dracula's spell.

Once again, Browning does not show the actual consummation of the Count's lust. After the shadow of his body has merged with her dreaming face he cuts away from Bela Lugosi's lips just as they are about to touch the neck of Frances Dade and moves instead to the anatomical theatre in Dr Seward's clinic. In a long shot we now see Lucy's corpse, lying on a dissecting table. While Dr Seward explains to the other doctors, as well as the medical students sitting in the auditorium, that the transfusions had not helped save the patient, who had died of an inexplicable loss of blood, he leans over her lifeless body and in so doing assumes the very same position Dracula had in the previous scene. Lucy has not only become the object of a collective gaze; she has also been transformed into a text, which the doctor must interpret on this public stage for a select audience. If, in a previous scene, we saw her as a spectator at The Royal Albert Hall, as a corpse she is now herself the centre of the performance. If, furthermore, while sitting in the theatre box she had recited a poem about how the dead haunt the living, she is now herself a revenant. Finally, if before going to sleep she had taken a book with her to bed, the feminine reader has now been turned into a sign, indeed into a text dictated by Dracula himself. As the gazes of the doctor and his students displace that of the Count, the perspective of the latter comes to be replaced by that of modern science. This transformation, however, significantly occurs over the body of a beautiful dead woman, which has now become a contested object between the representatives of enlightened science and those of superstition. Sitting in Dr Seward's office in a subsequent scene, Van Helsing offers an interpretation of both Lucy's corpse based on an ancient tomb about vampires, from which his helper is reading aloud. The transformation of Lucy Weston into a vampire thus entails a series of readings, beginning with Lucy herself, reading aloud at the theatre. Van Helsing immediately recognises her sign of transformation—the wound on her throat—as the signature of a vampire. Through the glasses of his anti-enlightened knowledge he is able to produce a reading of his own, meant to convince Dr Seward that, in the manner proposed by Horkheimer and Adorno, enlightened science can revert back to superstition. While Dr Seward continues to hold onto his belief that modern science does not acknowledge the existence of vampires, Van Helsing replies that yesterday's superstition can seamlessly turn into the scientific reality of today. It is his words, one might surmise, which produce the vampire as a thinkable object that Count Dracula can then give a body to in the follow sequences. In so doing, the vampire also materialises a dream for Van Helsing; namely the superiority of his mythically inflected interpretation of the word.

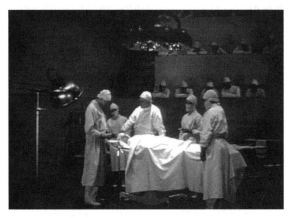

Reading Dracula's text, Lucy's corpse.

It is those that are positioned on the cultural and social margins, then, that are fascinated by the vampire: Renfield traveling through strange lands, Lucy dreaming of a past elegance, Van Helsing opposed to modern science. Only because they are willing to engage with him—as a representative of all that has no place in bourgeois modernity—can Count Dracula assume power in London. Indeed, precisely in the scene revolving around the infection of the psychiatrist's daughter Mina, Browning renders explicitly visible that we are to conceive of this vampire first and foremost as a phantom, giving body to the dreams and desires of the marginal members of this community. Mina's sudden illness is explicitly staged as an attack of hysteria, given that in the late nineteenth century this psychosomatic illness was predominantly conceived as a splitting of consciousness, with the nocturnal self radically contradicting the diurnal one. In Mina's case we find this double consciousness, as Sigmund Freud called it, performed by virtue of the fact that at times she displays an erotically encoded euphoria, while in her so-called normal condition all recollection of this other state is gone. Bram Stoker, familiar with French psychiatrist Jean Martin Charcot's writings on hysteria, was not the only novelist who had recourse to such reference. Given his interest in the murky interface between reality and dream as well as all indirect articulations of forbidden or hidden desires, he was, furthermore, also fascinated with the method of hypnosis developed by Charcot and Freud. Particularly useful for the dramaturgy of the vampire story was, of course, the fact that hysterics were famous for speaking with their bodies what they could not articulate in the symbolic language of everyday speech. The suggestibility of Count Dracula's victims, allowing them to fall into a trance almost immediately upon his gaze falling on them, their oscillating between excitation and exhaustion, as well as their dramatic performance of the strange stories about being attacked by magical creatures, are all gestures readily found in the psychiatric literature of the time. Indeed, the medical discoverers of the unconscious share with the authors of vampire stories the wish to explore those aspects of the psychic apparatus that cannot be thought by modern positivism. With the reversion back to superstition one finds in all vampire narratives, what also returns are all those aspects of the psyche that have no place in the world of utilitarian economic progress—anxiety, desire, ecstasy, and self-expenditure.

⌖ THE VAMPIRIC SCREEN ⌖

What, however, does it mean to make the claim that Count Dracula gives body to the dreams of those on the cultural margins? With the attack on Renfield, a rhetoric of hysteria sets in, which will repeat itself with all the other characters. Hypnotised by the gaze of the vampire, each one of the afflicted characters will open his or her window and immediately lose consciousness. The appearance of the vampire is thus made possible by virtue of the fact that these young Westerners listen to a 'different' voice; which for the language of cinema is significantly that of the gaze. It is to this speaking gaze that they submit themselves to—in all cases, however, with closed eyes. Appearing before Renfield, Lucy or Mina, Dracula is perceived by them only as a dream figure; which is to say as a figure with whom they communicate while they are in an unconscious state. At the same time the victims of the vampire are also a cipher for the film audience, which allows itself to be transposed into the position of dreaming, while sitting with open eyes in a dark film theatre. Tod Browning places this analogy at the

Dracula communes with his victims whilst they are in a receptive, unconscious state.

centre of his staging of the first attack on Mina. Initially we see her sleeping body, then in the reverse shot Dracula, who has suddenly emerged at her bedside. He is about to lean over her, but in contrast to the parallel scene with Lucy we do not see both together in one frame. Instead, Bela Lugosi leans forward towards the camera, until we arrive at a close-up of his face, distorted by lust, completely taking over the film screen. Seamlessly, the audience has been translated into the position of Mina, so that the vampire's threatening face is actually approaching the audience as well. The visual logic of this shot sequence suggests that Mina's dream is also ours; the bite she will receive, once the image has become dark, is also meant for us.

Mina covering her wound, the representation of a desire that she cannot express.

In the following scene Tod Browning cuts to the library in Dr Seward's home. Mina is trying to recount for her fiancé the nocturnal event we have just witnessed—the pale face with piercing red eyes approaching her through a foggy night. She is unable to describe the bite we were not shown, and brings her narration to a sudden halt. Jonathan, trying to calm her, insists that everything was only a dream, which she should try to forget. Van Helsing, however, sits down next to her. Once more at stake is the question of reading, because Mina, placed directly in front of a bookcase, is as much an object of interpretation for him as Lucy was. While Mina's father and fiancé look on, he discovers the familiar marks on her throat. Like Lucy she is also staged as the object of the gaze of men, who are in the process of deliberating her condition. In response to Jonathan's query how these wounds came about, a maid announces Count Dracula. This comic ploy might well also be taken as a dramatic performance of the fact that the vampire appears in response to a request. To the three men, he embodies their need to find someone to hold responsible for the fact that Mina is hiding something from them. As in many classic case histories of hysteria, the wound on her throat can be seen as a psychosomatic articulation of a desire, for which she can find no symbolic language, because she is not allowed to speak about it directly. Furthermore, like the patients Freud writes about, she becomes more animated once the Count has entered the sitting room, as though her body were giving voice to something her conscious mind forbids her to admit to herself. At the same time, as was the case with Lucy, her body also emerges as a text written by him. Dracula openly admits that the nightmares she has been having could well be the result of stories he has been telling her. In so doing he is, of course, equating the transfusion of blood, which Browning never shows us, with an exchange of fantasies.

Mina speaks to Dracula, but he has no reflection in the mirror.

In contrast to the static camera with which most of this dialogue scene is visually presented, Browning at this point includes one of the very few montage sequences of the entire film. While Mina, still sitting on the couch, continues talking to the Count, Jonathan and Van Helsing unintentionally point the mirror of a cigarette case in her direction, only to discover that the Count cannot be seen in the reflection. It is, of course, a commonplace of folklore that vampires have no mirror image; that as dead bodies returned to the living, they contain no corporeal substance. What this staging highlights, however, is Count Dracula's status as a phantom. While the three male onlookers intently follow the conversation between Mina and her guest, Browning offers a montage of what they see in the mirror as opposed to what they see in reality—a framed image of Mina speaking with herself. This image within the film image visualises that Dracula is not just to be understood as a concrete threat, but also as a monstrous body, emanating from Mina's imagination; a figure of fantasy she projects outside herself, so as to discover in conversation with him something she would otherwise have no access to.

The danger of Browning's vampire thus consists precisely in the fact that it isn't corporeal but spectral; a figure without concrete substance, present and absent at the same time. Given the fact that in this sequence of images the character, whose name the film bears in its title, can be made to appear and disappear by virtue of the trick of montage, what is suggested is that the spectral presence of the vampire may well also be read as a self-conscious reference to the phantomatic aspect of the film medium itself; the cinematic image, too, is nothing more than a projection from an internal light outside—present or absent, depending on the flicking of a switch.

After the father has sent away his daughter, a battle of wills ensues between the Count and his contestants. Van Helsing shows him the mirror and, with one of the melodramatic gestures Lugosi was to become famous for, Dracula throws it to the ground, regaining his composure before leaving the room. Van Helsing, who now believes he has enough evidence to disclose the true identity of the mysterious tenant of Carfax Abbey, finds the other men still doubting his superstitious code of interpretation. His insistence that the power of the vampire lies precisely in the fact that people will not believe in him once more gives voice to the performative aspect of the vampire—which is to say that Dracula gains reality by virtue of a belief *in* him and the attribution of the signifier vampire *to* him. At the same time the equation between the vampire and an act of faith, cinematically performed in the mirror scene, also discloses how much cinema in general owes to superstition. After all, the film screen also draws its affective power from the fact that it allows characters mysteriously to appear whose existence we do not rationally believe in. Apodictically put, precisely because we don't believe in these phantoms, cinema works. In Browning's staging Mina thus emerges as the point of negotiation for his own artistic medium. While the men argue with Van Helsing over the existence of vampires, she quietly leaves her father's house, only to walk straight into the arms of the Count, who envelopes her in his dark veil. At stake for her is neither a rational rejection *of*, nor a fantastic belief *in* his existence. Instead she is drawn by a force of attraction which cannot be explained, which pulls her along only to leave her exhausted once its power wears off.

A few minutes later, Jonathan will carry an unconscious Mina across the dark lawn back into the house. But the nebulous influence Count Dracula asserts over her—as a cipher for the demonic aspect of cinema itself—not only brings about exhaustion. It also calls for a rejuvenation, which allows those willing to submit themselves to this power to test emotions and roles they couldn't have devised on their own. At the *peripeteia* of the film's narrative, Mina appears in a tight silk dress on the veranda of her father's house. Jonathan calls her a "changed girl" and she herself admits to feeling strangely inebriated. In the seduction scene that ensues we recognise in Helen Chandler's gaze and gestures the transformation of the inhibited bourgeois daughter into a self-conscious glamour star.

To her fiancé she praises the night, while beckoning him with her eyes to come sit next to her on the bench and allow her to bite his neck. Long before Van Helsing puts an end to this unholy spell we recognise the demonic aspect of

Bela Lugosi in full flow as Dracula.

her charm, even while its attraction is fundamentally ambivalent. As she leans toward Jonathan, Browning cuts to a close-up of her face so that we see her enticing gaze coming ever closer to him, but also to us. What fills up the screen by virtue of this approach is, of course, the glamour star; the objectified body around which Hollywood's narrative code revolves. At the same time Mina now also assumes the position the vampire had in the scene of Lucy's seduction, although she immediately falls out of this new role once she sees the cross Van Helsing is holding in his hand, only to confess to Jonathan the blood she has exchanged with Dracula. What ultimately interrupts the scene is the sound of a shotgun—one of the servants had tried to shoot a bat hovering above the veranda; whereupon Van Helsing assures Jonathan that this is entirely impossible. In the reverse shot we see the servant, who is the only one not susceptible to the suggestive power of the vampire. "They are all mad", he explains to the serving girl standing next to him, and indeed inside the house everyone has been afflicted by the mass hysteria called forth by the Count's presence. Either they succumb to his gaze, like the maid in front of Mina's door, who allows him once more to enter her mistress' bedroom, or they run through the dark night toward Carfax Abbey, so that the final showdown between the vampire and his hunters can take place there. Once the infectious fantasy has set in, one might surmise, there can be no outside to the haunting.

Perhaps because all subsequent adaptations of this novel inevitably involve a complex return of things past, Browning's *Dracula* has become one of the most resilient ciphers for the cinematic fantastic. If the publication of Bram Stoker's novel fell into the same period in which cinema was born, its stage version brought with it a rejuvenation of the *Dracula* story that ultimately came to precipitate a long series of cinematic revenants. Because of these films, popular culture has become one of the privileged sites for defining our relation to late Victorianism as a vampiristic exchange; with each remake, the lost world depicted in Stoker's novel returns to haunt us. At the same time, cinema itself emerges as the site of a dialectic exchange with the dead. Owing to its play with light and shadow, phantoms can take shape and the dead can return to the living. Furthermore, the cinematic medium also bears the sign of the vampire insofar as it belatedly invokes, and this reinvigorates on screen, a world of film production which no longer exists—in the case of Tod Browning's *Dracula* the actors and sets of the early 1930s. The hypnotic gaze of Bela Lugosi has become coterminous with this self-reflexive moment, as it so explicitly refers not only to the visual as the sense privileged above all others by the cinematic apparatus, but also to its technical correlatives—the camera's lens, focusing the actor's performance, as well as the eye of the viewers, enchanted by what they find unfolding before them in the dark with the help of white light on a white screen. And it is precisely about the seductive power of cinema itself that Count Dracula speaks with these eyes, in all his cinematic embodiments since Tod Browning's first horror talkie.

⚐ NOTES

1. Joslin, Lyndon, *Count Dracula Goes to the Movies. Stoker's Novel Adapted*, 1922–1995, Jefferson and London: McFarland and Company, 1999, p. 27.

2. Jung, Uli, *Dracula. Filmanalytische Studien zur Funktionalisierung eines Motivs der viktorianischen Populärliteratur*, Trier: Universitäts Verlag, 1997, p. 111.

3. See David J Skal, *Hollywood Gothic. The Tangled Web of Dracula from Novel to Stage to Screen*, London and New York: Norton, 1990; and also Alain Silver and James Ursini, *The Vampire Film. From Nosferatu to Interview with the Vampire*, New York: Limelight Editions, 1997.

4. Skal, *Hollywood Gothic*, p. 130.

5. See Mark A Vieira, *Hollywood Horror from Gothic to Cosmic*, New York: Harry N Abrams, 2003.

6. Edwards, Larry, *Bela Lugosi. Master of the Macabre*, Bradenton: McGuinn and McGuire, 1995.

7. Skal, *Hollywood Gothic*, pp. 139 and 142.

8. Thomas, Ronald R, "Dracula: Novel and Cinema", *Nineteenth-Century Contexts. An Interdisciplinary Journal*, Special Issue: "Postmodern Victorians", vol. 22, no. 1, 2000, p. 78.

9. Jung, *Dracula*, p. 109. See also Elisabeth Bronfen, *The Knotted Subject. Hysteria and its Discontents*, Princeton: Princeton University Press, 1994.

TOD BROWNING'S

THEMATIC CONTINUITY AND
STYLISTIC DEVELOPMENT

Leger Grindon

IN IRON MAN

Iron Man, 1931, is an important but neglected film in Tod Browning's career, made after *Dracula*, 1931, but before *Freaks*, 1932—that is, in between the filmmaker's two most celebrated productions. As a result, it deserves attention. The film has been neglected in the critical literature, probably because it lacks the macabre quality for which Browning's films are known. *Dark Carnival*, the 1995 biography of Browning by David J Skal and Elias Savada, devotes less than a page to the film, and fails even to mention the title in its index.[1] Neither Stuart Rosenthal nor Elliottt Stein discusses the picture in their profiles of the filmmaker.[2] Nonetheless, *Iron Man* appears to have been profitable. Though box office figures are unavailable, the boxing drama was remade twice by Universal during the Hollywood studio era as *Some Blondes Are Dangerous*, 1937 and *Iron Man*, 1950, a testimony to its success.

The film stars Lew Ayres, in the year following his big success in Lewis Milestone's *All Quiet on the Western Front*, 1930, as Kid Mason, a lightweight boxing champion whose affection is divided between George Regan, his friend and manager (Robert Armstrong in an excellent performance), and his double-crossing wife, Rose (Jean Harlow). The movie is based on a popular novel of the same name by WR Burnett, an author of 'tough guy' fiction also responsible for the source novels for Mervyn LeRoy's *Little Caesar*, 1931, and John Huston's *The Asphalt Jungle*, 1950.

Iron Man is a cautionary tale about the boxer as a physically powerful man brought down by a woman. Kid Mason supplies the muscle in the ring, and George Regan directs his training and strategy. The film opens with Mason being knocked out, having abandoned his manager's advice in order to impress Rose. As a result of his defeat, Rose, a gold-digging vamp, leaves the Kid because he cannot provide the apartment and furs she demands. George comforts his buddy, who soon blossoms under Regan's direction to become a contender. Learning that Mason has signed to fight for the lightweight title, Rose returns. After the Kid wins, she comes between him and his friends from the gym. Now Mason dresses in elegant clothes, maintains a luxurious apartment, and

Iron Man: Kid Mason (played by Lew Ayres) in action in Tod Browning's underrated film.

frequents the theatre instead of the poker table. After George finds Rose snuggling up to Paul Lewis (John Miljan), a theatrical producer, he cautions the Kid. But the boxer remains oblivious to the vamp's adultery. Eventually a confrontation between George and Rose ensues and Mason, defending his duplicitous wife, slugs his pal. Rose takes the opportunity to put forward Paul Lewis as the Kid's new manager, and George agrees to give up his contract if the Champ will fight his new prospect for the title. Just before the bout Mason learns of his wife's betrayal. Heartbroken and abandoned, he is defeated.

Iron Man raises key questions regarding Tod Browning's authorship. First, are the themes and motifs evident in Browning's more famous tales of horror apparent in the boxing film? Second, Iron Man arises at an important juncture in the evolution of Browning's mise-en-scène. Commentators such as Elliott Stein have noted that during the silent era Browning maintained a stationary camera and depended upon editing and composition as expressive tools.[3] However, his collaboration on Dracula with the famous German cinematographer Karl Freund resulted in the conspicuous use of camera movement, a Freund trademark. In his first production after this collaboration, does camera movement become a key element in Browning's style?

Beyond superficial appearances, *Iron Man* displays thematic continuity with Browning's other films. Stuart Rosenthal argues persuasively that moral and sexual frustrations are Browning's principal subjects. Furthermore, he highlights four subsidiary motifs: appearances hiding truth (particularly physical beauty as a mask for villainy), sexual frustration, opposing tendencies within a protagonist that are often projected onto alter egos, and finally an inability to assign guilt.[4] In a similar vein, Elliott Stein calls attention to Browning's portrayals of physical suffering and a "sympathetic vulnerability" that become manifest in a predatory sexuality and masochism.[5] All of these factors are at play in *Iron Man*.

(left) The plot of *Iron Man* centres around the battle for Kid Mason between his manager, George Regan (Robert Armstrong) and his adulterous wife, Rose (Jean Harlow).

(right) Jean Harlow's gold-digging vamp is avaricious, aspiring and sexually predatory.

Rosenthal notes that Browning first establishes his characters and then allows the plot to arise from their interaction.[6] *Iron Man* builds its drama around the conflict between George and Rose for control of Kid Mason. Indeed, George and Rose represent opposing tendencies in Mason that are developed through these alter egos. Rose embodies pretence, greed, and predatory sexuality. She is a cousin to Dracula's fiendish daughters and Cleopatra in *Freaks*. Jean Harlow's beauty thinly veils her treachery, but her allure is enough to deceive the boxer, whose own physical prowess hides his weakness—a sexual vulnerability verging on masochism. First walking out on the boxer because he lacks money, and then betraying him for a more sophisticated companion, Rose excites sexual frustration and fears of inadequacy.

Paul Lewis embodies Rose's aspirations for wealth, culture and class. He appears in formal dress, does an elegant turn on the dance floor, and casts Rose in his stage revue. Lewis and Rose are both deceitful posers who betray their spouses. It is the divorce proceedings initiated by Mrs Lewis that finally open Mason's eyes to his wife's liaison. Theatrical artifice fosters duplicity and social arrogance as opposed to the frank and equal confrontations in the boxing ring. Later, the film crosscuts between Mason's defeat in the ring and a meeting between Lewis and Rose. When Rose resists his demand that they depart together, Lewis socks her on the jaw just as the film cuts to Mason taking a blow.[7] Equally decadent, unscrupulous, and cruel, Lewis and Rose crystallise the film's suspicion of beauty as deceit.

Iron Man develops the competing alter egos typical of Browning's work. George Regan embodies the brains, Kid Mason, the brawn. In many respects,

George Regan represents simplicity and loyalty in contrast to Rose's scheming.

George functions like Van Helsing in Dracula or Phroso, the sad clown in *Freaks*. He is an honest, insightful friend who uncovers deception. George's keen intelligence serves him in his work and his personal relations. He sees through Rose's schemes, but nonetheless loses the Kid to the vamp. Dismayed by their separation, he turns to drink to sooth his melancholy. George remains apart from women and sophisticated culture. He plays poker and solitaire, drinks and eats with his buddies, and fondly remembers fishing with the Kid in their early days. His habits are hardy and unadorned, his character marked by loyalty, understatement, and resilience. Though George has a sharp edge, his speech peppered with wisecracks, he remains caring toward his friend even after their estrangement. In the suggestive, unresolved closing scene, George visits Mason after his defeat and finds the boxer in tears, slumped on the dressing table. The manager chases the others from the room, stares into the Kid's eyes, and then prods him back to life with his habitual, caressing rebuke, "Put your robe on. Whatya wanna do, catch pneumonia?" In its closing line, the film portrays the ambivalent dynamics of male bonding, attack restrained and refashioned into affection.

The relationship between Kid Mason and George Regan is characterised by the ambivalence of male bonding, as in the film's closing scene.

In Kid Mason's fall, Tod Browning presents a cautionary tale. Whereas many of Browning's protagonists are deformed grotesques, the boxer displays physical perfection, but a flawed character. Kid Mason is related to the naïve Jonathan Harker, or more closely still to the subservient Renfield in *Dracula*, and the pathetic Hans of *Freaks*. Mason's nickname points to his immaturity. With women he is helpless. Shortly after Rose's initial departure, George protects the Kid from another woman trying to take advantage of him, and Mason gratefully assures his manager that "I'm through with women for life." But when Rose reappears, he immediately succumbs.

At Rose's behest, Kid Mason is transformed from physically robust boxer to fey dandy.

The boxer's fall is conveyed in his transformation from an image of unadorned physical health into a dandy. In the early scenes, when the Kid is close to George, Mason freely displays his muscular body, and not only in the ring; he also appears bare-chested out of the shower and half dressed in his hotel room. After he wins the title, Rose dresses him in formal clothes, with a cane, gloves and a flower in his lapel. The contrast between body and dress highlights the physical as the basis of the boxer's strength; by contrast fashion, manners, and class pretence debase his power. Simplicity and health, the physical training for sport, are associated with a power that is corrupted by the erotic.

Naturally trusting and in need of support, the Kid moves from a dependence upon George to a subservient and demeaning relationship with Rose. One of George's tactics in training is to incite Mason's anger against his ring opponent, egging him on by claiming that he will bet against him. When gamblers approach the manager with a proposition to fix the Prince Pearl fight, George sends them to talk to Mason, knowing that the scheme will enrage the boxer and prepare him for the bout. Left to himself the Kid appears malleable and naïve; yet it is that very vulnerability that excites our sympathy. Three incidents highlight his weakness. When George, drunk and forlorn, finally attacks Lewis and calls Rose a "double crossing wife", the Kid knocks him out. At this point Rose triumphs over George for the control of the Kid's emotions. Almost immediately Mason, confused and at a loss, apologises to George: "I didn't mean to go so far. I had to do it." Just before the final bout the Kid discovers Lewis' duplicity, lunging at him only to be restrained by his trainers. Without guidance he cannot redirect his rage and goes down for the count. George is downcast at the Kid's failure, but doesn't blame him for his fall. Mason's childlike nature absolves him of guilt.

Camera movement is central to the *mise-en-scène* of *Iron Man*. Elliott Stein describes Browning's camera during the silent era as "leaden", but, under Freund's influence, that is certainly not the case by 1931.[8] The variety of camera movement in *Iron Man* is impressive. Frequently the camera pans and/or dollies to reframe characters, or to recede before them down passageways. This allows for an expansive and fluent figure movement. Browning regularly uses a moving camera to establish a scene, beginning with a close-up or long shot, and then having the camera retreat to reveal the setting, or advance to capture figures in medium shot. Similarly, he frequently closes scenes by dollying into a thoughtful face for psychological emphasis. George, in particular, is privileged

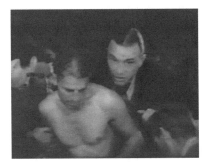

While under George's direction, Kid Mason's muscular physicality is evident.

with this treatment. In other cases, the director establishes setting by having the camera move independently of the characters. For example, he begins a scene with a close-up of a liquor bottle, pans to George asleep on a couch, and then moves to the door where a knock sounds. In a shot that anticipates the wedding feast in *Freaks*, the camera pans from a tight composition of the Kid at the head of a banquet table, celebrating his victory over Prince Pearl, down the table to reveal the boxer's entourage enjoying the feast. Later in the same scene, George rises from his seat and the camera follows him around the table. In *Iron Man*, then, fluent camera movement accents the drama in a variety of ways.

The climactic confrontation between George and Rose at a party in the Kid's luxurious apartment is also the high point of mobile camera *mise-en-scène* in the film. The scene opens with a close-up of the strings of a piano. The camera tilts up and pans to find Rose and Lewis dancing, and then follows the couple as they glide to the music around and behind the piano for a lustful exchange of glances. The shot then cuts to the Kid and follows him to the door to greet George. The two walk to the bar as cuts and camera movement are interspersed. Later the camera underlines George's suspicions by ominously following behind him as he moves to the bedroom to find Rose alone with Lewis. When the final confrontation comes, it is camera movement rather than editing that serves as a major expressive tool to accent the film's emotional showdown.

George perceives Rose's infidelity where Kid Mason cannot.

Iron Man is not an anomaly in Tod Browning's career; rather, it is a work that testifies to the continuity of his thematic concerns, as well as showcasing his growing facility with the camera after his work with Karl Freund. As such, the film testifies to the director's achievement in the maturity of his career.

⌖ NOTES

1. Skal, David J, and Elias Savada, *Dark Carnival: The Secret World of Tod Browning*, New York: Anchor Books, 1995, p. 157.

2. Rosenthal, Stuart, *The Hollywood Professionals: Tod Browning, Don Siegel*, New York: AS Barnes, 1975, pp. 7–66; Stein, Elliott, "Tod Browning", *in Cinema: A Critical Dictionary*, vol. 1, Richard Roud ed., New York: Viking Press, 1980, pp. 156–166.

3. Stein, "Tod Browning", p. 159.

4. Rosenthal, *The Hollywood Professionals: Tod Browning*, pp. 23–24.

5. Stein, "Tod Browning", p. 158 and throughout.

6. Rosenthal, *The Hollywood Professionals: Tod Browning*, p. 23.

7. Sid, "Iron Man", *Variety*, 22 April 1931, p. 18. The review chides the film for being "pretty rough" in this incident and notes that it elicited a scream from a woman in the audience. I should note that a 16mm television print and the VHS tape that I viewed had cut out this blow.

8. Stein, "Tod Browning", p. 159.

THE MONSTROUS BODY/POLITIC OF FREAKS

Bernd Herzogenrath

Tod Browning's 1932 movie *Freaks* has survived numerous appropriations and readings. From its original conception as a horror movie exceeding all expectations, something more disturbing than anything seen so far, via Dwain Esper's exploitation of it under dubious and misleading titles such as *Forbidden Love*, *Monster Show* and *Nature's Mistakes*, to its revival as an avant-garde movie in the tradition of Buñuel and Robbe-Grillet, *Freaks* has covered the range of horror, art-house and documentary. On the whole, however, it has remained a somehow under-appreciated and under-theorised movie; previous analyses have read it largely in the context of disability and gender studies.[1] Though there are definitely are points of convergence, I will try a somewhat different approach, relating *Freaks* to psychoanalytical theory—specifically a blend of Freudian and Lacanian concepts, and a concept of 'political self-organisation'—a Deleuzian Body/Politic.

Film and psychoanalysis—from their respective beginnings—have enjoyed a relationship which can be defined as both elective affinity and dangerous liaison. Cinema as a popular medium, as well as psychoanalysis as a 'popular science', both saw a rise to prominence in the first half of the last century. After all, both deal with dreams and fantasies. Thus, aspects of the dream-work such as displacement and condensation, free association, Oedipal situations and traumatic constellations became important elements for both the narrative structures and imagery of the cinema. On the other hand, films have made (and more often than not distorted) psychoanalytic terminology into everyday household concepts. Freud himself was very skeptical about the ability of cinema to deal effectively with the subject. Freud was so famous in 'Dream Factory' circles that Samuel Goldwyn in 1924 planned sailing to Vienna on a mission to produce the greatest love story from the world's most famous doctor of love—an attempt to get Sigmund Freud to write a screenplay for a love story about Anthony and Cleopatra. Although the offer of $100,000 was more than generous, Freud kindly declined.[2]

Michel de Montaigne states that "Dreams are faithful interpreters of our inclinations; but there is art required to sort and understand them."[3] *Freaks*,

I argue, is such a sorter of the dream-work, attempting to provide an understanding of our inclinations or self-images, an understanding that may not always be easy or pleasing—in fact, in Browning's circus sideshow, dreams turn out to be not Montaigne's 'wishful thinking', but its opposite. As Louella Parsons, Hollywood gossip columnist, commented after seeing *Freaks*: "I came into the Criterion Theater from the gayety of Mrs Gardner Sullivan's luncheon party and I felt as if I had suddenly fallen asleep and were having a weird nightmare...."[4]

Freaks: the film's opening titles.

    Freaks opens with a carnival barker displaying a sideshow freak. Realism is introduced by the barker tearing apart the opening film title from within the diegetic space, thus attempting to fuse extradiegetic reality with the narrated universe, peopled by 'real freaks'—when casting the movie, Browning had a large conglomeration of professional freaks applying for a role. The use of 'real freaks' somehow denied actors and audience the safe assurance that what was shown onscreen was 'just a fiction'. The 'life on screen' has always had the tendency to seem 'more real' than reality itself, but with the make-up tricks and special effects that would leave open the possibility of differentiation removed, the already fragile distinction seemed to collapse completely. It was as if the audience were back in the time of Auguste and Louis Lumière, trying to escape the train arriving at the station and invading the safe space of reality and the self—the audiences screaming and leaving the theatres at screenings of *Freaks* is a case in point.

    The barker addresses the spectators: "Friends, she was once a beautiful woman...."[5] The freak is revealed to his audience (but not to us), to the screams of the women watching, and as the barker begins to tell her story, the narrative of the film proper ensues, set within this frame. Cleopatra (Olga Baclanova), a beautiful trapeze artist with the carnival, is adored by a dwarf named Hans (Harry Earles). Frieda (Daisy Earles), his fiancée (also a dwarf), warns Hans that Cleopatra is only interested in him because he gives her money and expensive presents. Cleopatra has an affair with Hercules (Henry Victor), the circus' Strong Man, and when Frieda confronts her to stop making a fool of Hans, she mistakenly reveals to Cleopatra that Hans has inherited a fortune. Cleopatra and Hercules plan to get the money by having Cleopatra marry Hans and then poison him. During the wedding reception, while Cleopatra is openly flirting with Hercules, the freaks all gather around the table and begin a ritual of accepting Cleopatra to their circle. When a dwarf passes around a large loving cup for a communal toast, he is rebuffed by Cleopatra. She seals her fate by recoiling in disgust, pouring the champagne over the dwarf's head, mocking their acceptance ceremony, calling them "Dirty, slimy freaks!" and ordering them to leave. Back in Cleopatra's carnival wagon, she poisons Hans' drink, but Venus (Leila Hyams), one of the sympathising 'big people', confronts her former lover, Hercules, and threatens him unless he tells the doctor who is treating Hans about the poison. Cleopatra attempts to slip poison into the medicine the doctor prescribes, but this time she is surrounded by all the freaks, who band together and attack her.

Meanwhile, in the heavy rain, Hercules goes after Venus, who is pulling her carnival wagon out to escape from his fury when Phroso, the clown (Wallace Ford), comes to her rescue. He can't handle Hercules by himself, so the freaks throw a knife at Hercules. Reportedly, in the original version of the film, he was castrated—however, that scene has been cut if indeed it did exist. After that, we return to the sideshow barker. In the beginning, we left the audience after they have seen the "most amazing, the most astounding living monstrosity of all time". The film audience is denied the sight of the "living monstrosity" until this moment. Now we see the result of the freaks' revenge on Cleopatra: she has been turned into a legless, half-blind stump, a squawking Chicken Woman. A final scene, tacked on later as the studio insisted on a happy ending, shows Hans living like a millionaire in an elegant house; Phroso and Venus bring along Frieda, and the two lovers are reconciled.

Some of the inhabitants of Tod Browning's carnival.

A constant throughout his work, sexually charged mutilations play a dominant role in Browning's movies. This points to the fact that the body as such is already libidinally charged. In the body, as a kind of 'primary fact of existence', the human subject encounters itself as both subject and object. As Freud has shown, the agency and formation of the ego reveal a close complicity with the notion of the body. For Freud, the "ego is first and foremost a bodily ego… the projection of a surface".[6] In fact, Freud argues that it is only through this investment that the body becomes accessible to us at all: "The ego is ultimately derived from bodily sensations", a point where the body and the social collide, and which gains the utmost importance by being the first 'object' to which the human being's libidinal resources are attached.[7] This peculiar status of the human being as speaking being also turns the body into metaphor. Since the speaking human subject *qua* signifier is always already inscribed in the symbolic, the body is always more than just a biological given or natural fact.

Cleopatra, the trapeze, artist and the besotted Hans.

Jacques Lacan develops Freud's notion of the ego as bodily projection, connecting the question of identity to the relation of the human being to its body (image) and showing that the image of wholeness is an illusion attempting to cover a basic lack. In his essay on the 'mirror stage', Lacan reveals the ego to be not a pre-reflexive entity, a stable core of the self that gradually evolves; in fact, the ego itself is already based on reflection.[8] Constructed within visual space, the ego is the result of various identificatory processes, of the constant oscillation between self and other: there is no chance of perceiving one's own identity as separate from what is exterior to it. The ego is not so much the source of self-knowledge but the result of a fundamental *"méconnaissance"*.[9] There exists what Lacan calls the effect of a physiological "prematurity of birth" characteristic of the human newborn, which shows itself in its "motor incapacity and nursling dependence".[10] The child experiences the body in terms of incompleteness, insufficiency and lack of motor coordination. What follows is the anticipatory identification with the image of one's own body in the mirror. The promised and illusory totality of the ego is always threatened by phantasmatic returns of images of incompleteness. Thus, the mirror stage is a "succession of phantasies that extends from a fragmented body-image to a form of its totality that I shall call orthopaedic—and, lastly, to the assumption of an alienating identity".[11] Lacan thus shows how identity is constructed—is an effect rather than a cause, forever situated in a precarious balance between the complete and the fragmented body. Every identity is a "fictitious invention" and rests on a fundamental misconception. By "jubilatory" identification with the imaginary mirage of the whole body, the "real" of the fragmented body is repressed. However, this sense of unity is very frail, and the images of the fragmented body haunt and thus subvert any illusion of wholeness—"This fragmented body… appears in the form of disjointed limbs—the very same that the visionary

Hieronymus Bosch has fixed, for all time, in painting...."[12] Ultimately, for Lacan, these two body images are inseparable.

In Browning's movies, the body—in particular its dismemberment—plays a crucial role in his understanding of horror. It is here that Freud's essay on "The Uncanny" might present a fruitful theoretical foil against which to situate *Freaks*. Freud's essay, I argue, in marked contrast to its seeming datedness when it comes to modern horror, still provides a rich ground for analysis, precisely because it adds a further dimension to the oft-quoted cathartic effect of horror —the "return of the repressed". David Skal and Elias Savada have speculated in their book *Dark Carnival* that Browning himself—or via one of his scenario writers, Herman J Mankiewicz—might have been familiar with Freudian concepts. Mankiewicz is portrayed as being equipped with "both the cynical literary sophistication of a mid-20s Manhattanite and an awareness of the literary/dramatic implications of Freudian theory".[13] Having lived in Berlin in the 1920s, Mankiewicz was likely to be "familiar with the currents of psychoanalytic thought swirling about the German capital".[14] Whether through Mankiewicz's influence or otherwise, the Oedipus complex as a narrative structure, as well as aspects of the Freudian 'uncanny', dominate Browning's work.

Freaks: The Siamese Twins (Daisy and Violet Hilton) with Hercules, the Strong Man (Henry Victor).

In his essay, Freud refers specifically to bodily fragmentation as providing powerful images of the uncanny: "dismembered limbs, a severed head, a hand cut off at the wrist".[15] According to Freud, "[this] uncanny is in reality nothing new or alien, but something which is familiar and old-established in the mind and which has become alienated from it only through the process of repression".[16] The horror and repulsion associated with the sight of the freaks—the screaming audience within the film acts as a stand-in here—can thus be seen as a result of the repression of the primal fragmentariness of the body. What has to be stressed, then, is the relation of the uncanny to the 'normal': "the *unheimlich* is what was once *heimisch*, home-like, familiar; the prefix 'un' is the token of repression".[17] If these findings are connected to Lacan's view of the body-image, there is much that makes a psychoanalytical reading of *Freaks* worthwhile. Read together with Freud's essay, what has to be stressed then is the fact that the fragmented body emerges as the 'real(ity)' of the whole body.

The contrast between the 'whole' body of Hercules and the *unheimlich*, 'freak' body of Roscoe in drag. Courtesy of Paul Meienberg.

Not its utterly other, but its 'dark self'. The narcissistic 'big people' Cleopatra and Hercules are tied to the dwarfs and Living Torsos as inseparably as Daisy and Violet Hilton, the Siamese Twins, are tied to each other.

It is this relation of "what once was heimisch, familiar", with respect to the monstrous Body/Politic that I want to show in the following—on one level, *Freaks* takes up a political discussion that resonates through the whole history of (American) politics.[18] One of the most prominent visual representations of such a Body/Politic is the frontispiece of Thomas Hobbes' 1651 *Leviathan*. Here, we are confronted with an already altered version of the traditional Body/Politic, a Renaissance face representing a new, human-centred line of thought, showing greater attention to the abilities—and the needs—of the people.[19] Hobbes argued that government was not divine or 'natural' at all, but was an invention of mankind, for mankind. His was a model of a 'monarchical contract', a contract entered into not because of moral obligations, but because of self-interest and social agreement alone; not because of man's inherent striving for goodness and peace, but the contrary—to restrain violent and aggressive impulses. The Leviathan consists of a multitude of smaller bodies, all directing their gaze towards the head—the only organ that is not a "composite member", thus the place where a privileged metonymical part represents a complex body, where a potential multiplicity, a Many, is resolved and channeled into a One, a hierarchical fixture of authority and wholeness.

(left) Frontispiece from Thomas Hobbes' *Leviathan*, 1651.

(right) The physical perfection of Hercules was used to represent the unity and fortitude of the USA.

This miraculous bodily wholeness was realised in one of the suggestions for the Great Seal, commissioned by Congress on July 4, 1776. John Adams proposed the figure of Hercules. Although it was ultimately rejected, the figure of Hercules resurfaced in Franklin's design for the *Libertas Americana* medal of 1783. On this medal, commemorating the Revolutionary War, the figure of Hercules represents the strength of the Young Nation, as it did in Marquis de Barbi-Marbois' 1784 *Allegory of the American Union*. The monolithic and phallic figure of Hercules—a much more rigid version of the Body/Politic than Hobbes' *Leviathan*, where the constituting multiplicity is at least still visible—perfectly illustrates the solidity of the *Gestalt* in the mirror, which is one of its most important features. As Lacan states: "It is the stability of the standing posture, the prestige of stature… [which] sets the style for the identifications in which the ego finds its starting point and leave their imprint in it forever."[20]

In *Freaks*, it is the characters of Hercules, the Strong Man, and Cleopatra, the beautiful trapeze artist, that reveal the extremity of American individualism and the greed of American society. In comparison to the imaginary illusion of a whole, autonomous body, monstrous, grotesque bodies such as the freaks' can only be made sense of in the belated fiction of the Lacanian fragmented body-image; that is, as a "primary organisation that is subsequently disassembled", something (temporally) "before" and (spatially/logically) "outside", something perhaps faintly familiar, but something long forgotten as well.[21]

However, as a repressed that *returns*, I want to link the rhetoric of the grotesque body to an incident in American history that shows the use of this metaphor from another perspective. In contrast to the belated story of the fragmented body, another conception is possible—a conception that does not start with unity, but with multiplicity; which does not follow the logic of belatedness and representation, but of emergence and becoming—a logic that is proposed rigorously by the 'intelligent materialism' of Gilles Deleuze and Félix Guattari. They replace the belated fiction of the fragmented body by the 'becoming body', what they call the "Body without Organs" (or "BwO"), where the body's partial objects do not presuppose an original wholeness or a hope for a totalising Unity (as in Hobbes). The BwO, rather, is an assembly of dispersed partial objects that are "not the expression of a fragmented, shattered organism, which would presuppose a destroyed totality or the freed parts of a whole".[22] The BwO is thus the corps *morcelé* 'under opposite signs':

> It is not at all a question of a fragmented, splintered body, of organs without the body (OwB). The BwO is exactly the opposite. There are not organs in the sense of fragments in relation to a lost unity, nor is there a return to the undifferentiated in relation to a differentiable totality.... The error of psychoanalysis was to understand BwO phenomena as regressions, projections, phantasies, in terms of an image of the body.[23]

The fragmented body as BwO is thus not to be understood in terms of regression, or lack, but as a capacity for new connections, for dynamic openness and growth.

The body as bounded territory (the nation/body, the state/body) follows the logic of a unified organism, where all parts relate to one another in a hierarchically structured manner. The BwO, on the other hand, is a body not subjected to such constraining limits and definitions of its various parts, and of each part's meaning and function. Bodies, according to Deleuze and Guattari, are self-organising systems, non-hierarchic, where the head is no more important than the other members. Bodies are only ever in states of becoming, entering relations with their *milieu*, which in turn is always a part of a larger body of particles, *ad infinitum*. In such a pure state of multiplicity, the Body without Organs is a deterritorialised body, "the unformed, unorganised.... Body and all its flows... pure intensities", not (to be) shaped, informed and brought to life by an intelligent spirit or a divine One, since it carries with it the potential of self-organisation.[24]

In the times before the Civil War, one particularly popular spectacle in the sideshows were the brothers Chang and Eng, best known as the original Siamese Twins. As Allison Pingree has convincingly argued, Americans saw their own political struggle embodied in the twins at a time when questions of unity

The 'original' Siamese Twins, Chang and Eng.

and/or separation became more and more pressing.[25] The grotesque body of the Siamese Twins offered a potent metaphor of an American ideal, reflecting a basic democratic urge, yet at the same time questioning the concept of individuality and its concomitant distinction between self and other so dear to American individualism, in particular in its more capitalistic guise—as embodied, I would argue, in Hercules, both in 'Herculean' political rhetoric and iconography, and in the figure of Hercules in *Freaks*. As the principle question Chang and Eng posed for the spectator was whether they were two separate individuals jointed at the chest, or one person equipped with extra head, arms, legs, so the Young Nation struggled with its own governmental structures (divided states? a united nation?). Two of the pamphlets distributed at the performances of Chang and Eng focus upon the important metaphor that their conjoined body/bodies provided for the American Body/Politic. Under the title of these handbills, there was an American Eagle with shield, emblazoned with the phrase "*E Pluribus Unum*"; "United we stand". On another pamphlet, the motto reads "Union and Liberty, one and inseparable, now and forever", quoting and calling into mind Massachusetts Senator Daniel Webster's 1830 speech directed against the separatists in Congress, warning of the damaging effects of secession for the Body/Politic:

> When my eyes shall be turned to behold, for the last time, the sun in heaven, may I not see him shining on the broken and dishonoured fragments of a once glorious Union; on States dissevered, discordant, belligerent; on a land rent with civil feuds, or drenched, it may be, in fraternal blood! Let their last

feeble and lingering glance, rather, behold the gorgeous ensign of the Republic, now known and honoured throughout the earth, still full high advanced, its arms and trophies streaming in their original lustre, not a stripe erased or polluted, nor a single star obscured, bearing for its motto no such miserable interrogatory as, What is all this worth? Nor those other words of delusion and folly, Liberty first and Union afterward; but everywhere, spread all over in characters of living light, blazing on all its ample folds, as they float over the sea and over the land, and in every wind under the whole heavens, that other sentiment, dear to every true American heart—Liberty and Union, now and forever, one and inseparable![26]

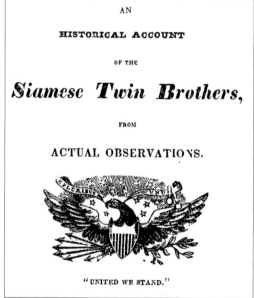

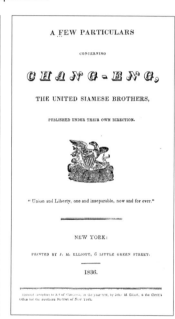

Before the Civil War, Americans drew comparisons between the physical duality of Chang and Eng and the question of their country's unity.

The close and almost self-explanatory conjunction of the twins with paroles and mottoes of American Democracy—*E Pluribus Unum*, United We Stand, conflates the brothers' inseparability with a Unionist discourse urging fusion among the States, in almost utopian hope of not losing one's 'individuality' in the process, thus embodying one of the central dilemmas of (not only American) democracy. From its beginnings onwards, the United States have—or has—been driven by debates concerning the paradoxical issues— and the means for their possible solution—of division versus unity, democratic egalitarianism versus extreme individualism. Thus, as Allison Pingree argues, the rhetoric tying Chang and Eng's body to antebellum politics has to be read against the background of the symbolism of "The House Divided", of "brother fighting against brother"—and it is really interesting to see how Lincoln later, in the course of the Civil War, forged the metaphor of the grotesque and monstrous body into his rhetorics of amputation:

The paramount idea of the constitution is the preservation of the Union. It may not be specified in so many words, but that this was the idea of its founders is evident; for, without the Union, the constitution would be worthless. It seems clear, then, that in the last extremity, if any local institution threatened the existence of the Union, the Executive could not hesitate as to his duty. In our case, the moment came when I felt that slavery must die that the nation might live. I sometimes used the illustration in this connection of a man with a diseased limb, and his surgeon. So long as there is a chance of the patient's restoration, the surgeon is solemnly bound to try to save both life and limb; but when the crisis comes, and the limb must be sacrificed as the only chance of saving the life, no honest man will hesitate.[27]

On the whole, however, from its beginning onwards, American mythology had been preoccupied with the strong, whole, autonomous, beautiful body—and the American movie industry followed suit. As Richard Watts Jr, in a positive review of an earlier Browning movie, *The Show*, 1927, pointed out: "Where every director, save Stroheim, breathes wholesomeness, out-of-door-freshness and the healthiness of the clean-limbed, Tod Browning revels in murkiness."[28] In *Freaks*, Browning continues his subversion of "clean-limbed-ness" both on the level of content and form, or visual aesthetics. In contrast to the stylish, glossy and optimistic "grey" tones of typical MGM productions, Browning was more inspired by the cinema of German Expressionism, the harsh black and white contrasts of films such as FW Murnau's *Nosferatu*, 1922, and Robert Wiene's *The Cabinet of Dr Caligari*, 1920. Browning was about to bring shadow its due attention in the movies. No wonder for a director whose "psyche was an attic, a crypt, a trunk, it was terrorised by sunlight, fields, deserts, woods and open spaces…. Tod Browning, the agoraphobic director *par excellence*."[29] On another level, the complex complicity between fragmentation and wholeness is repeated in the filmic medium itself. The 'unseen' filmic cut represses the fragmentation of its images in favour of the 'illusory wholeness'—the unity and coherence of the filmic image, its propelling forward, is in fact an effect of its inherent fragmentation. Also, the 'dismemberment' of characters by use of certain shots—decapitation as a consequence of a close up, dismembered limbs in detail shots—as well as their subsequent re-membering in the mind of the audience, relating all fragments to the image of the depicted character, can be read in the same way, as a kind of identification with images of wholeness akin to Lacan's mirror stage, which is indeed not just a developmental phase, but a foil underlying all subsequent identifications, and ultimately the visual realm as such. Finally, *Freaks* itself was mutilated, cut, censored because of its obvious opposition to wholeness, unity and "clean-limbed-ness."

In a scene early on in the movie, the freaks are shown playing around at a pastoral lakeside under the surveillance of Mme Tetrallini, the benevolent matron of the circus. A passing gamekeeper has seen them and, terrified, reports to the owner of the property, describing them as "a lot of horrible, twisted things, crawling, whining, globbering… there must be a law in France to smother such things at birth, or lock them up". Arriving on the scene, the proprietor and the gamekeeper—and we, the audience—for the first time see the freaks as a group: the "pinheads" Zip, Pip, Schlitzie and the Snow Twins; the half-boy Johnny Eck, who moves forward on his hands because the lower half of his body is missing; a Skeleton Man (Pete Robinson), Angelo Rossito, the dwarf, and the "Hindu Prince Randian", the Living Torso—a trunk and a head, no arms, no legs. When the two men arrive, the freaks seem to be frightened and run for shelter to Mme Tetrallini. She explains to the proprietor, "When I have a chance I like to take them into the sunshine and let them play like children. That is what

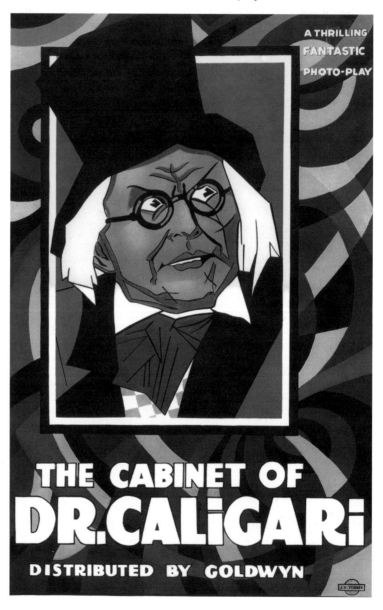

Promotional poster for *The Cabinet of Dr. Caligari*, 1920, directed by Robert Wiene.

(opposite) *Nosferatu*: Max Schreck in the 1922 film directed by FW Murnau.

most of them are—children." After the owner of the property has allowed them to stay, Mme Tetrallini says to the freaks, "How many times have I told you not to be frightened. Have I not told you God looks after all his children?"

Yet, it is exactly mistaking the freaks for children, naïve—or minor—that will prove dangerous for those who do. Constantly treating Hans like a child, and not as a man, as he insists, Cleopatra's misconception reaches its fatal climax when she and Hercules plan to poison Hans to get hold of his inheritance. Cleopatra's fate is sealed by her mistaken belief that "Midgets... are not strong ... They could get sick." Georges Bataille, in an essay on *Wuthering Heights* in his book *Literature and Evil*, has commented on the realm of childhood as posing a serious threat to the restrictions and laws of society. By equating benefit with profit, the good with reason, Bataille claims that what is at stake is a "revolt of Evil against Good".[30] It is not a question of the immoral against the moral: evil is understood here as something amoral rather than immoral (and 'moral' can be taken here in the Nietzschean sense of a thinly disguised craving for profit— Cleopatra and Hector would definitely subscribe to that). With the freaks, however, things change. *Their* law, their moral code, is based on different premises— "Their code is a law unto themselves. Offend one, and you offend them all." This is a law based not on individualism, but on group strength, on mutual support, that also remarkably recalls the Pauline metaphor on which the early Puritan Body/Politic was founded—"And whether one member suffer, all the members suffer with it; or one member be honoured, all the members rejoice with it. Now ye are the body of Christ, and members in particular."[31] The wedding banquet, with its eucharistic motif, reinforces and stresses this connection.

Freaks: Phroso hears from the Stork Woman of the birth of the bearded lady's baby.

Thus, I argue, any conventionally 'moralistic' reading of *Freaks* misses the point—although such a reading has certainly been invited by the awkward preamble of the film:

Before proceeding with the showing of this HIGHLY UNUSUAL ATTRACTION, a few words should be said about the amazing subject matter.... The revulsion with which we view the abnormal, the malformed and the mutilated is the result of long conditioning by our forefathers. The majority of freaks themselves are endowed with normal thoughts and emotions. Their lot is truly a heartbreaking one…. Never again will such a story be filmed, as modern science and teratology is rapidly eliminating such blunders of nature from the world. With humility for the many unjustices done… we present the most startling horror story of the ABNORMAL and the UNWANTED.

However, this preamble was tacked on to the movie by exploitation mogul Dwain Esper for his re-release of *Freaks*. As a consequence of the fact that this preamble appears on copies to this day, Skal and Savada explain, "audiences and critics have assumed it is some kind of position statement of Browning himself, instead of a distributor's cynical attempt to position the picture with a moralistic, 'educational' defense—just like the pictures about sex and drugs".[32]

Previous critiques have noted that the movie attempts to 'normalise' the freaks by showing them engaged in everyday actions—hanging up the washing, lighting cigarettes, having conversations—and never in their show acts, as spectacles. Such readings extract from this the obvious (and seemingly obviously stated) message that "the normals are the monsters, and the freaks are normal": "Browning has turned the popular convention of horror topsy-turvy. It is the ordinary, the apparently normal, the beautiful which horrify—the monstrous and distorted which compel our respect, our sympathy, ultimately our affection. The visible beauty conceals the unseen evil, the visible horror is the real goodness."[33] This view would parallel, say, the Dickensian question of 'true gentlemanhood' discussed in *Great Expectations*, or, for that matter, in David Lynch's *The Elephant Man*, 1980, which actually quotes Browning's movie. But *Freaks*, I argue, goes much further than that. Not only are they like us (our self-image), but we are like them (our image of the other). It is in fact this undecidable oscillation that makes *Freaks* a truly uncanny work of art. In Robin Wood's view, "horror films… are progressive precisely to the degree that they refuse to be satisfied with… [the] simple designation of the monster as evil".[34] *Freaks* is progressive precisely in that way. It has often been pointed out that Browning's use of real freaks instead of make-up and the contortionist-like stunts of 'able-bodied' actors like Chaney made for its uneasy (to say the least) reception. Yet, the Freak Show, the Dime Museum, PT Barnum's American Museum showing deformed people, had been a continuous presence in the life of nineteenth century America.[35] The cinema can in fact be seen as having developed out of fairground attractions, circuses and sideshows—many of the early cinema people were, like Browning, associated with the fairground. What was truly shocking was not the cast, but the (a)moral implications of the movie's message. On a political level, "*Freaks* is asking a Depression audience to identify not with the Beautiful people… but with the sideshow mutations, a total underclass. As a reflection of the time, it's almost revolutionary. But Depression audiences were not prepared for this kind of thing."[36] Instead of giving a reassuring categorisation of us and them (as the Freak Shows had still done), *Freaks* showed that, somehow, the very distinction between us and them does not hold, since both are two sides of the same coin. Thus, Cleopatra as the Chicken Woman is the repressed truth of her incarnation as the narcissistic Peacock of the Air—or, in other words, the Peacock is only the dream, or "orthopaedic armour", of the Chicken Woman.[37]

The two seemingly separate realms of freaks and 'big people' is in fact being constantly both reassured and opened up in the movie. In the beginning of *Freaks*, the barker announces: "You'll laugh at them, shudder at them, and yet, but for the accident of birth, you might be even as they are." Later, when the freaks suspect that Cleopatra is simply misusing Hans' feelings for her, Frances, the Armless Girl, declares: "Cleopatra ain't one of us. Why, we're just filthy things to her. She'd spit on Hans if he wasn't giving her presents." One of the climaxes of the movie (and a crucial scene where the two realms are on the verge of collapsing—either as an invitation or a threat, or both simultaneously) is the wedding banquet scene. Cleopatra has finally married Hans. During the banquet, she openly kisses Hercules. Hans watches, beginning to suspect that he has been taken for a fool. His fault, in the economy of the complex interplay of the fragmented and the whole body, is that he has momentarily given in to the illusion and seduction of wholeness, given in to the promise of being accepted, loved, taken seriously by a 'big person'.

The freaks begin their ritual of acceptance, passing a large goblet of champagne and finally offering it to Cleopatra, while singing "Gobble, gobble, we accept her, we accept her, one of us, one of us." Though always read as an openly stated peace offering, a ceremony of acceptance, it cannot be denied that there are violent undertones to this ambiguous scene. In the light of what's to come, the threat can already be felt, underlined by the fact that the freaks are beating a rhythm to their chant—with knives. After shouting "You dirty, slimy freaks!", Cleopatra almost desperately tries to keep the realms separate—"You filth! Make me one of you, will you!" The opening up of the two realms—and in fact their complicity—is most clearly voiced by the characters of what I call the 'middle realm'—most notably Venus and Phroso.

After the wedding banquet, when Cleopatra and Hercules have already begun to carry out their plan of slowly poisoning Hans, Venus confronts Hercules and demands that the plot against Hans is revealed, "or I'll tell the coppers". Hercules is furious: "So, you'd tell on your own people." Venus replies, "*My* people are decent circus folks, not dirty rats that would kill a freak to get his money." In a scene between Venus and Phroso, the clown replies to Venus' compliment that he is "a pretty good kid" with the unexplained line "You should have caught me before my operation." Within the Browning universe, such a remark more likely than not refers to a missing limb—given Phroso's flirtatious and sexually charged manner, it might even refer to a missing penis. Thus, Phroso most clearly voices Lacan's contention that in order to gain our entry into society, we have to accept castration—the loss of unlimited individuality.

We, the audience, have followed the subject's vicissitudes between the fragmented body and the whole body as well. Our gaze starts with the identification with the intradiegetic audience, then comes to an abrupt stop

The freaks' feast to celebrate the wedding of Cleopatra and Hans, where she and Hercules humiliate him.

—the camera starts to descend into the cage where Cleopatra, the Chicken Woman, sits, but then stops short—and is shifted to the perspective of Hans, viewing the Peacock of the Air from below.[38] We thus adopt the initial position of the child in Lacan's mirror stage, wishing for and identifying with the illusory wholeness posed before us. In the end, then, having come full circle, we are placed in the position of the 'big people' again, looking down at the Chicken Woman from above—a position, however, which by now is revealed as at least precarious, with respect to both individual psychology, and a cultural history of the monstrous Body/Politic.

Parts of this essay were published as *"Join the United Mutations: Tod Browning's Freaks"*, *Post Script: Essays in Film and the Humanities*, vol. 21, no. 3, Fall 2002, pp. 8–19. This essay is a revised and extended version.

⋈ NOTES

1. See Joan Hawkins, "'One of Us': Tod Browning's *Freaks*", in *Freakery. Cultural Spectacles of the Body*, R Garland Thomson ed., New York: New York University Press, 1996, pp. 265–276; and Martin Norden, "Violence, Women and Disability in Tod Browning's *Freaks* and *The Devil Doll*", in *The Horror Film Reader*, A Silver and J Ursini eds, New York: Limelight Editions, 2000, pp. 151–165.

2. See Ann Douglas, *Terrible Honesty: Mongrel Manhattan in the 1920s*, New York: Farrar, Straus and Giroux, 1995.

3. de Montaigne, Michel, *Essays*, London: Penguin, 1976, p. 385.

4. Quoted in Jack Stephenson, "Freaks—A Movie Undead", http://hjem.get2net.dk/jack_stevenson/freaks.htm, accessed 9 March, 2006.

5. All quotations from the movie are taken from the online transcript of the screenplay of *Freaks*. See http://www.angelfire.com/in3/jasonv/freaks.htm, accessed 5 October, 2005.

6. Freud, Sigmund, "The Ego and the Id", *On Metapsychology. The Theory of the Unconscious*, The Penguin Freud Library, vol. 11, London: Penguin, 1984, pp. 339–407, p. 364.

7. Freud, "The Ego and the Id", p. 364 n. 2.

8. Lacan, Jacques, *Écrits: A Selection*, A Sheridan trans., New York: Norton, 1977, pp. 1–7.

9. Lacan, *Écrits*, p. 6.

10. Lacan, *Écrits*, pp. 4 and 2.

11. Lacan, *Écrits*, p. 4.

12. Lacan, *Écrits*, p. 5.

13. Skal, David J, and Elias Savada, *Dark Carnival: The Secret World of Tod Browning, Hollywood's Master of the Macabre*, New York: Anchor Books, 1995, p. 103. This book has provided most of the biographical information and history referred to in this essay.

14. Farber, Stephen, and Marc Green, *Hollywood on the Couch. A Candid Look at the Overheated Love Affair between Psychiatrists and Moviemakers*, New York: William Morrow & Co, 1993, p. 27.

15. Freud, Sigmund, "The Uncanny", *Art and Literature*, The Penguin Freud Library, vol. 14, London: Penguin, 1990, pp. 335–376, p. 366.

16. Freud, "The Uncanny", pp. 363–364. For an evaluation of 'the uncanny' as a conceptual tool for the analysis and taxonomy of the horror movie, see Steven Schneider, "Monsters as Uncanny Metaphors: Freud, Lakoff, and the Representation of Monstrosity in Cinematic Horror", in *The Horror Film Reader*, Silver and Ursini eds., pp. 167–191.

17. Freud, "The Uncanny", p. 368.

18. The notion of the monstrous Body/Politic is there already, for example in the Antinomian Controversy, placing the 'monstrous births' of Anne Hutchinson and Mary Dyer against the 'closely-knit' communal body envisioned by Governor John Winthrop.

19. See Ernst H Kantorowicz's seminal study *The King's Two Bodies. A Study in Mediaeval Political Theology*, Princeton, New Jersey: Princeton University Press, 1957, for an analysis of the "curious legal fiction of the 'King's Two Bodies' as developed in Elizabethan England", p. vii.

20. Lacan, Jacques, "Some Reflections on the Ego", Nancy E Beaufil trans., *International Journal of Psychoanalysis*, no. 34, 1953, pp. 11–17, p. 15.

21. Berressem, Hanjo, *Lines of Desire. Reading Gombrowicz's Fiction with Lacan*, Evanston, Illinois: Northwestern University Press, 1998, p. 27.

22. Deleuze, Gilles, and Félix Guattari, *AntiOedipus. Capitalism and Schizophrenia*, R Hurley, M Seem, and HR Lane trans., Minneapolis: University of Minnesota Press, 1992, p. 326.

23. Deleuze, Gilles, and Félix Guattari, *A Thousand Plateaus. Capitalism and Schizophrenia*, B Massumi trans., Minneapolis and London: University of Minnesota Press, 1993, p. 165.

24. Deleuze and Guattari, *A Thousand Plateaus*, p. 43.

25. Pingree, Allison, "America's 'United Siamese Brothers': Chang and Eng and 19th Century Ideologies of Democracy and Domesticity", in *Monster Theory*, Jeffery Jerome Cohen ed., Minneapolis: University of Minnesota Press, 1996, pp. 92–114.

26. *Great Debates in American History*, vol. 5, New York: Current Literature Publishing Company, 1913, pp. 65–66.

27. Lincoln, Abraham, quoted in Francis B Carpenter, *Six Months at the White House with Abraham Lincoln*, New York: William Marshall, 1866, pp. 76–77.

28. Watts, Jr, Richard, "A Glance at Tod Browning, an Original of the Cinema", *New York Herald Tribune*, 20 March, 1927.

29. Stein, Elliott, "Tod Browning", in *Cinema: A Critical Dictionary*, vol. 1, Richard Roud ed., New York: Viking Press, 1980, pp. 156–166, p. 157.

30. Bataille, George, *Literature and Evil*, A Hamilton trans., London and New York: Marion Boyars, 1990, p. 19.

31. "The First Epistle of Saint Paul to the Corinthians", 12: 26–27, *The Holy Bible. King James Version*, http://www.bartleby.com/108/46/12.html, accessed 5 October, 2005.

32. Savada and Skal, *Dark Carnival*, p. 223.

33. Butler, Ivan, *Horror in the Cinema*, New York: AS Barnes, 1970, p. 65.

34. Wood, Robin, *Hollywood from Vietnam to Reagan*, New York: Columbia University Press, 1986, p. 192.

35. See Robert Bogdan, *Freak Show. Presenting Human Oddities for Amusement and Profit*, Chicago: University of Chicago Press, 1988.

36. Hobermann, J and J Rosenbaum, *Midnight Movies*, New York: Da Capo Press, 1983, p. 307.

37. And yet, the Peacock is as much a freak as the Chicken.

38. Compare Freud's observation in his essay on fetishism, that "the inquisitive boy peered at the woman's genitals from below". Freud, Sigmund, "Fetishism", *On Sexuality*, The Penguin Freud Library, vol. 7, London: Penguin, 1991, pp. 345–357, p. 354. Roger Dadoun rightly reads this as a "technical instruction to the film producer". Dadoun, Roger, "Fetishism in the Horror Film", in *Fantasy and the Cinema*, James Donald ed., London: British Film Institute, 1989, pp. 39–61, p. 40.

Mark of the Vampire

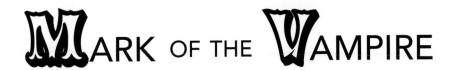

Matthew Sweney

Tod Browning's *Mark of the Vampire*, 1935, is not usually considered one of his best works, probably because of an ending which lets the audience down—way down—showing them the scenery is fake, the wings of the vampire mere props controlled by wires, the mark of the vampire made by fingernail scissors. The spectator feels like a carnival mark; he or she has been taken, had, robbed of the suspension of disbelief. But let's look at it again, for *Mark of the Vampire* is a densely composed film, and one of Browning's most mature and satisfying works. Satisfying with an unsatisfying ending? Yes—satisfying for its magnificent tracking shot on the stairwell, for its introduction of 'the Look' for female screen vampires, for giving us more Lugosi, for letting Lionel Barrymore chew the scenery, for its eerie soundtrack, for the invention of 'bat thorn'. *Mark of the Vampire*, like a good carnival sideshow, is greater than the sum of its parts.

The carnival sideshow, the freak show, brings to town the unusual. The Strong Man, the Fat Lady—these are extremes justly slightly beyond the realm of the ordinary. But the Two-Headed Calf, the Wolf-Boy, the Giant Sewer Rat of Paris, the Hermaphrodite—these you normally don't get to see until they come to your town with the carnies. The film spectacle works in a similar way. You don't get to see Count Dracula very often in the flesh. You pay your dime, you enter the dark tent. You know you're going to be fooled, but you've spent your money to suspend your disbelief.

    Mark of the Vampire is Tod Browning at his carnival master best. It is a film that repeated viewings only improve. Its melodramatic plot only enhances the surprise ending; its surprise ending, so patently false, does not negate what has come before it, but rather asserts the dream logic of the film itself.

    The story begins fairly straightforwardly: Baron Otto Von Zinden announces that his brother Sir Karell has died suddenly in the night. The local doctor, who believes in vampires, finds that the body has been drained of blood via two puncture wounds in the neck. Locals conjecture that it must be the work of the vampire Count Mora, a former owner of the abandoned castle still attached to the chateau. Inspector Neumann of Prague, who does not believe in superstition, arrives on the scene to investigate.

Sir Karell Borotyn's daughter Irena is to be married to a young man, Fedor Vincente, and the daughter becomes the ward of her uncle. A year passes; the wedding is nigh. Fedor succumbs to two bites in the neck, is weak. Then his fiancee also is bitten. An expert in the supernatural from Prague, Professor Zelin (played to the hilt by Lionel Barrymore) is called in by Inspector Neumann. He advises that the doors and windows should be firmly shut at night and protected by the application of 'bat thorn' to ward off vampires. But some windows are left open, and vampires get into the house....

Mark of the Vampire saw Tod Browning introduce 'the Look' for female screen vampires. Courtesy of Elias Savada.

The visual style of the film is what we pay our money for, and *Mark of the Vampire* delivers. The opening shot is of a cross atop a mediaeval church spire; the camera pans down, there is a split screen, and then we are at ground level where villagers are singing around a fire; we cut to an old woman indoors who affixes a bunch of dried herbs to a horse's neck; a mother prays to the Lord over her baby (in Czech; the working title of the film was *Vampires of Prague* and while the characters' names are misspelled in the credits, it is to the filmmakers' credit that the villagers and servants in the film speak Czech)—the baby also clutches a handful of herbs in his/her tiny fingers: belief starts in the cradle. We go back outside to the singing villagers around a fire, then cut to the old herb gatherer in the cemetery—she spies a man (we are soon to be introduced to him as Doctor Doskil) who speeds by, whipping his horse; cut back to an owl in a tree in the cemetery; and cut back to the woman gathering more herbs in the cemetery. A bat flies past her from behind and then circles round her, it startles her, she runs away, but the hem of her robe is caught by the fingers of a corpse.

The entire scene as just described is played out to a soundtrack of the 'villagers' dirge'; at the moment the bony hand clutches her, the soundtrack shifts to sounds of moaning and night creatures: an owl hoots, crickets chirp in the background. Then there is another split screen, and we meet a young couple at an inn, in modern dress (the woman wears a man's hat and tie and smokes a cigarette—compared to the women already shown she looks as if she dropped out of the sky). They are told to stay there—it is not safe tonight—and are instructed in the art of placing bat thorn at doors to protect oneself from "the demons of the castle".

This inn scene would mark the start of a typical horror film. *Mark of the Vampire* is not a typical horror film. The opening sequence (a tightly cut minute and a half), it signals a world of different traditions, one with a different language and beliefs we may not share nor understand. The world is split between what is

A publicity still from *Mark of the Vampire* he film showing Carol Borland, Bela Lugosi and Holmes Herbert as the fly caught in their web.
Courtesy of Elias Savada.

'real' and what is 'modern'. We have no reason not to doubt that the hand coming from the grave is fake, not at the beginning of the film, nor at its end.

The soundtrack of *Mark of the Vampire* contributes in no small part to the overall atmosphere, and deserves an essay of its own (Douglas Shearer, 12 time Oscar winner and brother of Norma, is credited as Recording Director); in addition to the slightly unsettling effect of many characters speaking a foreign language, the moaning sounds described above are slowed down and sped up to create a kind of Theremin wow which is extremely unsettling. Stuart Rosenthal has written that "*Mark of the Vampire* [relies] upon a minimum of mood music."[1] In fact there is no orchestral music in the film at all, except for the opening and closing credits (it is an MGM film). The only melodic music within the film is made by the performers: the singing and violin playing of the villagers, and the melodramatic organ (played by a dead man!). The only incidental music, the "mood music"—consisting as it does of groans and nocturnal animal sounds—is perhaps minimalistic, but it is not used minimally, occurring throughout the film expressly to score the vampire scenes. Frightening scenes are not punctuated by orchestral crescendos but by babies crying, women screaming, horses neighing, bells striking.

If Browning wanted to follow up on *Dracula*, he went to the right place. The screenwriters did their homework: Guy Endore and Bernard S Schubert, and (according to Savada and Skal in *Dark Carnival*) also HS Kraft, Samuel Ornitz, and John L Balderston (one of the writers of the play *Dracula*) set the film *Mark of the Vampire* in the countryside outside of Prague. In his first draft of Dracula, Bram Stoker originally placed Dracula's castle in Styria (part of Austria); he made the change to Transylvania so that Jonathan Harker could travel through the lands of the Austro-Hungarian empire, meeting Czechs, Slovaks, Wallachs, Romanies, and Magyars along his way. Transylvania was then part of that empire and it is rather in these lands—the former kingdoms of Hungary, Moravia, and Bohemia, and not what we think of as today's Romania—where the bulk of historical vampire sightings occurred and legends spread.

Why Count Mora? In Czech, *mora* is a creature of the night: a dialectical variant of today's *mura*. *Nocní mura* in modern Czech means 'nightmare' (*nocní* is the adjectival form of 'night')—literally it means 'night moth', but then nightmare is literally 'night horse'. Or is it? Actually 'mare' in the English word 'nightmare' is the same word as *mora*, an Old English word describing a demon of the night, sometimes drinking its victim's blood, other times suffocating its victim, sometimes taking the form of a moth or bat to fly away.

James Wong Howe is credited as the film's sole cinematographer. In Dark Carnival, Skal and Savada quote the MGM production manager JJ Cohn, who removed Howe from the film because "he wasn't getting the effects right".[2] Howe is quoted as saying Browning "had the actors play 'at' the camera instead of moving around it, so the picture was very stagy and he used cutting to get him through".[3] However, in fact there are a great many moving camera effects in Mark of the Vampire, although only in those scenes where the supernatural is at work, creating a visual tension in the film. The effects shots, indeed, make the film, and overpower the static shots in which the film's plot and denouement

Mark of the Vampire: the two night walkers on their home ground.

take place. (Skal and Savada also quote the actress Carol Borland, who played the female vampire Luna, as saying that the film's ingénue star (Elizabeth Allan in the role of Irena Borotyn) complained that Howe concentrated more on the effects lighting than on her close-ups—it's more likely the MGM star system that forced Howe's removal.)[4]

By far the most interesting part of the film is one such effect, its famous tracking shot, which occurs approximately 17 minutes into the film. The camera follows Count Mora and his daughter Luna as they cross a sort of landing and then glide down the stairs. What was originally probably an unbroken tracking shot is intercut with shots of creeping creatures (cockroaches, bats, a possum, a tarantula). As the Count and Luna move to the right of the screen a bat appears and flies through cobwebs and what looks like a wall: this is a process shot in which the barriers to the bat simply melt away; the bat continues its flight from behind the duo and then over and around them, casting its shadow upon them. The two continue their promenade out of the castle, into the night air facing the cemetery. All of this is accompanied by the mood music mentioned above.

This one-minute sequence is one of the greatest visual feasts in the cinema of the macabre. The motion of the two night walkers, the motion of the bat and the motion of the camera all combine in a fluid journey that takes the viewer down into the castle cellar and through its walls, out into the cemetery night. After this experience, it is the static plot scenes where everyone is jabbering which seem unreal and dreamlike. The vampire scenes are conducted without dialogue, and in contrast to the somewhat forced dialogues of the rest of the characters (concerning bat thorn and other plot devices), their silence lends a further tension to the film.

Of equal interest is another brief scene, almost immediately following: Luna, a bat trailing her, comes out of the cemetery and looks in at the window of Irena, who sees her, then arises and walks trance-like out of the room. There is a cut—Irena is outside, still moving as if in a trance; she sits down, the Count stares at her, looking on; Luna approaches, Irena gazes at her; Luna fixes Irena with a stare and Irena faints as Luna opens her arms wide and swoops down upon her, covering her in the folds of her robe/shroud. The Count looks on and smiles. Cut to the clock tower striking midnight. A woman screams. The editing, credited to Ben Lewis, is exquisite.

The sexual aspect, here a lesbian scene with male voyeur, is undeniable —it builds upon the sexual content of Browning's *Dracula* and that inherent in vampirism itself. Later in the film they embrace again, the fiancé Fedor watching —un-vampire-like, he does not condone the liaison and breaks it up. Luna hisses at him while Irena escapes. Their relationship is reflected in the 'modern' world during the denouement when we learn Fedor was not to be told that the vampires are not real: "Forgive me, Fedor, for they wouldn't let me tell you— they were afraid that you wouldn't let me go through with it."

The other great piece of cinematography comes at about 39 minutes into the film, when Luna flies from up near the ceiling down to the cellar floor, folding her wings behind her as she lands, in a sudden and extraordinarily convincing transformation from monster to human. The shot lasts all of five seconds, and according to Skal and Savada it took a day and a half to shoot (and certainly weeks of preparation), but the effect is worth it.[5] The scene is carried out so that Baron Otto can be witness to it: it makes him a believer as well. In the last five minutes of the film, the vampires are revealed to be actors, an ending that works on two levels at once. The first is to show the viewers of the film that they have been duped, that everything is make-believe. If you get to see the Two-Headed Calf in daylight, you can see the stitches holding the second head in place. This scene places *Mark of the Vampire* in the realm of Browning's carnival films, for he is showing the audience how easy it is to fool them. As we know, some freaks are born, and some are made. On the other hand, if we accept the plot of the film on its own terms, then the actors can't be acting, for the visual effects would not be possible except on a cinema soundstage where there is no ceiling. If this 'play' was really enacted within the castle walls, there would be no place to suspend the wires which hold the Bat Woman in place; no room for running the marionette wires which control the flapping wings of the bat. There would be no need for the lesbian seduction scene (as theatre), for there would be nobody to witness it. Real cobwebs could not cover a room overnight.

"Everything is getting cloudy, cloudy, do you understand?" These are the first words Professor Zelin says as he hypnotises Baron Otto in the last reel of the film, and we start to question the logic of what we have already seen and heard. When things are cloudy, we do not understand. We witness the murder of Sir Karell at this point, a recreation with the aid of hypnosis and with an actor playing the part of the victim. For Baron Otto the theatre is real: he goes through the motions just as if he were living through it.

For the Luna Bat Woman Theatre troupe are a corollary to the faked vampire murder in the beginning of the story. During the climactic hypnosis scene we learn that Baron Otto drugged his brother with tainted wine, then punctured two holes in his neck with nail scissors and drained the blood by suction, using a heated cup. He faked the death to frighten the superstitious locals and deflect suspicion from himself. And yet it is he, the modern scientific one, who finally succumbs to superstition, believing the actors are real.

And so where does theatre start—what is real about 'real life' in this film? Browning blurs these distinctions with an ending which purposefully makes viewers question what they have seen in the past hour and what they will see in the dark cinemas of their future. "Did you see me?" Lugosi asks his fellow actress in his one and only speech at the film's very conclusion, "I was greater than any real vampire!"

☙ NOTES

1. Rosenthal, Stuart, *The Hollywood Professionals. Tod Browning*, London: The Tantivy Press, 1975, p. 50.

2. Skal, David J and Elias Savada, *Dark Carnival. The Secret World of Tod Browning*, Hollywood's Master of the Macabre, New York: Anchor Books, 1995, p. 197.

3. Skal and Savada, *Dark Carnival*, p. 197.

4. Skal and Savada, *Dark Carnival*, p. 197.

5. Skal and Savada, *Dark Carnival*, p. 196. More than 70 years after the film's release, the transformation sequence does not at all seem old-fashioned, precisely because it relies on theatre rather than special cinematic effects; the sideshow runs in real time.

PLATES

PRISCILLA DEAN
SUPPORTED BY
LON CHANEY
IN
"Outside the Law"
BASED ON THE MOTION PICTURE STORY
by Tod Browning

ITS A
UNIVERSAL
JEWEL

"Popular Plays and Screen Library"
TRADE MARK

⋈ Plate I ⋈

CATCH
THIS WOMAN!
TRICKY EYES
DANGEROUS SMILE
EXQUISITELY
GOWNED
NIMBLE FINGERS
She's
"Outside
The Law"
Morgan

Plate II

UNIVERSAL JEWEL

CARL LAEMMLE OFFERS

Priscilla Dean
SUPPORTED LON CHANEY
in "Outside The Law"
by TOD BROWNING

⋈ Plate III ⋈

The Mocking Bird

An Underworld story of the London Limehouse District

BASED ON THE MOTION PICTURE STORY

By

TOD BROWNING

A Metro-Goldwyn-Mayer PICTURE

Starring

LON CHANEY

"Popular Plays and Screen Library"

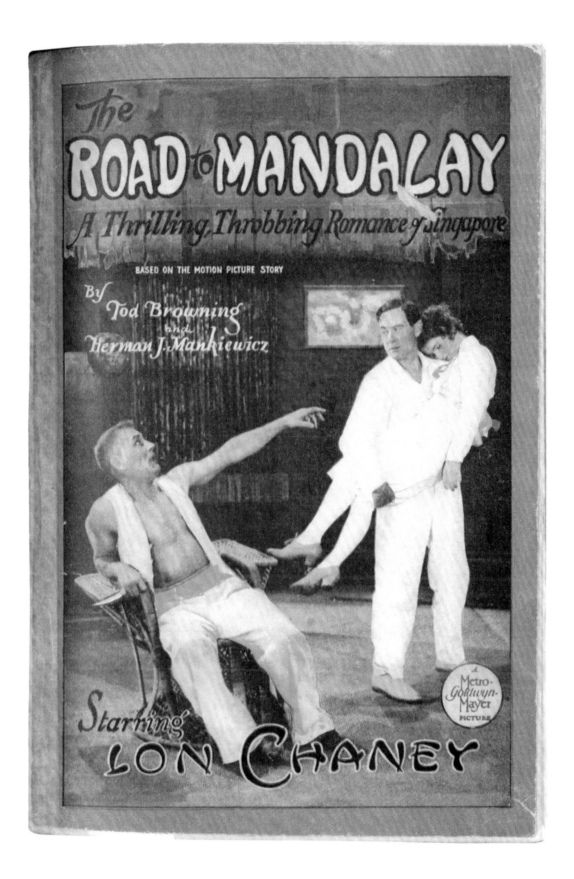

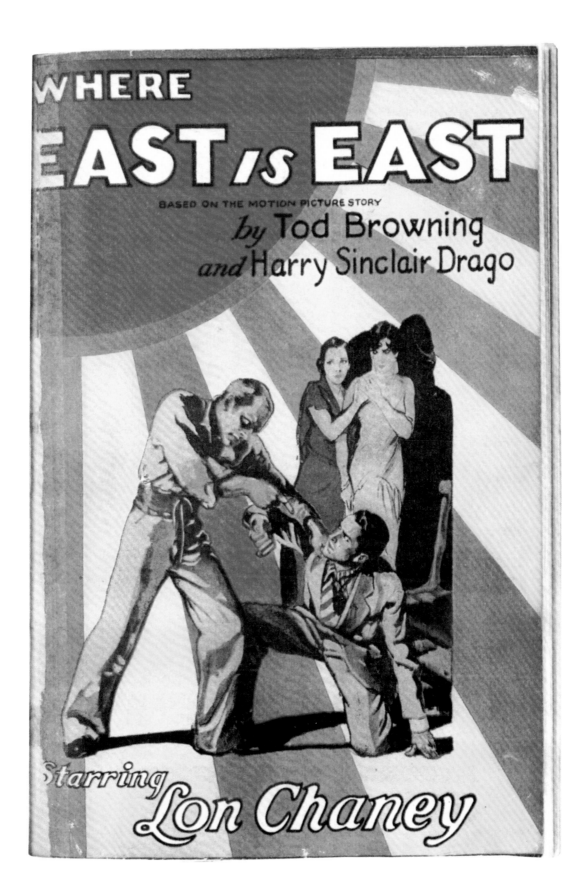

WHERE **EAST** *is* **EAST**

BASED ON THE MOTION PICTURE STORY

by Tod Browning
and Harry Sinclair Drago

Starring Lon Chaney

LON
CHANEY
in

WHERE
EAST
IS EAST

Brazenly she defied every threat

A Metro-Goldwyn-Mayer PICTURE
MADE IN U.S.A.

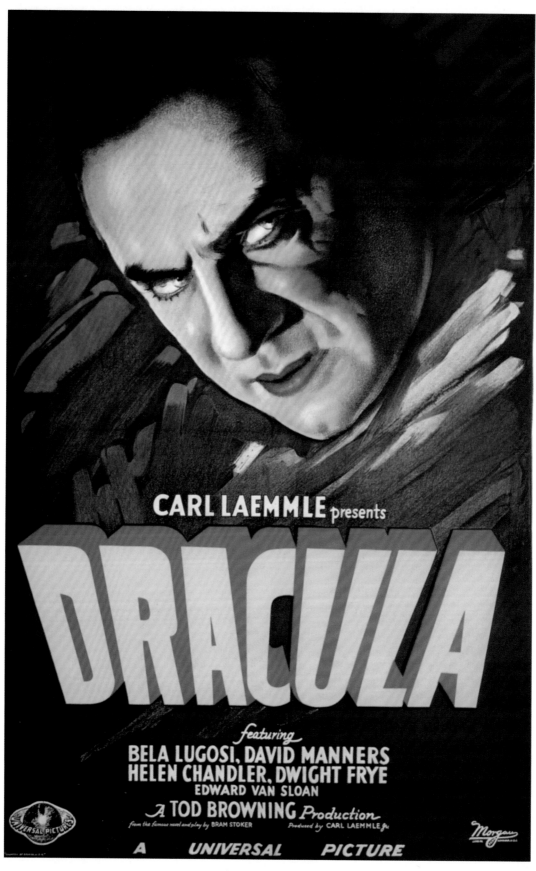

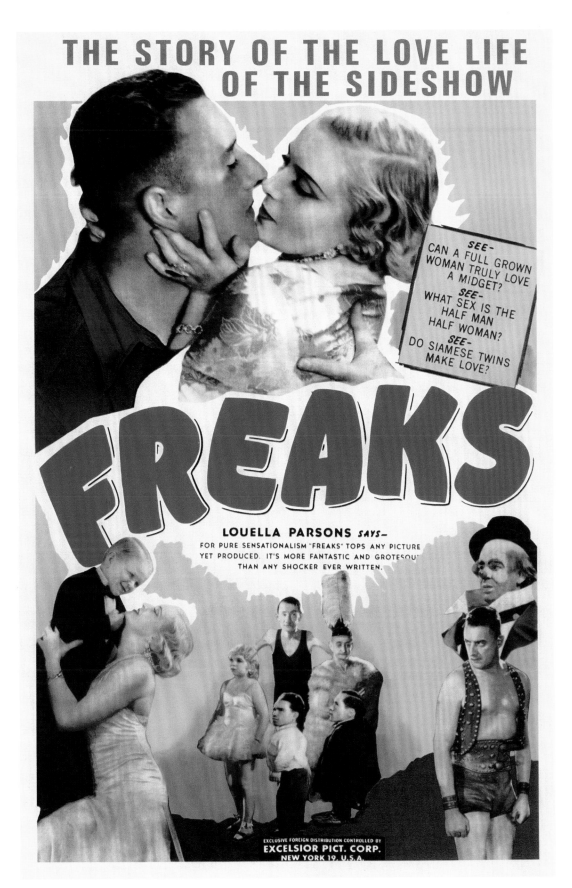

They brought terror to the living from the world of the "undead."

LIONEL BARRYMORE in "MARK OF THE VAMPIRE"

Plate XIII

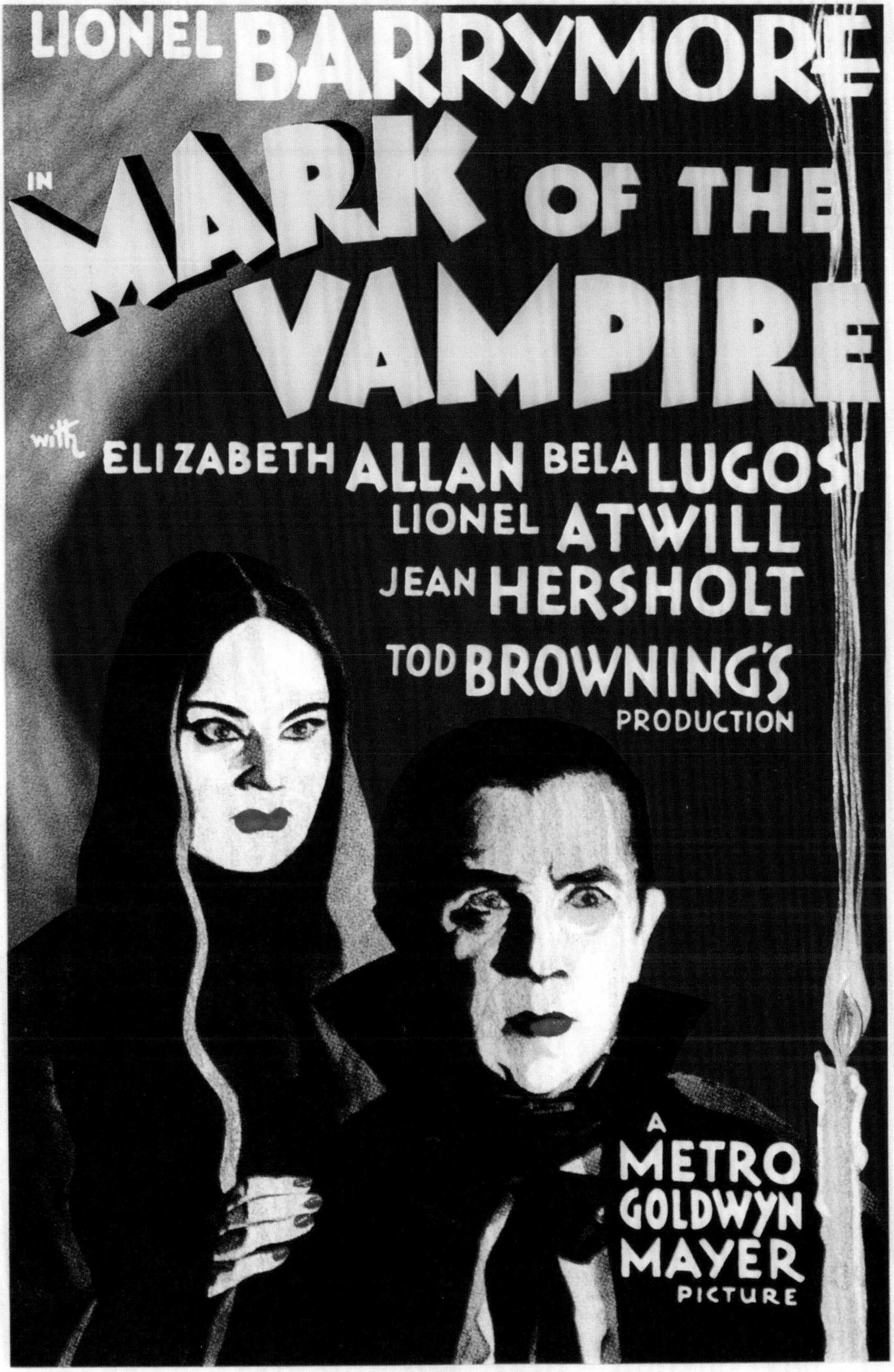
LIONEL BARRYMORE
IN
MARK OF THE VAMPIRE
with ELIZABETH ALLAN BELA LUGOSI
LIONEL ATWILL
JEAN HERSHOLT
TOD BROWNING'S
PRODUCTION
A
METRO
GOLDWYN
MAYER
PICTURE

Plate XIV

FILMOGRAPHY

1909

Ethel's Luncheon (actor)

1913

Bill Joins the Band (actor)

Scenting a Terrible Crime (actor)

A Fallen Hero (actor)

1914

An Interrupted Séance (actor)

After Her Dough (actor)

Victims of Speed (actor)

The Fatal Dress Suit (actor)

Nearly a Burglar's Bride (actor)

Izzy and the Bandit (actor)

The Scene of His Crime (actor)

A Race for a Bride (actor)

The Man on the Couch (actor)

Neil's Eugenic Wedding (actor)

An Exciting Courtship (actor)

The Last Drink of Whiskey (actor)

Hubby to the Rescue (actor)

The Deceiver (actor)

The White Slave Catchers (actor)

Bill's Job (actor)

Wrong All Around (actor)

How Bill Squared it with his Boss (actor)

Leave It to Smiley (actor)

Bill Takes a Lady Out to Lunch (... Never Again) (actor)

Ethel's Teacher (actor)

Bill Saves the Day (actor)

A Physical Culture Romance (actor)

Bill Organizes a Union (actor)

The Mascot (actor)

Business for Himself (actor)

Foiled Again (actor)

Bill Manages a Prize Fighter (actor)

The Million Dollar Bride (actor)

Bill Spoils a Vacation (actor)

Dizzy Joe's Career (actor)

Bill Joins the WWW's (actor)

Casey's Vendetta (actor)

Ethel's Roof Party (actor)

Out Again, In Again (actor)

Ethel Has a Steady (actor)

A Corner in Hats (actor)

Mr Hadley's Uncle (actor)

The Housebreakers (actor)

Bill and Ethel at the Ball (actor)

The Record Breaker (actor)

By the Sun's Rays (director)

1915

The Lucky Transfer (director)

The Slave Girl (director)

An Image of the Past (director)

The Highbinders (director)

The Story of a Story (director)

The Spell of the Poppy (director)

The Electric Alarm (director)

The Living Death (director)

The Burned Hand (director)

The Woman from Warrens (director)

Little Marie (director)

The Queen of the Band (story)

Sunshine Dad (story)

The Mystery of the Leaping Fish (story)

1916

Puppets (director)

Intolerance: Love's Struggle Throughout the Ages (actor, assistant director)

Everybody's Doing It (director)

The Fatal Glass of Beer (director)

Atta Boy's Last Race (story, scenario)

1917

Jim Bludso (director, scenario)

A Love Sublime (director, scenario)

Hands Up! (director)

Peggy, the Will O' the Wisp (director)

The Jury of Fate (director)

1918

The Eyes of Mystery (director)

The Legion of Death (director)

Revenge (director)

Which Woman? (director)

The Deciding Kiss (director)

The Brazen Beauty (director)

Set Free (director, scenario)

1919

The Wicked Darling (director)

The Exquisite Thief (director)

The Unpainted Woman (director)

The Petal on the Current (director)

Bonnie, Bonnie Lassie (director, scenario)

1920

The Virgin of Stamboul (director, scenario)

Outside the Law (director, producer, story, scenario)

1921

No Woman Knows (director, producer, scenario)

1922

The Wise Kid (director)

Man Under Cover (director)

Under Two Flags (director)

1923

Drifting (director)

The Day of Faith (director)

White Tiger (director, story, scenario)

1924

The Dangerous Flirt (director)

Silk Stocking Sal (director)

1925

The Unholy Three (director, producer)

The Mystic (director, producer, story)

Dollar Down (director)

1926

The Black Bird (director, producer, story)

The Road to Mandalay (director, producer, story)

1927

The Show (director, producer)

The Unknown (director, producer, story)

London After Midnight (director, producer, story, scenario)

1928

The Big City (director, producer, story)

West of Zanzibar (director, producer)

1929

Where East Is East (director)

The Thirteenth Chair (director, producer)

1930

Outside the Law ['remake' of Browning's 1920 version] (director, producer, story, scenario)

1931

Dracula (director)

Iron Man (director)

1932

Freaks (director, producer)

1933

Fast Workers (director, story)

1935

Mark of the Vampire (director, producer)

1936

The Devil Doll (director, story, scenario)

1939

Miracles for Sale (director, producer)

This filmography takes as its main source David Skal's and Elias Savada's *Dark Carnival: The Secret World of Tod Browning, Hollywood's Master of the Macabre*, but other works have also been referenced. We have done our best to ensure accuracy but some facts about Tod Browning's films are disputed and cannot be confirmed, as many of his films no longer exist or are inaccessible. The publisher and authors ask for your leniency should any of our information prove to be inaccurate.

FURTHER REFERENCES

Adorno, Theodor and Max Horkheimer, *The Dialectic of Enlightenment*, John Cumming trans., London: Verso, 1986.

Arata, Stephen "The Occidental Tourist: Dracula and the Anxiety of Reverse Colonization" in *Dracula*, 1897, David J Skal and Nina Auerbach edS., New York: WW Norton & Company, 1997.

Azoury, Philipe, "Browning Congele" in *Cahiers du Cinema* 576, 2003.

Balázs, Béla, *Theory of the Film*, E Bone trans., New York: Dover, 1970.

Balderston, John L and Hamilton Deane, *Dracula*, London: Samuel French, 1933.

Barnum, PT, *The Humbugs of the World*, Detroit: Singing Tree Press, 1970.

Barthes, Roland, *Mythologies*, Annette Lavers trans., London: Vintage, 1993.

Bataille, George, *Literature and Evil*, A Hamilton trans., London and New York: Marion Boyars, 1990.

Baxter, John, *Hollywood in the Thirties*, New York: Paperback Library, 1970.

Beckett, Samuel, *Waiting for Godot*, London: Faber, 1965.

Berenstein, Rhona J, "Spectatorship-as-Drag: The Act of Viewing and Classic Horror Cinema", in *Viewing Positions: Ways of Seeing Film*, Linda Williams ed., New Brunswick: Rutgers University Press, 1995.

Berressem, Hanjo, *Lines of Desire: Reading Gombrowicz's Fiction with Lacan*, Evanston, Illinois: Northwestern University Press, 1998.

Bhabha, Homi K, "The other question: The stereotype and colonial discourse", in *Visual Culture: A Reader*, Jessica Evans and Stuart Hall ed., London: Sage, 1999.

Bodeen, DeWitt, "Lon Chaney, Man of a Thousand Faces," *Focus on Film* 3, 1970.

Bogdan, Robert, *Freak Show: Presenting Human Oddities for Amusement and Profit*, Chicago: University of Chicago Press, 1988.

Bombaci, Nancy, *Freaks in Late Modernist American Culture: Nathanael West, Djuna Barnes, Tod Browning, and Caron McCullers*, New York: Peter Lang, 2006.

Bourget, Jean-Loup, *Hollywood, années 30: Du krach à Pearl Harbor*, Renens: 5 Continents/Hatier, 1986.

Braff, Richard E, "A Lon Chaney Index," *Films in Review* 21, 1970.

Brecht, Bertolt, *Brecht on Theatre*, John Willett trans., London: Methuen, 1978.

Brenan, Matthew C "The Novel as a Nightmare: Decentering of the Self in Bram Stoker's Dracula", *Journal of the Fantastic in the Arts* 7, 1996.

Brion, Marcel, *L'art fantastique*, Paris: Marabout Université, 1968.

Bronfen, Elisabeth, *The Knotted Subject: Hysteria and its Discontents*, Princeton: Princeton University Press, 1994.

Brottman, Mikita, *Offensive Films: Towards an Anthropology of Cinema Vomatif*, Westport: Greenwood Press, 1997.

Browning, Tod, *The Mocking Bird*, New York: Jacobsen Hodgkinson Corporation, 1925.

Browning, Tod, *Outside the Law*, New York: Jacobsen Hodgkinson Corporation, 1925.

Browning, Tod, *The Road to Mandalay*, New York: Jacobsen Hodgkinson Corporation, 1926.

Browning, Tod, *Where East is East*, New York: Jacobsen Hodgkinson Corporation, 1929.

Burch, Noel, *Life to Those Shadows*, Berkeley: University of California Press, 1990.

Butler, Ivan, *Horror in the Cinema*, New York: Paperback Library, 1971.

Chion, Michel, *The Voice in Cinema*, Claudia Gorbman trans., New York: Columbia University Press, 1999.

Christopher, Milbourne, *The Illustrated History of Magic*, New York: Thomas Y Crowell, 1973.

Clarens, Carlos, *Horror Movies: An Illustrated Survey*, London: Panther Books, 1971.

Clover, Carol J, *Men, Women, and Chain Saws: Gender in the Modern Horror Film*, Princeton: Princeton University Press, 1992.

Cook, James W, *The Arts of Deception: Playing with Fraud in the Age of Barnum*, Cambridge, Massachusetts: Harvard University Press, 2001.

Crafton, Donald, *Talkies: American Cinema's Transition to Sound 1925–1931*, Berkeley: University of California Press, 1999.

Crawford, Joan and Jean Kesner Ardmore, *A Portrait of Joan: The Autobiography of Joan Crawford*, New York: Doubleday & Co, 1962.

Creed, Barbara, "Dark Desires: Male Masochism in the Horror Film", in *Screening the Male: Exploring Masculinities in Hollywood Cinema*, Steven Cohan and Ina Rae Hark eds., London and New York: Routledge, 1993.

Dadoun, Roger, "Fetishism in the Horror Film", in *Fantasy and the Cinema*, James Donald ed., London: BFI, 1989.

Davidson, Michael, "Phantom Limbs: Film Noir and the Disabled Body" in *GLQ: A Journal of Lesbian and Gay Studies* 9, 2003.

Davis, Janet M "Freakishly, Fraudulently Modern" in *American Quarterly* 55, 2003.

Deleuze, Gilles, *Cinéma 1: l'image-mouvement*, Paris: Minuit, 1983.

Deleuze, Gilles, and Félix Guattari, *Anti Oedipus: Capitalism and Schizophrenia*, R Hurley, M Seem and HR Lane trans., Minneapolis: University of Minnesota Press, 1992.

Deleuze, Gilles, and Félix Guattari, *Mille plateaux: capitalisme et schizophrénie*, Paris: Minuit, 1980.

Deleuze, Gilles, and Félix Guattari, *A Thousand Plateaus: Capitalism and Schizophrenia*, B Massumi trans., Minneapolis and London: University of Minnesota Press, 1993.

Deleuze, Gilles, *Présentation de Sacher-Masoch*, Paris: Minuit, 1967.

Derrida, Jacques, "Living on-Border lines", in *Deconstruction and Criticism*, James Hulbert trans., Harold Bloom et al eds., New York: Continuum, 1979.

The Devil Doll, VHS, directed by Tod Browning, 1936, MGM Warner, 1996.

Doane, Mary Ann et al, *Re-Vision: Essays in Feminist Film Criticism*, Los Angeles: AFI/University Publications of America, 1984.

Douglas, Ann, *Terrible Honesty: Mongrel Manhattan in the 1920s*, New York: Farrar, Straus and Giroux, 1995.

Dracula, DVD, directed by Tod Browning, 1931, Universal Studios, 1999.

Dyer, Richard, *The Matter of Images: Essays on Representations*, New York: Routledge, 1993.

Edwards, Larry, *Bela Lugosi: Master of the Macabre*, Bradenton, Florida: McGuinn and McGuire, 1997.

Evans, Henry Ridgely, *Edgar Allan Poe and Baron von Kempelen's Chess-Playing Automaton*, Kenton, Ohio: International Brotherhood of Magicians, 1939.

Farber, Stephen, and Marc Green, *Hollywood on the Couch: A Candid Look at the Overheated Love Affair between Psychiatrists and Moviemakers*, New York: William Morrow & Co, 1993.

Fiedler, Leslie, *Freaks: Myths and Images of the Secret Self*, New York: Simon and Schuster, 1978.

Freaks, DVD, directed by Tod Browning, 1932, Warner Home Video, 2004.

Freud, Sigmund, *Art and Literature*, James Strachey trans., Harmondsworth: Penguin, 1985.

Freud, Sigmund, "The Economic Problem of Masochism", in *The Standard Edition of the Complete Psychological Works of Sigmund Freud*, vol. XIX, London: The Hogarth Press/The Institute of Psycho-Analysis, 1961.

Freud, Sigmund, "The Ego and the Id", in *On Metapsychology: The Theory of the Unconscious*, The Penguin Freud Library, vol. 11, Harmondsworth: Penguin, 1984.

Freud, Sigmund, "Fetishism", in *On Sexuality*, The Penguin Freud Library, vol. 7, Harmondsworth: Penguin, 1991, pp. 345–357.

Freud, Sigmund, "The Uncanny" in *Art and Literature*, The Penguin Freud Library, vol. 11, Harmondsworth: Penguin, 1990, pp. 335–376.

Gandini, Leonardo, *Tod Browning*, Milano: Il Castoro, 1996.

Garsault, Alain, "Tod Browning: à la recherche de la réalité", *Positif*, no. 208–209, 1978.

Gates, Henry Luis Jr, "Writing 'Race' and the Difference it Makes", in *'Race,' Writing, and Difference*, HL Gates Jr ed., Chicago and London: The University of Chicago Press, 1985.

Geltzer, George, "Tod Browning", *Films in Review* 4, 1953.

Gifford, Denis, *A Pictorial History of Horror Movies*, London: Hamlyn, 1973.

Giles, Dennis, "Conditions of Pleasure in Horror Cinema", in *Planks of Reason: Essays on the Horror Film*, Barry Keith Grant ed., London: Scarecrow, 1984.

Glover, David, "Bram Stoker and the Crisis of the Liberal Subject," *New Literary History* 23, 1992.

Gordon, Mel, *The Grand Guignol. Theater of Fear and Terror*, New York: Amok Press, 1988.

Gunning, Tom, "An Aesthetic of Astonishment: Early Film and the (In)credulous Spectator", in *Viewing Positions*, Linda Williams ed., New Brunswick: Rutgers University Press, 1997.

Halbertstam, Judith, *Skin Shows: Gothic Horror and the Technology of Monsters*, Durham: Duke University Press, 1995.

Hand, Richard J and Michael Wilson, *Grand Guignol. The French Theatre of Horror*, Exeter: University of Exeter Press, 2002.

Hansen, Miriam, *Babel and Babylon: Spectatorship in American Silent Film*, Cambridge and London: Harvard University Press, 1991.

Harrington, Curtis, "Ghoulies and Ghosties", in *Sight and Sound* 21, 1952.

Harris, Neil, *Humbug: The Art of P.T. Barnum*, Chicago: University of Chicago Press, 1973.

Hawkins, Joan, "'One of Us:' Tod Browning's *Freaks*", in *Freakery. Cultural Spectacles of the Extraordinary Body*, R Garland Thomson ed., New York: New York University Press, 1996.

Hawkins, Joan, "Horror Cinema and the Avant-Garde" Ph.D. dissertation, Berkeley: University of California, 1993.

Hennelly, Mark M, "Dracula: The Gnostic Quest and the Victorian Wasteland" in *English Literature in Translation: 1880–1920*, 20, 1977.

Higham, Charles, *Merchant of Dreams: Louis B. Mayer, MGM, and the Secret Hollywood*, New York: Dutton Books, 1993.

Hobermann, J and J Rosenbaum, *Midnight Movies*, New York: Da Capo Press, 1983.

Hoffmann, ETA, *Tales of Hoffmann*, RJ Hollingdale trans., Harmondsworth: Penguin, 1982.

Huss, Roy and TJ Ross, *Focus on the Horror Film*, Trenton: Prentice-Hall, 1972.

Hyde, Lewis, *The Trickster Makes his World: Mischief, Myth and Art*, New York: Farrar Strauss and Giroux, 1998.

Hynes, William J and William G Doty, "Mapping Mythic Tricksters", *Mythical Trickster Figures: Contours, Contexts, and Criticisms*, Tuscaloosa: University of Alabama Press, 1993.

Jackson, Rosemary, *Fantasy*, London: Methuen, 1981.

Joslin, Lyndon, *Count Dracula Goes to the Movies: Stoker's Novel Adapted 1922–1995*, London: McFarland & Company, 1999.

Jung, Uli, *Dracula. Filmanalytische Studien zur Funktionalisierung eines Motivs der viktorianischen Populärliteratur*, Trier: Universitäts Verlag, 1997.

Juranville, Alain, *Lacan et la philosophie*, Paris: PUF, 1988.

Kaplan, E Ann, *Woman and Film: Both Sides of the Camera*, New York and London: Methuen, 1983.

King, Noel, "The Sound of Silents", in *Silent Films*, Richard Abel ed., New Brunswick: Rutgers University Press, 1996.

Koch, Gertrud, "Between Two Worlds: von Sternberg's The Blue Angel", in *German Film and Literature: Adaptations and Transformations*, Eric Rentschler ed., New York and London: Methuen, 1986.

Kracauer, Siegfried, *From Caligari to Hitler*, Princeton: Princeton University Press, 1974.

Král, Petr, *Le Burlesque ou Morale de la tarte à la crème*, Paris: Stock, 1984.

Král, Petr, *Les Burlesques ou Parade des somnambules*, Paris: Stock, 1986.

Lacan, Jacques, "Seminar on The Purloined Letter" in *The Purloined Poe*, Jeffrey Mehlman trans., John P Muller and William J Richardson eds., Baltimore: Johns Hopkins, 1988.

Lacan, Jacques, *The Four Fundamental Concepts of Psychoanalysis*, New York: Norton, 1988.

Lacan, Jacques, *Écrits: A Selection*, A Sheridan trans., New York: Norton, 1977.

Laplanche, Jean, *Vie et mort en psychanalyse: suivi de dérivation des entités psychanalytiques*, Paris: Flammarion, 1970.

Laplanche, J , J-B Pontalis, *The Language of Psycho-Analysis*, Donald Nicholson-Smith trans., New York: WW Norton and Company, 1973.

Larcher, Jerome, "Tod Browning, d'une voix a l'autre" in *Cahiers du Cinema* 564, 2002.

Larsen, Robin and Beth Haller, "Public reception of real disability: the case of Freaks" in *Journal of Popular Film and Television* 29, 2002.

The Legion of Death, VHS, directed by Tod Browning, 1918, Quality Video, 1998.

London After Midnight, DVD, directed by Tod Browning, 1927, Warner Home Video, 2003.

King, Noel, "The Sound of Silents", in *Silent Films*, Richard Abel ed., New Brunswick: Rutgers University Press, 1996.

Kristeva, Julia, *The Powers of Horror: An Essay in Abjection*, New York: Columbia University Press, 1982.

MacDonald, Beth E, "The Vampire as trickster Figure in Bram Stoker's Dracula" in *Extrapolation* 33.2, 1992.

Manon, Hugh S, "Seeing Through Seeing Through: The Trompe l'Oeil Effect and Bodily Difference in the Cinema of Tod Browning" in *The Journal of Cinema and Media* 47, 2006.

Mark of the Vampire, VHS, directed by Tod Browning, 1935, MGM Warner, 1998.

Metz, Christian, *The Imaginary Signifier*, Celia Briton et al trans., Bloomington: Indiana University Press, 1982.

Montagu, Jennifer, *The Expression of the Passions*, New Haven and London: Yale University Press, 1994.

Montaigne, Michel, *Essays*, Harmondsworth: Penguin, 1976.

Moretti, Franco, *Signs Taken for Wonders*, Susan Fischer et al trans., London: Verso, 1997.

Morrison, Toni, *Playing in the Dark: Whiteness and the Literary Imagination*, Cambridge: Harvard University Press, 1992.

Musser, Charles, *The Emergence of Cinema I: The American Scene to 1907*, New York: Scribners, 1991.

Nordau, Max, *Degeneration*, New York: D Appleton, 1895; Lincoln: University of Nebraska Press, reprint, 1993.

Oates, Joyce Carol, "Dracula: the Vampire's Secret" in *Southwest Review* 76, 1991.

Outside the Law/Shadows, DVD, Directed by Tod Browning, 1920/1922, Universal, 2000.

Pearson, Roberta E, *Eloquent Gestures. The Transformation of Performance Style in the Griffith Biograph Films*, Berkeley: University of California Press, 1992.

Pick, Daniel, *Faces of Degeneration: A European Disorder, c. 1848–1918*, Cambridge: Cambridge University Press, 1989.

Pierron, Agnès, et al, *Le Grand Guignol*. Le Théâtre des peurs de la belle époque, Paris: Robert Laffont, 1995.

Poe, Edgar Allan, "Maelzel's Chess-Player", *The Complete Tales and Poems of Edgar Allan Poe*, New York: Vintage Books, 1975.

Rapp, Augustus, *The Life and Times of Augustus Rapp: The Small Town Showman*, Glenwood, Illinois: Meyerbooks, 1991.

Reik, Theodor, *Masochism in Modern Man*, New York: Grove, 1957

Riley, Philip J, *London After Midnight*, New York: Cornwall Books, 1985.

Risterucci, Pascale, "Reine et Poule: a propos d'un plan de Freaks" in *Art Press* 20, 1999.

Robert-Houdin, Jean-Eugène, *Memoirs of Robert-Houdin, King of the Conjurers*, trans., Lascelles Wraxall, New York: Dover Publications, 1964.

Robinson, David, *Hollywood in the Twenties*, New York: Paperback Library, 1970.

Romer, Jean-Claude, "Tod Browning," *Bizarre*, nos. 24–25, 1962.

Rosenthal, Stuart, *The Hollywood Professionals: Tod Browning, Don Siegel*, New York: A.S. Barnes, 1975.

Sabatier, Jean-Marie, *Les Classiques du cinéma fantastique*, Paris: Balland, 1973.

Sadoul, Georges, *Dictionary of Films*, Peter Norris ed., Berkeley: University of California Press, 1972.

Said, Edward W, *Orientalism*, New York: Vintage Books, 1978.

Sarris, Andrew, *The American Cinema*, New York: EP Dutton, 1968.

Savada, Elias, "The Making of freaks," in *Photon* 23, 1973.

Schmid, Hans, "Children of the Night: Das Kino des Tod Browning", in *Tod Browning's Freaks*, Jack Stevenson ed., Munich: Belleville, 1997.

Schilder, Paul, *The image and appearance of the human body: studies in the constructive energies of the psyche*, New York: International Universities Press, 1950.

Schneider, Steven, "Monsters as Uncanny Metaphors: Freud, Lakoff, and the Representation of Monstrosity in Cinematic Horror", in *The Horror Film Reader*, A Silver and J Ursini eds., New York: Limelight Editions, 2000.

Shipman, David, *The Great Movie Stars: The Golden Years*, New York: Crown, 1970.

Silver, Alain, and James Ursini, *The Vampire Film: From Nosferatu to Interview with the Vampire*, New York: Limelight Editions, 1997.

Silverman, Kaja, *Male Subjectivity at the Margins*, New York: Routledge, 1992.

Silverman, Kaja, *The Subject of Semiotics*, Oxford: Oxford University Press, 1984.

Skal, David J and Elias Savada, *Dark Carnival: The Secret World of Tod Browning*, Hollywood's Master of the Macabre, New York: Anchor Books, 1995.

Skal, David J, *Hollywood Gothic: The Tangled Web of Dracula from Novel to Stage to Screen*, London, New York: Norton, 1990.

Snyder, Sharon L, "Re-engaging the Body: Disability Studies and the Resistance to Embodiment" in *Public Culture* 13, 2001.

Spadoni, Robert, "The Uncanny Body of Early Sound Film" in *The Velvet Light Trap* 51, 2003.

Spivak, Gayatri Chakravorty, "Can the Subaltern Speak?", in *Marxism and the Interpretation of Culture*, Cary Nelson and Lawrence Grossberg eds., Urbana, Chicago: University of Illinois Press, 1988.

Stallybrass, Peter and Allen White, *The Politics and Poetics of Transgression*, Ithaca: Cornell University Press, 1986.

Stam, Robert, *Film Theory: An Introduction*, Oxford: Blackwell, 2000.

Standage, Tom, *The Turk: The Life and Times of the Famous Eighteenth-Century Chess-Playing Machine*, New York: Walker and Company, 2002.

Stastny, Peter, "From Exploitation to Self-Reflection: Representing Persons with Psychiatric Disabilities in Documentary Film" in *Literature and Medicine* 17, 1998.

Stoker, Bram, Dracula 1897, Nina Auerbach and David J Skal eds., New York: WW Norton & Company, 1997.

Stein, Elliott, "Tod Browning", in *Cinema: A Critical Dictionary*, volume one, Richard Roud ed., New York: Viking Press, 1980.

Studlar, Gaylyn, *In the Realm of Pleasure: Von Sternberg, Dietrich, and the Masochistic Aesthetic*, Urbana and Chicago: University of Illinois Press, 1988.

Studlar, Gaylyn, *This Mad Masquerade: Stardom and Masculinity in the Jazz Age*, New York: Columbia University Press, 1996.

Tesson, Charles, "L'extemite de l'amour" in *Cahiers du Cinema* 569, 2002.

Thompson, Rosemarie Garland, "Introduction: From Wonder to Error—Genealogy of Freak Discourse in Modernity" in *Freakery: Cultural Spectacles of the Extraordinary Body*, R Garland Thomson ed., New York: New York University Press, 1996.

Truffaut, François, *Hitchcock*, New York: Simon & Schuster, 1985.

Ulmer, Edgar G, "Karloff, Lugosi, Browning et Whale", in René Predal, *Le Cinema Fantastique*, Paris: Éditions Seghers, 1970.

The Unknown, DVD, directed by Tod Browning, 1927, Warner Home Video, 2003.

Vieira, Mark A, *Hollywood Horror from Gothic to Cosmic*, New York: Harry N Abrams, 2003.

Williams, Linda, "'Something Else Besides a Mother': Stella Dallas and the Maternal Melodrama", in *Home is Where the Heart is: Studies in Melodrama and the Woman's Film*, Christine Gledhill ed., London: BFI, 1987.

Wood, Robin, *Hollywood from Vietnam to Reagan*, New York: Columbia University Press, 1986.

Wood, Robin, "Burying the Undead: The Use and Obsolescence of Count Dracula", *Mosaic* 16, 1983.

Zizek, Slavoj, *Everything You Always Wanted to Know about Lacan (But Were Afraid to Ask Hitchcock)*, London: Verso, 1992.

Zizek, Slavoj, *The Metastases of Enjoyment: Six Essays on Woman and Causality*, London: Verso, 1994.

INDEX

FILMS

OTHER WRITTEN AND VISUAL MATERIAL

ACKNOWLEDGEMENTS

Bernd Herzogenrath would like to thank Black Dog Publishing for making this book possible, in particular Amy Sackville for her meticulous editing work and for making this a joyful experience! Thanks also to: Nicole Brenez, Vivian Sobchack, and Elisabeth Bronfen for being the wonderful people they are.

Boris Henry would like to also thank Nicole Brenez, and Corinne Oster; Matthew Solomon thanks Jeanine Corbet; and Nicole Brenez would like to thank Pierre-Jacques Brenez, Pierre Hecker and Stéphane du Mesnildot.

Elias Savada and Laurent Preyale are owed special gratitude for opening their collections of Browning images and generously providing us with much appreciated jewels from their crypts.

Black Dog Publishing would like to thank Eliana Sousa Santos whose research on the text and illustrations for the book greatly contributed to its content.

Black Dog Publishing
Architecture Art Design Fashion History
Photography Theory and Things

Designed by Emilia López @ bdp with the assistance of Evdokia Topouri

Black Dog Publishing Limited
Unit 4.4 Tea Building
56 Shoreditch High Street
London
E1 6JJ

Tel: +44 (0)20 7613 1922
Fax: +44 (0)20 7613 1944
Email: info@bdp.demon.co.uk
www.bdpworld.com

All opinions expressed within this publication are those of the authors and not necessarily of the publisher.

British Library Cataloguing-in-Publication Data.

A catalogue record for this book is available from the British Library.

ISBN-10: 1-904772-51-X
ISBN-13: 978-1-904772-51-4

Every effort has been made to trace the copyright holders, but if any have been inadvertently overlooked the publishers will be pleased to make the necessary arrangements at the first opportunity.

Printed and Bound by J. H. Haynes & Co. Ltd., Sparkford